A HISTORY OF
WORLD POTTERY

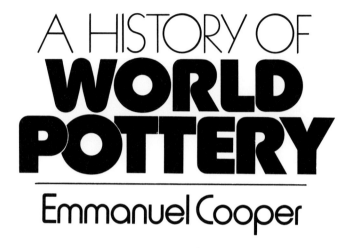

A HISTORY OF WORLD POTTERY

Emmanuel Cooper

Chilton Trade Book Publishing
Radnor, Pennsylvania

Acknowledgment

The author wishes to thank the many museums and individuals throughout the world for responding so generously to requests for photographs, and also the staff of *Ceramic Review* magazine for kindly putting their archives at his disposal.

© Emmanuel Cooper 1972, 1981

First published 1972
Second Edition 1981
Third Edition 1988

Published in Radnor, Pennsylvania 19089, by Chilton Trade Book Publishing

ISBN 0-8019-7982-X
LC 88-63366

Filmset in Monophoto Univers by Servis Filmsetting Ltd, Manchester

Printed and bound in Great Britain by Anchor Press Ltd, Tiptree, Essex

CONTENTS

INTRODUCTION

Since the second edition of *A History of World Pottery* there have been many exciting and far-reaching changes in the ceramic world. This new edition discusses these recent developments; the opportunity has also been taken to increase the number of colour illustrations, and to replace some of the earlier ones with examples which better illustrate current work. Yet, despite the changes in the world of pottery, what is evident is that working with clay continues to hold its attraction, whether in making pots for use in the home, in forming vessels, or in creating hard-edged or figurative sculptural forms.

Pots not only reflect technological development at particular times but they are often beautiful objects in their own right, over and above the demands of function. Such pots have been made ever since clay was first moulded, and this gives them added interest. Pots are also fascinating because of the way in which they were made, decorated and fired, as well as the forms which were chosen. These are the sorts of pots which are described in this book.

Changes in style and type of pottery occurred in response to social, economic and technical demands, and therefore pottery is closely integrated with the development of different civilizations from the earliest times to the present day. For this reason I have attempted to fit pottery into its historical and technical background, providing information to help the reader form a picture of society rather than taking the pots out of context with the place in which they were made and used.

Major countries have been dealt with more or less as a whole, and the pottery developments followed chronologically. After a brief introduction to the basic pottery processes, different techniques are explained as they occurred and are related to those which existed in other places at the same time.

It has not been possible here to deal with all the uses to which clay has been put, such as the manufacture of bricks, tiles and drainpipes, or the great industrial development of the pottery industry during the nineteenth century when the use of the machine enabled the mass production of pottery for expanding home and overseas markets; soft paste porcelain, too, is referred to only when its development influenced that of pottery. Instead, I have concentrated on pots made largely for use by individual potters or by small pottery workshops.

Today there is a great interest in the art and craft of pottery throughout the world. This is partly due to the activities of such bodies, as, in the UK, the Crafts Council or, in the US, of the American Crafts Council or the National Endowment for the Arts. The appearance of magazines about new ceramics has also been important. All serve to improve communication between potters and the public.

Like many other writers in the field of history I have tended to follow convention and refer to the potter as 'he' meaning both men and women. With a new awareness of the need to use language more precisely and to avoid imposing interpretations based on behaviour in our society onto earlier and very different societies, it does not now seem sufficient to use only the male pronoun. Women as well as men have made, and continue to make, some of our finest pots. Consequently I have revised the text to refer to potters in the plural unless a particular potter is being mentioned.

In one sense there is not a history of pottery, for different countries developed techniques, shapes and glazes at different times; instead there are many jumps in time and place for a variety of reasons. However, there is a common thread of styles, techniques and skills which link countries and people in a fascinating way. These I have attempted to pick out. Sufficient detail has been included to interest the more knowledgeable reader, yet this book is essentially an introduction to one of our oldest and most exciting art forms, and as such will, I hope, serve as a springboard for further investigation.

Emmanuel Cooper

	6000	5000	4000	3000	2000	1000

NEAR AND MIDDLE EAST

Anatolia / Syria / Asia Minor: Earliest pottery known. Painted pottery with white pigment on red body. Wares generally showed influences from Crete and Mesopotamia. Decorated wa[re]

Mesopotamia: Incised ware. Painted ware. Painted Samarra ware. Wheel developed and kiln improved. Olive coloured pottery. Richly painted style. Glass made. Lead glaze used. Glaze in general use. Unglazed wares still generally made

Egypt: Badarian pottery. Finely made, well considered form, carefully prepared clay. Red burnished ware with black (smoke reduced) top. FAIENCE. Wheel introduced Meydum ware. Extensive trade brought foreign pottery and stylistic changes. Rich painted style developed. Wheel more efficient. Faience developed. Roman Occupati[on]

Persia: Richly painted wares from Tepe Giyan, Susa, Tepe Sialk. Development of form and decoration for use in rituals

Crete: Minoan civilization. Richly painted style based on naturalistically painted decoration

FAR EAST

India: Indus Valley. Very well made. Painted decoration

China: Neolithic Period. Urns, made out of red clay, richly painted swirling patterns in red, black and brown. Kansu Province, Yellow River. Bronze Age metalwork had strong influence on form of pots. Cooking vessels in grey clay with tripod feet. Experiments with more carefully prepared clay a[nd] high firing temperatures

Korea: Little is known about early pottery but it is assumed to follow that of China

Japan: Hand-built methods followed. Joman style. Coil-built urns with impressed decoration of cords

EUROPE

Greece: Mycenaean culture. Minyan ware. Highly refined. Classical Greek Period. Geometric style. Black-Figure style. Red figu[re] style

Italy: Villanovan civilization. Hard, grey pottery. Etruscan grey ware. Rome established

Byzantium:

Spain: Beaker folk (?) emigrated to other parts of Europe. Iberians. Painted style influenced by Greek export ware. Coarse pottery in Roman style

Netherlands: Bowls and urns with incised decoration. Wheel introduced. Pottery made in imitation of iron forms. Impressed decoration

Germany: Hand-built wares.

AMERICA

North:

Central: Archaic Period. Jars and bowls found. FORMATIVE PERIOD. Wide range of forms, mainly for domestic use – cooki[ng] pots, storage vessels, water pots. Decoration – slip. painted and resist. Burnished surfaces. Incised pattern[s]

South: Earliest pottery found in Ecuador. Archaic Period. Chavin and Cuprisnique style. Mould-made ware. Stirrup handle. Incised decoration. Northern Andes region

GREAT BRITAIN

Pottery introduced from the Continent. Hand-built bowls for holding seeds etc. Cooking pots. Beaker folk. Hand-built forms with incised forms. Cinerary urns with incised and applied decoration. Iron Age. Simple wheel introduced. Forms imitated more closely thos[e] of iron. Incised decoration

100 200 300 400	500 600 700 800 900	1000 1100 1200 1300 1400	1500 1600 1700 1800 1900
n unglazed			Isnik wares
	ISLAMIC RELIGION Unglazed ware Lead-glazed ware Tin-glazed ware Lustreware	Underglaze painting Lustrewares	
an upation Christian influence Coptic		Rich lustre-ware made Painted wares	
Large storage vessels often moulded Rich turqoise alkaline glaze	East Persia painted style Sgraffito wares	Kashan, Rayy } Centres Seljuq wares Artificial body Decorated and lustrewares	Blue and white wares Gombroon wares Kubachi wares
ade with Roman npire brought ad glaze heel used extensively. oulds used onze still most teemed material d forms imitated Kilns improved Unsettled period. Trade disrupted. Further improvement in high temperature firing	Settled period. Trade with Islamic Empire brought lead glaze. Rich lead-glazed ware with splash decoration developed. Yueh, green, white, and many other high-temperature wares developed	Classic period for pottery. Stoneware and porcelain made Ting and Ch'ing pai wares Chun wares Northern Celadons Ju ware Tz'u-chou wares Lung-ch'uan wares Chien wares, etc. Ching-te Chen. Imperial porcelain factory established Blue and white wares Copper-red decoration Enamel decoration	Large export trade Influence on form and decoration "Famille verte" enamel decoration Swatow wares Yi-hsing wares Blanc-de-chine Porcelain wares very refined but forms dull
High fired glazes developed Strong Chinese influence	Celadon ware Fine white wares	Style shows marked differences to that of China Closed country. Develoment of free, peasant type of decoration of free and vigorous brushwork	
Strong Chinese influence via Korea Olive-green stoneware glazes and lead-glazed ware		Stoneware made in Japanese style at six main centres	Pottery made for tea ceremony Porcelain made at Arita (Imari) Exported to West. Raku made Studio potters Hamada etc.
an upation			
an Empire -gloss wares se wares l glazed wares	Domestic pottery Lead-glazed and unglazed	Imported Islamic decorated wares Tin-glaze wares Archaic style – Formal – Renaissance Lustre Sgraffito wares – North Italy	Porcelain Influence of Chinese
Constantinople established as capital. Influences from West and East Lead-glazed and painted wares on buff body Applied and sgraffito decoration on red body			
Visigoths Painted wares Impressed decoration	Fine pottery imported from Islamic countries	"Cuerda-seca" technique used Blue and white painted bowls Lustre developed at Malaga Blue, white and gold wares of Manises	Alcora Underglaze decorated ware at Talavera de la Reina
		Red earthenware made Tin-glazed earthenware in Italian style	Delft-ware similar to imported blue and white style Fine red unglazed stoneware
an upation -gloss wares se wares -glazed wares	Higher fired wares developed Pingsdorf and Badorf kiln sites Buff ware with red vitreous slips	Ware exported in Europe SALTGLAZE DEVELOPED Raeren and Cologne brown wares Siegburg white wares Genzhausen coloured wares. Kreussen enamel wares	Bauhaus influenced much of European design
olo Indians settle in south-east n undecorated pottery orated pottery made in Eastern odlands	Plain grey ware in form of gourds and baskets. Built in coils Cooking pots White slip decoration	Finest pots made Black and white slip decoration Many individual styles of decoration Polychrome decorative style developed. Patterns of geometrical forms as well as natural objects. Glaze used only for decorative purposes	Spanish Conquest. but many styles continued to be made in many areas NORTH AMERICA 1800 Industrial firms producing a wide range of functional and decorative wares in earthenware and low-temperature porcelain 1900 "Art" pottery produced, e.g. Newark, New Jersey 1950 Studio pottery produced. Strong Japanese influence Free use of clay for objects and sculpture, e.g. Voulkos "Pop" influence
SSIC PERIOD er development of basic forms and growth. dividual style. Teotihuacan, Maya chrome style developed	POST CLASSIC PERIOD Break-up of peaceful city states. Pottery forms continued much as before. Designs less vigorous	Aztec domination Montezuma Mazipan style Cholula pottery Spanish Conquest	Redware Saltglaze ware
hica: fine mould-made wares, additional incised and modelled ration. South Andes: Nazca; mould e, wide range of rich painted decoration. y other styles		Chimu pottery – continued earlier. Mochica style. Chancay pottery – simple forms, added human figures Incas Limited pottery range but technically excellent	
an Occupation se pottery made at y centres – Castor, Forest, Aldgate, hester, St Albans and wheels introduced Anglo-Saxon urns. Well made with impressed and incised decoration. Dark firing body Cooking pots	Technical improvements introduced mainly from the Rhineland St Neots Ipswich Thetford Stamford glazed ware Fast wheels Improved kilns Lead glazes Saxo-Norman wares	Medieval style Jugs and pitchers. Wheel-thrown, thin bodied, finely thrown wares. Lead glazes dusted on unfired pots. Simple incised and slip-trailed decoration. Made mainly in south-east Domestic pots Tudor wares with bright green glaze imitating metalwork Cistercian wares. Dark brown glaze over hard red body. Made principally in monasteries	Tin-glazed earthenware London, Liverpool and Bristol Red earthenware. Mainly for local areas. Slipware decoration. Especially in Staffordshire Saltglaze stoneware Art pottery Doulton, etc. Martin Brothers Creamwares Wedgwood Industrial pottery Porcelain Studio pottery Leach, Cardew, Staite Murray

100 200 300 400 500 600 700 800 900 1000 1100 1200 1300 1400 1500 1600 1700 1800 1900

1 THE EARLY CIVILIZATIONS

The invention of the processes of pottery –
modelling and shaping the plastic clay, drying
it out and then baking it in the fire to turn the
clay into pot – is lost in the obscurity of time.
From archaeological discoveries we can trace
the use and development of different making
techniques and the wide variety of patterns
and designs used on the pots, all of which tell
us much about the nature of the society in
which they were made. In later periods more

Jar with painted decoration in a scarlet red, black
and cream pattern, from Ur, Jemdet Nasr period,
3100–2900 BC, South Mesopotamia. (British
Museum)

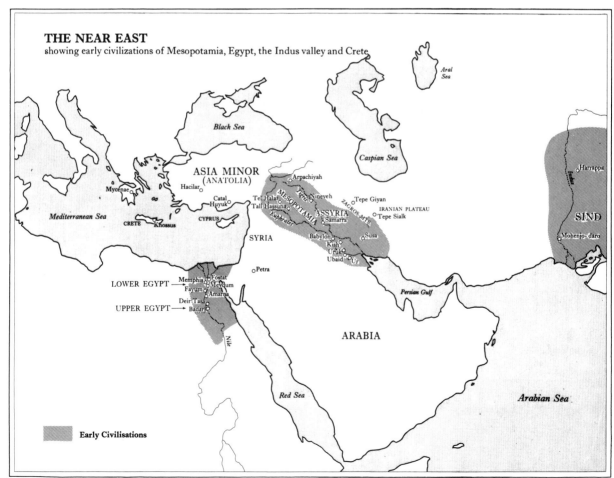

THE NEAR EAST
showing early civilizations of Mesopotamia, Egypt, the Indus valley and Crete

Early Civilisations

sophisticated firing techniques were developed; kilns became more efficient and eventually the ability to produce a shiny waterproof surface, known as glaze, on the pot, was invented. This chapter describes the basic processes of the potter and their use and development in early civilizations.

Basic materials and processes

The qualities which make plastic clay immediately attractive to children are probably qualities which attracted early peoples who, as far as we can tell, shaped simple pots and modelled small figures. What could seem to be more natural than to pick up a lump of clay from a river bed or by the side of a lake and press it into shapes with the fingers? From very early times myth and magic has played an important part in the life of different communities and societies and it is more than probable that symbolic figures were modelled in clay at this stage as part of fertility rituals and ceremonies. Only later, as societies became more settled, were pots made as con-

tainers for food or seeds or religious purposes.

Clay itself has no characteristic form. Depending on the amount of water present in the clay, it occurs naturally as a dry, powdery solid, as a sticky but plastic mass or as a lumpy liquid. All these states are useful to the potter in different ways, but the plastic state is the one which responds most quickly to the potter's hands.

Clay is made up of tiny particles that are flat and plate-like, each with an electrical charge on the surface which causes them to cling and hold together. The addition of water enables the particles to slide over one another without breaking apart. Too much water results in a formless mess while too little prevents any movement. As the water in the clay evaporates, the clay shrinks in size and becomes hard and brittle, but it will soften if water is added. Unlike materials such as wood or ivory, clay itself does not impose any restriction on the shapes which can be made. Nevertheless, some shapes are much better and easier to make than others. It would, for example, be possible to make a pair of scissors in clay, though they would have little mechanical strength. The limits on form which clay imposes can only be extended at the risk of structural weakness.

The major factor determining the form and shape of the pots has always been, until the introduction and development of industrial methods of production, the method of manufacture. Wheel-made pots, for example, which came relatively late in the evolution of pottery, must be round and their shape can only be modified by further processes. Pots made from slabs of clay will have flat or curved sides in a flat base, while pots made from pinching out shapes from a lump of clay are limited to a certain size and will probably be round. Early potters often used simple moulds such as shells, gourds or old pots as a base for the pot. Ropes, coils or rings of clay were built up on this base and then smoothed over to form an even wall.

Female figure modelled in terracotta. Taxila 2000–3000 BC (Victoria & Albert Museum, London)

Far right: Slab-built heating pot from Pompeii

Ant-eater water pot from the Omagua tribe, Brazilian Indian (British Museum)

Most pots are circular, and even before the wheel was invented the majority were rounded as a result of the method of making rather than the demands of the clay. It is much easier, for example, to squeeze out a round pinch pot than a square one. In spite of this there are, however, many surviving pots which are not circular: rectangular dishes, oval bowls and, from Crete, rectangular troughs divided into partitions.

Because clay itself has no defining form and no intrinsic value, objects made from clay have often taken on the form and appearance of things made in other materials. Throughout the whole history of pottery the imitation in clay of other objects and materials has been evident. There are many examples of this: some pots have imitated natural forms, such as gourds, ostrich eggs and bamboo, and many have copied objects made from materials which impose a strong form such as basketry. Such things as wooden trays, leather bags and bottles have all been copied at some time. Later, as bronze and metal-working developed, these objects were the predominant forms which were imitated.

Early discoveries

We can only speculate on the earliest uses of clay such as for tribal identification marks, as material for building or strengthening shelters; none of it had been hardened by fire. Only with the discovery that heat changes clay into a material which is unaltered by water can we say the history of pottery begins.

The use of clay seems to have been developed independently by different people in different parts of the world. Nomadic races would have little time or use for fragile pottery and so it was with the beginnings of the more

Two small drinking urns, handbuilt, with dark brown glaze. Tibet, mid-nineteenth century. (Victoria & Albert Museum, London)

settled life of the New Stone Age that the making of pots started. Before then images of men, women and animals were modelled in a clay and were used for magical or religious purposes. Mother goddesses with enlarged sexual organs have been excavated in various parts of the world, including the Indus Valley and Mesopotamia, and date back to prehistoric times. These were part of the religious cult encouraging fertility for the birth of babies and good-sized crops. As the tribes settled the ritual figures and objects were hardened in the fire, and now give us important information about the societies of the time. It is possible that such figures, along with shells and coloured stones could have been used for trade.

How the discovery was made that dried clay, subjected to red heat, about 600°C (1112°F), would become hard and not disintegrate in water, is not known. It is probable that the idea developed over a considerable period of time and there are two theories to

Earthenware cistern with moulded decoration and green-coloured lead glaze. England, sixteenth century. (Victoria & Albert Museum, London)

Lidded pot in the form of a snake. Stoneware with cream-coloured glaze. Chinese Sung Dynasty. $4\frac{1}{2}$ inches tall. (Victoria & Albert Museum, London)

account for it. The first, and possibly the more valid, is the hearth theory. Fire was a valuable and vital part of early societies and cultures, providing warmth and light, as well as frightening away animals; it was also used for cooking food. It would be carefully tended and maintained. Holes were made in the ground and these could well have been lined with clay. The fire kept in such a hearth would turn the clay into pot and when the fire was eventually put out a crude vessel would be left.

The second theory is that baskets would have been lined with wet clay to render them waterproof and in due course, as the clay dried out and contracted, a simple pot would be formed which could have held fire.

Such clay-lined baskets could also have been burned in the fire, which would have left a simple fired pot behind. Such a theory presupposes the existence of basketry. In some early cultures basketry existed without pottery but in others pottery without basketry. All that

can be assumed is that a successful combination of social, technical and economic factors resulted in the discovery that clay changes to pot when heated sufficiently.

Clay preparation

Clay occurs over most of the earth's surface and, while some of it may be more plastic or of a different colour, the basic working qualities are much the same, though in early civilizations, as well as today, good usable clay was highly valued. Some tribes travelled many miles to collect workable clay or clay of a particular colour. Much of the success of the Athenian and Corinthian potters of Ancient Greece was due to a large extent to the fine smooth clays readily available to them. The Pueblo potters of Zuni in south-west North America brought clay from the top of a mountain because of its workable qualities. In Ancient Egypt the smooth red Nile clays resulted in the finely made Badarian wares. During the seventeenth century clay was taken from East Anglia to Holland to be used for Delftware because it was better suited to the needs of fine white maiolica. As pottery became a more specialist activity the availability of good clays became a major factor; the clay had to be easily accessible, relatively clean, free from impurities or foreign matter such as stones or vegetation and the right colour. It had to be plastic so that it could be moulded and worked, and able to withstand the heat of the fire without collapsing. The pottery industry which developed in Britain in the eighteenth century depended on making a fine white body from clays brought from different regions of the country.

Clay which was used for handbuilding pots would have been carefully prepared. First, any stones or other foreign bodies which would cause the pot to crack as it dried or to explode in the firing would have been removed, and secondly, it would have been made even throughout by a process called wedging. This was a combination of banging and kneading which was done either with the feet or hands. If large pots were to be made, some sort of filler, such as broken up shells, sand or grit, would be added to the clay to open it, making it easier to control when modelling and, in the case of cooking pots, more able to withstand the rapid expansion known as thermal shock which had to take place when the pot was placed on the fire.

Making methods

Before the invention of the wheel, pottery was made entirely by hand by one of several methods or by a combination of methods:

1 Pinch pots were made in the hand by

Coil-built pot with a splashed resin glaze, Africa.

squeezing and manipulating clay between the fingers.

2 Coil or ring pots were made by placing lengths of clay on top of each other, joining them together and smoothing them over. This enabled the construction of much larger pots.

3 Pots were made using a mould or a former. Clay was made into slabs, or laid in rings

Press-moulded pot from the Middle East, bearing a Chinese motif. About 6 inches tall. (British Museum)

either over natural forms such as gourds, or forms such as baskets or other pots; sometimes the clay was smeared on the inside of a mould such as a basket or on the outside in the case of solid moulds such as stones.

4 Slabs of clay, made by cutting or beating a block of clay, were built up to form flat-sided 'troughs' or other angular forms.

5 Pots could also be made by patting out clay from a lump using an outside beater and an inner support often shaped like a mushroom. These tools are sometimes known respectively as the paddle and anvil; they were also used, as in the Indus Valley, to complete the form of a pot thrown on the wheel.

Most of the early potters sat on the floor and probably used either the inside of their thighs to support the pot or rested it on a disc or mat on the floor in front of them. This enabled the pot to be turned round much more easily. Such concave discs have survived from the Indus Valley. In some societies it was the women who were the potters: along with caring for the living area they prepared plots of land, ground and cooked the grain, spun, wove, made clothes, prepared ornaments and magical articles as well as fashioned and baked pots. It was probably the men who cleared the land, built huts, tended the livestock, hunted, and manufactured the tools and weapons. In other societies it was the men who were the potters. With the evolution of more urban societies and the establishment of fairly large groups of skilled workers, when pots were made on a wheel, pottery became highly specialized work which was probably done by the men and women as an industry.

The wheel was invented in Mesopotamia around 3–4000 BC, and was adopted for use by the potter. At first the stone or wooden wheel, pivoted in the ground, was used; this enabled pots to be made much more quickly. The wheel was either pushed or kicked round and the impetus of the wheel was sufficient to enable pots to be made. This completely new technique not only speeded up production but meant the clay had to be more plastic to enable it to be smoothed into shape; it also had a strong influence on the form, as all pots made by this method had to be round and no sharp curves or angles were possible. Because the pots had also to be made quickly to prevent the clay from collapsing, they developed a new freedom and spontaneity, though the forms generally became more standard. Decoration, too, was affected; horizontal bands could be drawn quickly and easily on the revolving pots and this method of decoration began to predominate.

As technology developed, the wheel became more sophisticated. The pivot was

The god Khum depicted working on a kick wheel.

An Indian potter pushing a pottery wheel round with a stick.

improved and eventually a shaft was fitted to the wheel-head and a flywheel added at the base, so that a faster, smoother action was obtained. This basic wheel is still used in some Middle East countries.

Finishing the pots

Pottery fired to the fairly low temperatures obtainable by simple kilns and hearth firings was porous and sometimes fragile. Until the waterproof covering known as glaze was in widespread use other methods had to be used to render the pottery impervious and give it strength. Different finishes were obtained by various methods, many for practical reasons such as to make pots stronger and smoother, as well as to make them more waterproof. One common method was to burnish the clay when it was not quite dry. The surface was rubbed with a smooth stone or pebble which pressed the surface flat, giving it a dull, attractive shine and making it less porous. The shine remained after firing. The other most popular method was to cover the surface of the pot with a slip of fine clay, prepared by removing the larger particles, such as was used by the Greeks on their red and black painted ware to give a decorated as well as a smooth surface.

Pots could be blackened during the firing to make them more attractive. Towards the end of the firing the pots were covered with wet leaves which produced smoke that penetrated the pores and made the whole pot a black colour in the process known as 'carbon smoking'.

On other pots a vegetable 'glaze', made by boiling leaves or bark until a strong solution was obtained, was applied to the pot still hot from the fire. Though the results were not as permanent as a true glaze, the pot was made more waterproof. Some African potters still use this method.

Firing

Clay is changed into pot by heating it as evenly as possible to red heat and above (about 600°C, or 1112°F). The earliest firings were probably carried out in the domestic hearth though open bonfires would also have been used and this method can still be seen in, among other places, Nigeria. In this method the fire is slowly started round the thin-walled and rounded-shape pots, gradually built up, and then the whole is covered with grass, reeds or cattle dung to protect the contents from cold air. Only comparatively low temperatures can be obtained by this method and glaze cannot be used. The colour of the pots is affected by the flames and smoke, giving uneven results.

Kilns were fairly specialized pieces of basic equipment and it was only with the establishment of pottery centres that they were developed. They were, at first, simple updraught kilns built from clay; the fire was made underneath an arrangement of arches which supported the pots in the kiln. Pots were stacked in the kiln from the top and this was then covered over with broken pots, mud or earth, leaving a small hole for the smoke. Even so simple a kiln gave much more control than an open bonfire; it retained the heat and kept fire and pots separate; it allowed for a controllable draught and kept the pots together in one place.

Later, more sophisticated kilns developed: the flames were made to stay inside the kiln longer by directing them first to the top and then to the exit flue at the bottom. This latter arrangement is called a 'downdraught' kiln; it had the advantage of retaining more heat and enabled higher temperatures to be reached.

The earliest pots

On our present knowledge the earliest pottery comes from Anatolia; it is associated with cave-dwelling communities of the late Mesolithic period and dates to not later than 6500 BC though recent researches suggest that the date may be earlier. The earliest wares were undecorated and made from the local reddish-brown clay. This was followed in the same area by a group of painted wares which date from around 5000 BC. Designs painted in red pigment on to a cream slip in geometrical patterns were the most common. The designs were put onto the pots after they had been fired. The whole pot was burnished to give a rich and pleasing effect. The painting on the pots reflected the contemporary interest in wall paintings. Similar pigments could

Pot in form of tortoise, incised decoration, clear vegetable glaze over red clay. Melanesia, nineteenth century. Length 7 inches. (Anthropological Museum, University of Aberdeen)

Anthropomorphic vase from Haçilar, Turkey, c 5000 BC. Height 6 inches. (Ashmolean Museum, Oxford)

have been used for the pots and for painting and were derived from local clays of different colours.

From these early beginnings the basic style of Middle Eastern pottery developed which remained basically unchanged until the use of the wheel and of glaze became widespread some time after 2000 BC. Hand-building methods were used and the surface of the pots was often burnished to give a smooth, slightly shiny appearance. Some pots were left plain while others were decorated, sometimes with impressed designs but more often painted with clays and pigments in simple geometrical patterns. Undoubtedly, potters of the Mesopotamian civilization owed a great deal of their skill to the Anatolian potters.

Mesopotamia

In the fertile land between the rivers Tigris and Euphrates known as Mesopotamia, the earliest known civilization developed.

Hassuna period (5000–4500 BC)

Early settlements in which the peasants lived in farmhouses, cultivated crops, kept cattle and sheep, wove materials and made pots date back to between 5000 and 4500 BC. This is known as the Hassuna Period. The pots of the time were well developed and fall into two

main types. The first group, from north Mesopotamia, comes from the area which was later to become Assyria. Bowls and globular jars have been found at, among other centres, Nineveh and Tell Hassuna. What makes the pottery characteristic is the simple incised linear designs. Samarra ware, named after the site where it was found, forms the second group. It is characterized by painted rather than incised decoration. Simple geometrical designs were painted in red and purplishbrown pigment on to a matt cream slip. Occasionally semi-stylized natural motifs of human and animal figures were incorporated into the designs. It is probable that Samarra ware originated in the Iranian plateau to the east and was either imported or brought by people moving into the more fertile country of Mesopotamia.

Halaf period (c 4500–4000 BC)

In the Halaf Period, c 4500–4000 BC, named after Tell Halaf, two technological developments were made which were to influence the

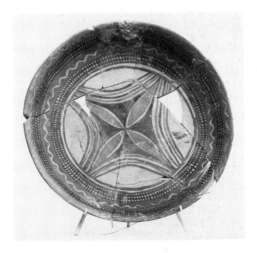

Painted bowl from Arpachiyah, Mesopotamia. Polychrome design painted in black and red on a buff slip. Halaf Period, c 4500–4000 BC. (British Museum)

manufacture of pottery and culminate in one of the richest wares in the Near East. The first was the development of kilns which enabled pots with painted decorations to be fired so that they retained their clear colours. In earlier kilns the pots came into contact with the flame and smoke which coloured them red, black and brown; any painted decoration would, to a large extent, be lost beneath these firing colours. The use of a kiln in which the chamber for the pots was kept separate from the fire-box was a great step forward.

The other development was the making of a pottery glaze which resulted from attempts to reproduce the stone lapis lazuli. Probably because of its bright ultramarine colour and attractive surface it was highly prized. Its natural occurrence was rare, and efforts were made to reproduce it synthetically by carving small objects such as beads in soapstone (a form of talc stone) covering the surface with powdered ores of copper such as azurite or malachite, and heating them until the surface melted and formed a simple glass. Though only indirectly related to pottery, it was probably in this beginning that the origins of glass and glaze lie.

Pottery now became more varied and complex: thinner walls and flaring shapes suggest metal prototypes. Rims, for example, were made which curled over in a way more suited to metal, and the profile of the pots often seemed to echo metal shapes. This was the beginning of the Bronze Age period during which time metal-working became highly developed and metal products highly valued. Clay was more carefully prepared and the kiln-fired pots, having reached a high temperature, were quite hard and much stronger. Thin-walled bowls, jars with rounded rims and sharply curved sides and a variety of round-bottomed vessels indicate the range of shapes. Red and black pigments were painted on to the pots before they were fired. Designs included geometrical shapes and floral and natural motifs which often developed into complete schematic patterns such as the so-called 'Bull's Head' and 'Double Axe'. Samarra ware continued to be made throughout this period and many modelled female figures of this date have also been found. These were made in limestone and pumice as well as in fired clay.

Ubaid period (c 4000–3500 BC)

During the Ubaid Period, c 4000–3500 BC, Sumer at the head of the Persian Gulf became the principal city and main pottery centre. Ur, Uruk and Kish were other main cities. Stone was rare and clay bricks were made with which to build cities. It was during this period that the axle was developed which was later adapted for use on the potter's wheel permitting faster speeds and smoother action.

The potter's wheel was not the fast, smooth machine we know today. It developed slowly: first the pot was set on a movable base such as a mat or potsherd; this base was then pivoted to enable it to turn more easily, and finally the slow wheel was developed. A heavy wheelhead of stone or wood was pushed round to enable the pots to be built up. It was not until much later that the free and fast-running wheels came into use. However, the effect of even a simple wheel was considerable as pots could be made much more quickly and with greater uniformity.

Improvements in kiln design continued and the first excavated kiln dates from this period. These two developments – the slow wheel and kiln – changed the whole nature of pottery. Clay which had been suitable for hand-building methods of manufacture now had to be more carefully prepared. Coarser particles of stone had to be removed as they hindered the working of the clay on the slow wheel. This was done by reducing the clay to a liquid state which enabled the finer particles to be tapped off while the coarser pieces sank to the bottom, in the process known as levigating. This process is also important as it was the basis of the decorative technique used on Greek and Roman pottery which will be explained more fully in the next chapter.

Pottery from this period has a characteristic pale olive-green colour; the shapes were more uniform than before and as the area developed were manufactured over a wider area. Extensive intercommunication over much of the Near East encouraged the distribution of techniques as well as of the pottery itself. Brushwork decoration became much more fluid and alive and the designs became more intricate and ambitious. The pots themselves were more finely made.

From around 3500–2800 BC, Uruk ware was produced in the south of Mesopotamia at Warka (Uruk) in the area which was later to become Babylonia. A rich, painted pottery style developed in which complex designs were carried out in black, red and brown in ornate patterns including geometrical and stylized naturalistic motifs. In the north, pots were decorated with either painted decoration of animals in a single colour or incised with ornate geometrical patterns.

Discoveries during the period c2000–1000 BC in Mesopotamia eventually led to the production of a proper glaze which was used first on bricks and later on pots. Around 2000 BC true glass was made by melting sand, quartz and alkaline fluxes together; though it was not moulded or blown while it was a hot liquid, but was carved and polished like stone

Stone pottery wheel-head from Ur, Mesopotamia. *c* 2200 BC. (British Museum)

Two finely made and painted beakers from Susa, Persia. *c* 3500–2800 BC. Height 6 inches. (British Museum)

when solid, it was a major development. During the period 2000–1000 BC glass was produced which could be worked while still hot and fluid; it was also discovered that the glass could be coloured by the addition of metal oxides of copper to give turquoise, cobalt to give blue and tinstone to make it opaque white. All these metal oxides were later used to colour glazes. For the first time lead was added to the glass frit and it was found that this not only gave greater brilliance and enabled the glass to be worked more easily, but also reduced the shrinkage when the glass was cooling. This meant that the glass frit could, when ground up, be used as the basis for glaze, and that, for the first time, glazing was possible. The main difficulty in using glazes containing alkalis like soda as a flux to cause the sand to melt had been the amount the liquid glass contracted on cooling. This usually prevented the glaze from staying on the surface of the clay. From the discovery of the benefits of lead the Mesopotamians seem to have developed a lead glaze suitable for use on pottery. An ancient glaze recipe on a clay tablet found in northern Iraq and dating back to 1700 BC is, in modern notation:

Glass	243.0	Saltpetre	3.1
Lead	40.1	Lime	5.0
Copper	58.1		

The amount of lead is significant in that this particular proportion enabled the glaze to be applied successfully to clay. Pots with a blue-green glaze have been found in northern Syria and date to the period 1700–1400 BC.

Bricks and tiles were decorated with the lead glaze which was rendered white opaque by the addition of the tinstone. Metal oxides were painted on to the surface to add colour. The decorated tiles were used with great effect on the doorways and gates in Babylon. Little effort seems to have been made to apply this glaze to pottery in general.

Alkaline glaze made from soda potash and sand seems to have been used on pots throughout the Near East at this time with moderate success.

Persia

Persia, lying to the east of Mesopotamia on the Iranian plateau, separated from Mesopotamia by the Zagros Mountains, has a long history of painted decorated ware.

Sites such as those at Tepe Sialk and Tepe Giyan have been excavated, and reveal that around 2500 BC pottery similar to that of the Ubaid culture of Mesopotamia existed in this area. The style may have originated here much earlier and been taken to Mesopotamia by the movement of the people from the more barren highlands to the fertile lowlands.

It is from Susa on the plateau that some of the finest pottery comes. Shapes were well thought out and achieved a high degree of technical ability. They included jars and bowls, as well as shapes like chalices and goblets which are made in two parts, as a bowl and a stem, which are then joined together. The designs, native to Iran, were finely painted and well related to the shape of the pot. Combinations of geometric and semi-stylized natural forms such as the leopard were used to decorate the pots.

Later at Tepe Sialk, around 1000 BC, a new series of ornate and sophisticated shapes developed. Long-spouted vessels, perhaps imitating birds, were produced and decorated with painted geometrical forms as well as animals. These spouted vessels were probably made for contemporary ritual purposes and could have been used to pour water in ritual (and practical) washing ceremonies. The designs on the pots owe a great deal to the earlier traditions of painted wares.

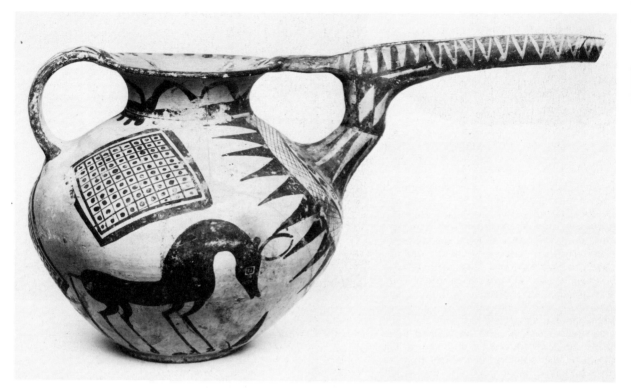

Spouted flask from Sialk, Persia. Long spouts and a rich decorative style characterize this ware which was probably for use in rituals. *c* 1000 BC. Height 14½ inches. (British Museum)

Glazed tiles with rich colours and imaginative designs were used at the Palace of Darius, Susa, for wall decoration incorporating turquoise, brown, yellow, green and white colours.

Syria and Anatolia

Syria, lying to the north-west of Mesopotamia on the upper reaches of the Euphrates, and Anatolia in Asia Minor, show developments similar to that of Mesopotamia. However the nature of the area as a landbridge linking east and west brought influences from both directions and it is more difficult to isolate and identify the pottery styles which show influences of shape, technique and decoration from countries over a large part of the Mediterranean and Middle East.

Finely made pottery, decorated with bold simple swirling patterns, dates from before 4000 BC in Anatolia, which has been referred to, and probably influenced later Mesopotamian pottery. Syrian contacts with Mesopotamia can be identified from as early as 3500 BC by, among other things, similarities in architectural detail and fresco painting and it can be assumed that these contacts extended to the exchanging of information about pottery. For example, the shape of chalices, bottles, bowls and beakers found in Syria show a marked Mesopotamian influence. Styles which developed in areas bordering on

the Mediterranean to the west can also be seen in some of the pottery. Bottles, found in Syria, dating back to 2500 BC, show influences from pre-Minoan Crete and the Aegean area. On some pottery the merging of the eastern and western styles can be seen.

All local styles were more or less destroyed when the Assyrian armies destroyed the Syrian cities in the ninth to the seventh centuries BC. A century later, in 538 BC, the Babylonians, who had conquered the Assyrians of north Mesopotamia, were defeated by the Persians in alliance with the Medes. So the whole area, including the Iranian plateau, fell under the control of a single ruler, which helped to unify styles and techniques. This area, with its long tradition of finely made and richly decorated wares, eventually saw the rise to power of the Islamic Empire which continued to favour decorated pottery with designs and motifs; these were one of the major characteristics.

Egypt
Early periods (*c 5000–3200 BC*)

The earliest Egyptian pottery was made in the central Nile Valley and forms one of the most aesthetically pleasing groups of wares made in Egypt. Between 5000 and 4000 BC the flourishing Badarian culture produced a range of highly accomplished, thin-walled pottery of which the earliest wares from Deir Tasa

Badarian bowl, from Egypt. Fine, thin, hard walls with 'chattered' decoration and blackened rim. One of the finest of the Nile Valley wares, c 4000 BC. Diameter 11 inches. (Petrie Collection, University College London.)

consisted of deep bowls with flat bases and angular sides narrowing towards the mouth. Beakers with flared rims were often decorated with incised lines filled with white pigment. Later on the Badarian wares became even finer; using carefully prepared red Nile clay the pots were very strongly made with thin walls, lightly burnished to give them a dull shine and well fired.

Forms were on the whole simple and combined well with the black, brown and red colours of the body and occasional combed decoration. The entire production seems restrained and uncomplicated, being mainly cooking pots with rounded bases and no rims or necks.

Fayum, in the west of the Nile Valley, was also an early production area though the pots were not as finely made as Badarian wares: the pots were fairly coarse and the body was filled with chopped chaff to increase the working qualities of the clay. No decoration seems to have been used and the shapes were irregular.

A typical Gerzean pot with lugged handles. Full, globular form with rounded rim and painted spiral pattern. Other designs copied rope patterns as well as natural stone patterns of alabaster. Egypt, c 3300 BC. Height 5 inches. (Petrie Collection, University College London.)

Gerzean jar. Dark painted designs on buff clay show ship with emblem, aloe and flamingos. Egypt, c 3200 BC. (Petrie Collection, University College London)

In pre-dynastic Egypt dating from around 3500 BC to 3200 BC pottery continued to be made much as in the early period. Essentially the style was monochrome and undecorated and made from the red Nile clay, though new shapes and techniques were developed. Undoubtedly the main product was the black-topped red wares. Tall storage jars with pointed bases, and beakers, all highly burnished, were made and were probably fired upside down with their mouths buried in ash to achieve the black-coloured top: the technique did not lend itself easily to shallow bowls and dishes. Occasionally animals in low relief were modelled on the pots and, rarely, animals were incised into the surface.

The red polished Badarian pottery continued to be finely made, and further technical improvements were achieved; the colour was more regular, the gloss was higher and the range was extended to include a wider variety of shapes. Dishes and bowls, narrow-necked vases, bulbous flasks and long-necked vessels were common. Double-lobed and spouted vessels were more rare. All the pots were hand-built and no evidence of the use of the wheel has so far been found.

Early dynasties (c 3250–2700 BC)

Egypt was united as a single country in 3250 BC by Menes. The country was tightly governed, scientific knowledge was carefully controlled, and art formed part of religious belief. Rigid rules about the way paintings and sculpture should be carried out ensured that in the following 3000 years little change was made. Paintings, executed according to strict rules on the walls of tombs, depicted scenes which would be useful to the deceased in the next world and were perhaps characteristic

scenes from the life of the dead person. Such a rigid and inflexible system did not allow, let alone encourage, much movement in art. Pottery made in this period lost much of the vitality it had had earlier.

Cream-coloured clay free from organic matter was used; it was found in desert valleys in Middle and Upper Egypt and, when fired, became grey or buff in colour. Decoration was painted on to the light-coloured pots with iron oxide, which became purplish-red when fired, and white slip. The natural stone patterns of alabaster were often copied and more elaborate designs of boats, men and women, birds, trees and other objects were carried out. Unlike the formal arts of painting and sculpture few if any rules defined the decoration of pots, which were often unsophisticated and lively. Little regard seems to have been paid to the symmetry of the designs. Some stylistic developments were made; handles, for instance, fixed on to the side of the pots, were made for the first time in Egypt. Forms became more cylindrical, imitating the results obtained from contemporary stone working.

Old kingdom (c 2700–2100 BC)

During the Old Kingdom, about 2700–2100 BC, two major developments, both inspired by discoveries in other countries were introduced. The first was the simple slow wheel

brought from Mesopotamia. The shapes of pots became finer and owe much to metal prototypes. Spouted ewers, lipped jugs, bowls with in-curving rims, tall libation vessels, tall stands for ritual vessels and low stands for domestic pots are characteristic. Around 2500 BC very fine bowls were produced at Meydum which reflected the contemporary interest in metal-working. These carinate bowls had rounded bottoms and sharply angled sides; the clay was carefully prepared and the walls were thin and highly burnished. The simple forms and decoration gave the bowls a refined, precise, quality which other contemporary pottery lacked.

The second development was the production of moulded glazed objects. Gold, copper, precious stones, ivory, alabaster and wood were all worked with great skill. There was much interest in producing an artificial paste to replace the soap-stone which had been used in the manufacture of small glazed objects in what is often known as Egyptian faience. This mixture was a development of the technique used in Mesopotamia and was made by putting together powdered quartz sand with an alkaline material known as a flux, which caused the quartz sand to fuse at a workable temperature. Potash, which occurs in wood-ash, and natron, which is a mineral containing sodium found in the western desert of Egypt, were the fluxes used. Small objects moulded in such a mixture would, when heated to a sufficiently high temperature, form a shiny surface; if small quantities of copper were present in the paste, rich turquoise colours were formed on the surface, while small quantities of manganese gave a purple surface.

The earliest faience objects in Egypt were made in Badari, Upper Egypt, in the form of beads. Small pieces of jewellery, figurines, amulets, vessels for precious liquids such as perfumes or oil, inlays for coffins, furniture and temple walls came later. Small pots made in moulds were fashioned in quite complex shapes, the range of which included baskets with lids and modelled pomegranates, though the objects rarely exceeded three inches in height until about 1000 BC.

Middle kingdom (c 2100–1320 BC)

As trade increased foreign influence became more pronounced, particularly in the manufacture of pottery in the period 2100–1600 BC. Imperial expansion overseas and imported ware from Mycenae, Cyprus and Crete began to affect the forms of Egyptian pottery. From the Mediterranean large numbers of small bottles with narrow necks and handles were imported which probably contained precious perfumes or oils; these in turn were imitated

Holy water jug, faience, from Tutenkamon period Egypt.

Thrown pot with a rich floral decoration. Egypt, 1380–1350 BC.

by the Egyptian potters. The wheel became more efficient, and potters shown at work on the wall of the Egyptian tomb of Beni Hasan *c* 1900 BC appear to make the wheel go round by pushing it with the hand. The geometric patterns easily obtained with the wheel began to be used by the Egyptians, and carefully thrown pots were joined together to produce quite complicated forms. Pots with pedestal feet were made for the first time, imitating those made in the Mediterranean.

In the ruins of Akhetaten (Amarna) large quantities of painted pottery made for the use of the court for special religious purposes, dated to the years 1380–1350 BC, have been found. Many of the pots were large and complex, some over three feet high, and demonstrate the skill of the potters. Painted designs were ornate and well related to the shape of the vessel. Motifs of garlands of flowers, geometrical patterns and tomb scenes were painted in red, blue, white and black pigment after the pots had been fired. The decoration seems to reflect the strongly naturalistic tendencies which inspired the art of the period.

Painted pottery continued to be made after 1350 BC, though changed in character. Designs on the pots were more crowded and less well painted. Decorated pottery that had been made specially for the use of the court was now made for a much larger group of people. Foreign influence continued and the loop handle came into general use. Amphora-type storage pots were made in large quantities.

Late period

Changes in burial customs during the New Kingdom (*c* 1320–750 BC) led to a reduction in the amount and nature of pottery placed in the tomb. It may be that pottery was not now specially manufactured for burial purposes as in the past and the pottery which has been found is on the whole more utilitarian and less exciting. In the late period *c* 750–325 BC a

Pot with stirrup handle and painted and banded geometrical designs shows evidence of foreign influences. Egypt, c 1000 BC. Height 4 inches. (Petrie Collection, University College London)

Above right: Pottery jar, Knossos, Crete, with painted octopus design. Late Minoan, c 1450–1400 BC. Height 18 inches. (Ashmolean Museum, Oxford)

renaissance of Egyptian culture affected most arts and crafts but was less apparent in pottery. Shapes became more complex and the use of lead glaze, already employed in some regions, became more general. The wheel, too, continued to gain in efficiency, lessons perhaps having been learnt from the Greeks. A tomb painting of about 300 BC shows the god Khum sitting at a potter's wheel making a human being; the heavy stone flywheel is shown being pushed round with the foot near the ground; the wheel-head is raised to a height of two feet. Such wheels were in use until the invention of the crank shaft in the late middle ages.

In 30 BC Egypt became a Roman province and the Romans introduced their own methods of making pottery. Around AD 350 the Coptic branch of the Christian Church became a dominant factor and ancient Egyptian designs were fused with classical elements. At the battle of Heliopolis in AD 640 the Islamic Arabs took control of Egypt and further styles and techniques were developed.

Crete

The Minoan culture on the island of Crete was the first civilization in Europe. It rose around 3000 BC and developed and survived for about 1800 years during which time a particularly distinctive and technically accomplished style of pottery was made. Pottery had been made in Crete before the Minoan period and continued to be made long after the civilization had finished but none had the same freshness of design and technical brilliance. Unlike the other early civilizations the Minoan culture developed not in a river valley but on an island. This affected it in a particular

way, for the sea, as well as protecting the islanders from attack, enabled an economy based on trade to develop: they exported oil and wine in pottery vessels, in exchange for corn. This open and free trade brought with it a very cosmopolitan atmosphere. Unlike the Egyptians, the Minoans had neither an oppressive priesthood nor a heavy and determined artistic style, and the culture which developed was rich, free and reflected many different influences.

Chronologically the Minoan civilization is comparable with Egypt, and while Cretan sculpture and architecture were not as technically accomplished as that of Egypt, the pottery was superior, being more varied technically and aesthetically. In contrast to Egyp-

Large coil-built storage jar with cord decoration. Height 45 inches, Crete.

tian pottery, the carefully observed and drawn natural objects used in the decoration of the Minoan pots give much of the work a freshness which is almost modern.

At various times immigrants from Egypt and Mesopotamia brought their skills, and such craftworkers as potters and metal-workers were received as honoured members of society. The nobility used the fine earthenware on their tables and special pots were often richly coloured and very attractive. At their best Minoan pots were thought good enough to bury in the tombs of Egyptian noblemen along with their other treasures.

A wide variety of forms were made: tallstemmed wine cups, imitating wooden chalices, handled vases, pitchers and large storage jars as well as a range of delicate drinking cups and bowls with thin rims and lively but delicate handles. Painted decoration was, however, the chief characteristic of Minoan pottery. Between 2000 and 1550 BC decoration derived from nature was used. At first the designs were stylized, but later during the middle Minoan period (1900–1700 BC) they became much more naturalistic. Several colours, including white, red, blue and black, were used and designs were often painted on to a dark ground. Vivid pictorial representations of plants, lilies, octopus, seaweed and marine life in general were painted with great vigour, often over the whole surface of the pot. The resulting patterns were fresh and naturalistically rendered and lay easily on the surface of the pots; some sources of Greek art are discernible here. The pots were unglazed and the free-flowing natural decoration echoed their smooth round forms.

The Minoan capital of Knossos was destroyed around 1400 BC either by the invading Mycenaeans from the Greek mainland or by an earthquake, or both, and it is only recent excavations which have revealed the enormous achievements of the Minoans.

Three-handled pot with painted design of marine motifs. Crete, late Minoan period, c 1450–1400 BC. Height 5½ inches. (British Museum)

Minoan pots seem, with their detailed observation and naturalistic decoration, to reflect a happy, almost naïve society. No human figures are shown on the pottery and, unlike the Greeks, the Minoans do not seem to have had an obsession with the past, nor did they make any attempt to record contemporary events. The designs are immediate, fresh and light and, unlike later Greek pots, demand little intellectual effort. Although in Crete we see the beginnings of Greek shapes and Greek vase painting there is none of the heaviness which Greek pots sometimes have; here are pictorial, lively, completely unsophisticated designs on sound practical shapes. The work is unique and the qualities it possesses are rarely found in combination. Only with the destruction of Minoan society around 1400 BC and the diminution of trade, did the standard of pottery decline and the decoration lose its vitality.

Indus valley

The Indus civilization, which developed in the alluvial valley of the Indus in north-west India, is thought to have started around 3000 BC and lasted until 1500 BC. It seems to owe much of its technology to Mesopotamia, and the immense cities of Harrappa and Mohenjodaro, now gigantic mounds, leave evidence of the relatively advanced development of the two cities. Carefully planned, they were complicated and well thought out with running water and sanitation. Buildings were made of mud and fired bricks, irrigation was practised, copper and bronze were smelted, Egyptian faience was made and stamped seals were used for identification. Developments in other fields were made independent of Mesopotamia. New crops such as cotton were cultivated, and animals such as the ox were domesticated.

The pottery was technically excellent and much of it has been compared to the wares produced by the Roman Empire and the Victorians: technically accomplished, but extremely standardized and with a general lack of aesthetic sensibility.

Three-footed tankard with painted decoration probably derived from plants. Crete, late Minoan period. c 1450–1400 BC. Height 3 inches. (Fitzwilliam Museum)

Modern Sind potters continue to use a foot-wheel which is almost certainly a legacy of the latter part of this period. Such wheels, which probably came from Mesopotamia, are still used in remote parts of Iran and north Africa. The arrangement of the wheel consists of a pit in which is set a central axis connecting a heavy fly-wheel at the base with a lighter wheel-head at the top, on which the pots are made. The potters sit on the edge of the pit pushing and controlling the fly-wheel with their feet.

Painted decoration took the form of natural motifs such as birds, fish, animals, plants and trees. Though the chemistry of glazing seems to have been understood, little use was made of it. At Mohenjo-daro many broken pots have been found by a water stall; the pots are roughly made and from the evidence it seems they were used once for drinking and then thrown away. Such pots must have been produced both quickly and cheaply by the potters.

Red earthenware jug, wheel-turned and polished. Ayum Chitral District, North-West India. (Victoria & Albert Museum, London)

Earthenware wheel-made pots with painted decoration. Baluchistan. (British Museum)

2 THE GREEKS AND ROMANS

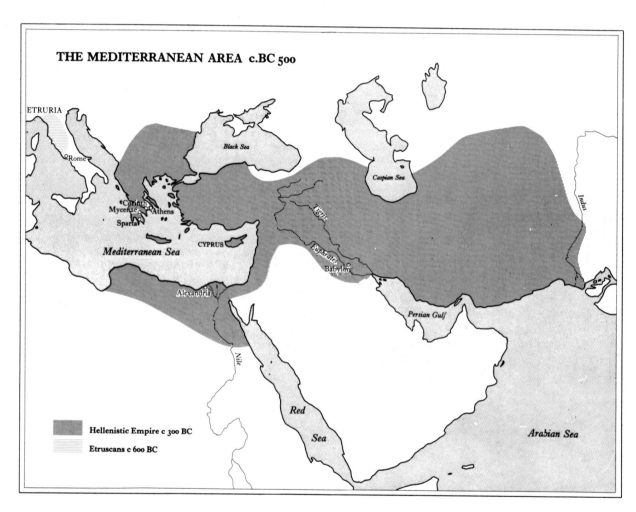

THE MEDITERRANEAN AREA c.BC 500

ETRURIA

Rome

Black Sea

Caspian Sea

Corinth
Mycenae Athens
Sparta

CYPRUS

Mediterranean Sea

Tigris

Euphrates

Babylon

Indus

Alexandria

Persian Gulf

Nile

Red

Sea

Arabian Sea

Hellenistic Empire c 300 BC

Etruscans c 600 BC

By 1500 BC the skills of the potter were well developed; they included the refining of clay, the use of the smooth wheel and the sophisticated kiln; with the rise of Greek civilization and emphasis on all the arts, we can see these skills developed to the full. The Romans adapted and built on these skills and eventually took them across much of Europe.

Mycenae

The mainland of Greece, unlike the Island of Crete, was much slower to develop a settled civilization. Mycenae, a city in southern

Goblet with formal and restrained painted design on buff background. Mycenaean, c 1300 BC. (Fitzwilliam Museum)

Stirrup vase for containing oil. Design mainly limited to formal bands. Mycenaean, *c* 1300 BC. Height 3 inches. (Hastings Museum)

Three-handled jar with ornate spiral decoration. Mycenaean. 21 inches tall. (British Museum)

Greece, flourished around 1500 BC and was strongly influenced by the Minoan and Anatolian cultures. Fierce and warlike, the Mycenaeans built cities with strong fortifications, very much in contrast to the Minoans who led a peaceful island existence. It was an attitude reflected in the pots they made. Gold was abundant and metal-working and ivory-carving were highly developed skills.

Pottery, in this society, was not regarded in the same way as in Crete. Metal was the chief source of wealth and pottery an inferior alternative. The early pottery was the grey Minyan ware, made around 1600 BC; the pots were soapy to the touch and the shapes closely reflected those made in metal. The influence of the warlike invading Achaeans from the north coast of the Peloponnese around 1500 BC was combined with the Minoan influence from the south Aegean to produce distinctive if unexciting pots. Natural forms of cuttlefish, seaweed and shellfish, such as were used by the Minoans, were some of the decorative motifs, all reflecting a sea culture, but no longer were the designs painted over the entire surface but placed more formally. The introduction of the wheel, probably from Egypt, led to the banding of lines on the pot and these bands were soon used to confine the designs to borders, chiefly on the neck and shoulders. Minoan potters had filled all the available space on the surface with painted designs and the results were fresh and immediate. Mycenaean pottery lacks this freshness, and with the Dorian invasion from the north around 1200 BC pottery decoration became more limited and the beginnings of designs using geometrical shapes appeared; the formal styles which incorporated the lozenge, chequers and the meander were used in border patterns.

Two-handled jar made in Cyprus about 1200 BC, with a lively but formally-painted design. Potters in the Mediterranean islands often felt much freer to paint such imaginative patterns. $10\frac{1}{8}$ inches tall. (British Museum)

The shapes were thinly made, reflected the influence of metal forms, and began to evolve as basically Greek, though they lacked the strength of those which were to develop later. With the Iron Age well under way the Dorians, with their severe and militaristic temperament and superior weapons and armour had a deadening influence on art as a whole. Artistic achievement seemed to decline in the entire Greek peninsula until the emergence of the Greek city states around 1000 BC.

Greece

From around 1000 BC the classical Greek culture as we understand it today began to emerge. Art in Greece was of the people: the community, religion and the arts were closely linked. The State was the main patron of the arts, acting as such through the assemblies, councils and magistrates. Art was completely enmeshed in daily living and was not exclusive to the wealthy. Pottery was thought of in much the same way. The careful and highly sophisticated painted pottery was as highly regarded as any other art form and was used at

Two-handled bowl with formal figure design in the geometric style. Greece, c 800–900 BC. (British Museum)

various times for grave monuments and as prizes for athletic success. Little pottery was produced merely for display; most of it had a clearly specified function. Undecorated pottery probably formed the largest part of the total production; as this pottery was not so highly regarded it has not survived to the same extent. Much of the undecorated ware, made for cooking and for use in the home and kitchen, was made locally, while the painted pottery was made in two special centres, Corinth and Athens, both of which have large beds of fine red or yellow clays.

Most of the Greek painted pottery now on show in museums has been found in graves, which indicates that it was highly prized and regarded. Painted pottery was valued both for the amount of work and skill such painting entailed and for the nature of the scenes depicted. These related to mythical as well as contemporary events though the pots were decorated to make them attractive rather than to turn them into works of art. Paintings on Greek pots which reflected the culture and tradition of Greek society are a vital source from which to learn about the history of the Greeks and for this reason they have been studied intently.

Greek pots have two unique characteristics, the form and the decoration. The forms were precisely designed and made, using crisp, clean shapes which owe much to metal-working. Yet each particular shape was worked out for a specific use, and was given a name which referred to this function. The decorative painting on the surface of the pot, as well as being both artistically and technically skilled, was closely related to contemporary Greek culture.

All the painted designs referred to particular incidents or told a story and used a complicated system of references to male and female gods which would have been under-

Jug, late geometric style, with stylized birds and geometric designs, and plastic modelling of snake on handle. Greek, eighth century BC. (British Museum)

stood by most people. Designs were not arbitrary but were carefully, and subtly, worked out to convey their message. Some scenes, such as were often used on the base of wine cups, were lewd and made sexual suggestions which needed no interpretation. Others were inspirational or commemorated important events, but all relied on the viewer having all the necessary information to read and interpret the tale.

Technique

Painting on pottery had been used earlier by the Mycenaeans but was developed to a new level of perfection around the mid to late sixth century BC by the Greeks. The pots are usually classified into four styles, based on the style of decorations used, and correspond to four roughly chronological periods, described later.

The use of the wheel was widespread throughout Greece around 1000 BC. Pots made from carefully and highly prepared clay were thrown on a wheel propelled by an assistant who was usually a young apprentice. The clay used for the decorated wares was highly workable and fired a yellow-red colour in a kiln with a clean oxidizing atmosphere. Attic clay used by the Athenian potters was dug from the borders of the city and fired rich red, while the yellower clays used by the Corinth potters were lighter in colour. Pots were thrown in sections which were joined together when the clay had become stiff enough to be handled yet soft enough to be moulded; this is known as the leather-hard stage. At this point the pots were placed back on the wheel and the pieces luted and joined together. In the process known as turning, surplus clay was shaved off the surface using either a metal or a wooden tool. In this way any finger marks made while throwing could be removed and the profile, so important to the Greek pots, could be sharpened. It should be remembered that by the time of the early Greek period the wheel had become much more efficient and smooth. Both the throwing of the large forms and the turning would have been very difficult without this improved wheel.

The painting on the surface was achieved by using fairly simple materials in a sophisticated way. Glaze had been discovered earlier, probably in Mesopotamia, and may easily have been known to the Greeks who, for some reason, chose not to use it, preferring instead a fine clay slip which lost its mattness and became slightly shiny and glass-like in the kiln. It was not completely waterproof and it could not be called a true glaze. The effect was achieved by using clay which consisted of very fine particles and contained a high

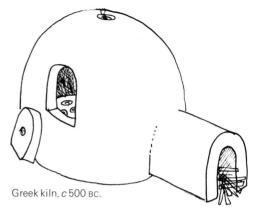

Greek kiln, c 500 BC.

percentage of iron oxide – ferric oxide (Fe_2O_3). In a kiln where there was plenty of oxygen the slip fired a dense red colour; if the oxygen content was reduced (by burning damp wood or closing the air inlets into the kiln) the flame, hungry for oxygen, would take it from the easiest available source – in this case the oxygen in the iron oxide contained in the clay which, with a reduced amount of oxygen, became ferrous oxide, FeO, which fired black. Using carefully prepared slip, red and black colours could be produced on the same pot by the following method:

1 The pot was made in finely prepared clay which fired red in an oxidizing kiln.

2 A slip was made from red clay and an alkali, such as wood ash, was added to break down the ability of clay particles to cling together; this caused the large clay particles to sink and the finer particles were then poured or siphoned off. Eventually a slip was made which contained only small particles. Acid, in the form of urine or wine, was added to make the mixture flowing yet firm. The slip was then applied to the surface of the pot either by painting or drawing, or, for the larger areas, pouring.

3 The pot was fired in the kiln with plenty of oxygen present (oxidized atmosphere) up to 900°C (1650°F); at this stage all the undecorated surfaces as well as the decoration areas of the pot would be red.

4 Air inlets would now be partly closed and damp fuel burnt in the kiln to create a smoky flame which would lower the oxygen content of the kiln (reduced atmosphere); all the surface of the pot including the decoration at this stage would turn black.

5 Finally a brief oxidizing period reintroduced oxygen into the kiln and lasting only a short time would finish the firing. The dampers would be opened and dry fuel used in the fire box. The body of the pot would turn back to red and the decoration painted in slip would remain black since it was much more dense – the clay particles were finer and there was a greater percentage of iron oxide; if this oxidizing fire lasted too long, the slip would also turn red as the oxygen began to penetrate its surface. Some pots have been found which show evidence of this.

Shapes

All the main shapes of the pots were evolved early on in the Greek culture and were a development of Minoan, Mycenaean and Dorian shapes. Most of the basic shapes were intended for holding liquid of some sort. Wine and water containers predominated, but smaller containers for oil and perfume were also made. It was the Greek custom to drink wine mixed with water and the necessary

Lekythos, black figure design of Satyrs on a drab ground painted with purple accessories. 9½ inches tall. (British Museum)

vessels were the crater or large mixing bowl, the narrow-necked amphora for the wine and the three-handled water pitcher or hydria for the water. A tall-handled ladle or kyathos was used to pour the wine into jugs known as oinochoai or into flat, two-handled cups known as kylikes. Sometimes the wine needed cooling and then a psyketer, a vessel with a tall stemmed foot, was filled with wine and stood in cold water in a lekane, which was a general purpose bowl. Personal toilet pots were also made. For the more precious liquids there were small bottles called aryballoi, lekythoi and alabastra.

The forms of the pots remained basically unchanged throughout the period of classical Greece, probably because they proved to be practical and convenient in use. The majority of pots were left plain or decorated with bands of black slip, or, later, covered entirely with black slip; decorated pots represent only a small proportion of Greek wares. Cooking pots of all kinds were produced very cheaply; metal was still an expensive luxury while clay products were not. Storage pots, saucepans, ovens, frying pans, stoves, cooking pots and braziers were all produced. Water clocks were made for the law courts. These consisted of a pot with a small hole which let out the water over a measured period of time; the force of the stream indicated the length of time left for the water to run out. Both plain and painted pots were exported in vast numbers as containers of olive oil or wine. Technically the ware was well fired and strong, but it chipped easily at the edges and these were often thickened to strengthen them.

Geometric style (c 1000–700 BC)

The earliest recognizable Greek painted style, known as proto-geometric, began to emerge roughly around 1000 BC. Forms developed at this time which, with some modifications, were to form the basis of shapes used throughout most of the Greek period. Decoration was clearly defined with light areas of clay and dark areas of slip forming simple balanced designs. Bands of slip were confined to shoulders and tops of pots; simple half-spiral designs and concentric circles were carefully drawn in slip and appear to have been done with mathematical precision. Completely abstract, the designs broke away altogether from the naturalistic style of the Cretans and the cramped convention of the Mycenaeans. Only black slip was used, though it occasionally fired dark brown.

Around 900 BC the geometric style emerged more fully, characterized by severely defined shapes with ornamental bands of patterns covering the entire pot. Decoration was still regular and mostly stylized abstract motifs, but, later, human and animal figures appeared also in very abstract forms and still confined to the borders. Burial scenes were also depicted. Very little is known about other art of this period and as not much has survived these pots may have been one of the main art forms; often used as monuments on graves, they have a formality of shape and design which gives them an austere beauty.

The mature geometric style had a still more balanced decoration which usually incorporated the handle into the design. Decorative motifs included not only concentric circles, chequers, triangles, zig-zags and the meander, but also the quatrefoil and swastika. Towards the end of the style plastic modelling was introduced and rims, for example on the oinochai or jug, were modelled.

Oriental or black-figure style
(c 700–550 BC)

Around 700 BC the Greek city states expanded, both geographically and artistically. The Greeks colonized much of the Mediterranean and came into much closer contact with the Near East and the oriental ideas of decoration. This influenced the decoration on the pottery and gave rise to the period known as oriental or black-figure because of the distinctive black figures painted on to the surface of the red pots. A wider range of ornaments, different animals and foreign plants were introduced into the designs; the curve of the pot became less restrained and there seems to be a great awareness of organic form. Experiments were made in drawing the human figure in a stylized form.

Later other colours besides black were introduced to heighten the designs. Small areas of purple, red, white and later yellow helped to break the designs away from the austerity of the geometric style.

Pots decorated with animals, which hitherto had included only the goat and deer, were now incorporating the lion, bull, dog, hare, eagle, cock and goose as well as the mythological sphinx and griffin. All the animals were shown in peaceful, formal poses with little movement and no signs of aggression. This animal style was brought to perfection in the seventh century BC by the Corinthian potters, using the local yellow clays. Detailed friezes beautifully carried out were shown in bands often no more than two inches wide. Incised lines were used in the designs to convey detail and the success of the designs was unequalled elsewhere in Greece. Bands of figures in complex arrangements were also shown.

It was in the study and drawing of the human figure that the potters of Athens found their greatest satisfaction; this was indigenous to the Greeks and owed little to oriental influence. Battles, races and processions were favourite themes and, later, scenes from mythology were introduced. No attempt was made to make the drawing absolutely anatomically correct; what seemed important was the recording of contemporary events. A profile was used for the head with a frontal eye view; limbs were shown in profile, while the torso was either in profile or front view. No attempt was made either to fit in a background or indicate depth.

Jug, proto-Corinthian, painted in the oriental style. c 700 BC. (British Museum)

Aryballos (Corinthian scent bottle). Exported in large quantities in the Mediterranean. Naturalistic decoration of lions and boar shows strong Egyptian and Assyrian influence. Painted in black and red pigment with incised details and outline. c 700 BC. Height 2 inches (Hastings Museum)

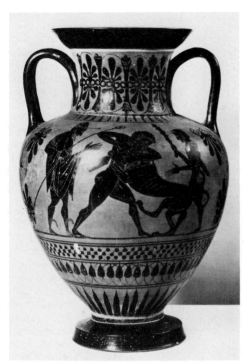

Amphora, black-figure design showing warrior fighting lion. Athens c 520 BC. Height 12½ inches. (Victoria & Albert Museum, London)

Amphora, black-figure style. Red panel shows scene of warrior in chariot. Double honeysuckle pattern round neck. Athens, c 500 BC. Height 13¾ inches. (British Museum)

Black figures were painted on to the red background and fine detail was scratched through the slip to reveal the red body. The finest designs were often restrained and masterful, without any of the heaviness which developed towards the end of the period. Early designs included many border patterns, but gradually these were simplified and occasionally eliminated altogether. Purple was no longer used and by convention black was adopted for male flesh, white for female and purple-red was confined to drapery and accessories. Generally the colours were more sombre than those used earlier by the Athanian or Corinthian potters. The work of individual painters can be recognized and among the greatest are Lydos, Nearchos, Exekias and the Amasis painter. While Corinthian potters developed a precise and elegant animal style, Athenian potters brought the black-figure style to its peak between 550 and 530 BC.

Red-figure style (c 530–330 BC)

The red-figure style was the last major Greek pottery painting style; it developed in Athens around 530 BC and may to some extent have been suggested by changes in contemporary art. Wall painting had become popular and painters were turning to this new and larger dimension in preference to the comparatively cramped and limited size and palette of the vase painter. Vase painting, therefore, required a technique which allowed greater emphasis to be placed on accuracy rather than stylization if it was to continue as a medium used by the best painters. The red-figure technique gave painters scope to practise their newly acquired skills. Economic reasons may also have encouraged the new stylistic development as overseas potteries set up by emmigrant potters were producing work almost identical to black-figure pots. An attractive alternative had to be produced in Greece or export markets would have been lost.

The human figure, hitherto depicted stylistically and with a minimum amount of ana-

Kylix, red-figure style. Exterior shows armed, satyrs. Interior shows black figure on horseback. Signed by Hischylos, potter, and Epictelos, painter. Athens, c 520 BC. (British Museum)

Red-figure crater painted during the finest period; purple is used for the inscriptions and details such as the snake's tongue, The youth Triptolemos is sitting in the winged car, in front of him stands Persephone with a torch in her hand. $8\frac{1}{4}$ inches tall. (British Museum)

Hydria, painted in the red-figure style at its late stage of development. Designs in red, white and yellow show Maenads, Satyrs and Erotes, by Painter of London. Athens. *c* 390–370 BC. (British Museum)

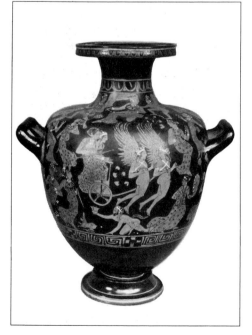

tomical detail, now became the object of serious study. The incised method of scratching through the black slip to show detail was no longer thought satisfactory and a finer, more precise method of drawing had to be invented. Instead of painting the figure black on a red background the process was reversed and the background was painted black leaving the figure red in silhouette; detail was painted on to the figure with a thin raised black line, or else a thinner brown line. The early red-figure style was founded on line drawing rather than shading.

As the style developed, the figures were no longer shown with such a strict regard for convention; a note of reality was added with attempts made to suggest depth, using three-quarter views and foreshortening; draperies were more detailed and ornate dots were used to suggest hair and texture; black-figure designs had had a solemnity lacking in the red-figure work which took a much more light-hearted view of life. As well as mythical subjects, scenes from daily life became popular subjects. The best work in the red-figure style was produced from about 530 to 500 BC; it expressed calm, refined, academic qualities and tended to reflect the best from the past rather than ape the contemporary vogue for free painting with its grandiose figures and compositions. In later designs figures were no longer planted firmly on the baseline, but, in a further attempt to suggest depth, moved over the surface of the pot, often in uneasy arrangements. Instead of limiting the colours to black and red other colours were introduced.

The red-figure style ceased to be used after 200 years or so. The overseas markets had been severely reduced both by emigrant Greek potters and the declining power of Greece; the industry failed to adapt itself to small production methods or to attract the better artists.

White-ground ware

Only one other distinctive style of decoration came into use. Around 580 BC potters started painting the background of the pot white and this was often supplemented by washes of colour, in red, purple or yellow ochre; this style, made in Athens, was known as Attic white-ground ware. Since the white slip ground was fragile the technique was reserved for rather precious pots – for example small oil-bottles or funeral pots. Scenes depicted on them tended to be of a peaceful nature and the pots as a whole were charming and delicate. Often small containers were hidden inside the larger outer pots.

Gradually, as the Greeks warred with Persia and the city states became less strong, the fine, high quality of Greek pottery declined. Eventually the Romans occupied much of Greece and took over those parts of the Greek pottery technique they required and adapted them for their own use.

The Italian peninsula
The Villanovans

Developments in the Italian peninsula came slightly later than in Greece. The first major state was Etruria, powerful, highly developed and war-like, situated between Rome, Florence and the Apennine Mountains. The Villanovans, who lived in the region of Etruria before the Etruscans, were both skilled metalworkers and potters; their dead were cremated and the ashes buried in urns. They made pots by a combination of throwing and handbuilding methods. Fairly coarse, iron-bearing clay was used and the surface was often burnished. Incised, often geometric designs decorated some of the pots, though towards the end of the eighth century BC an oriental influence was evident in the use of lotus flowers and mythological monsters.

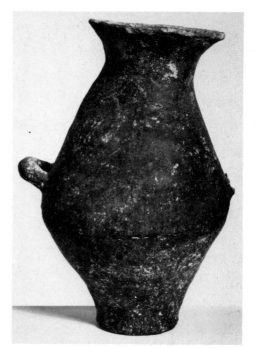

Urn, Villanovan, c eighth century BC.

Amphora. Bucchero ware with engraved and inlaid design. Etruscan, seventh century BC. (British Museum)

The Etruscans

Around 700 BC the Etruscan culture emerged. Many ideas from abroad, mainly from the Near East, were incorporated into their culture. They learned from Babylon how to

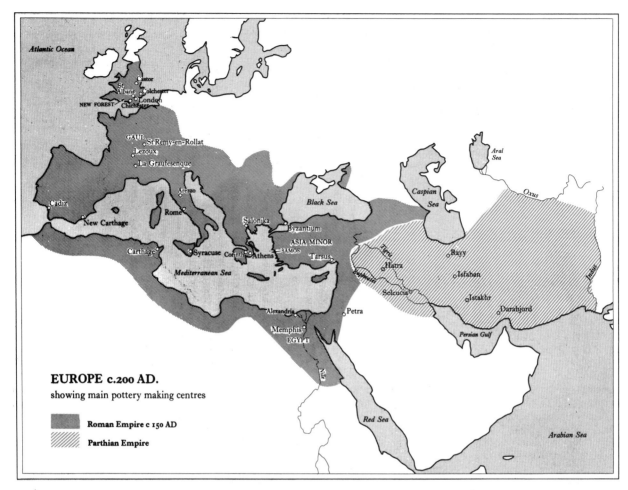

EUROPE c.200 AD.

showing main pottery making centres

Roman Empire c 150 AD

Parthian Empire

construct the vaulted arch, from Egypt how to make faience, how to work gold from Assyria and silver working from Phoenicia. Etruscan bronze-work is one of their finest achievements and was prized over the whole Mediterranean area. The early pottery was made from unpurified and roughly mixed clay which fired variable colours such as black, brown or red.

Around the middle of the seventh century BC grey-coloured pottery, often known as Bucchero Etruscan ware, was made. Technically the ware was sound and the shapes reflected the interest of the culture in metal objects. The forms were finely worked out and well executed. Decoration usually consisted of simple geometric designs, again boldly incised on a shiny black or grey surface.

In the early seventh and sixth centuries BC Etruscan pottery was influenced both by immigrant Greek potters and imports of Greek pottery; first by the Greek geometric style and

Skyphos with incised figure of a soldier. Etruscan. (Fitzwilliam Museum, Cambridge)

later by the red-figure style from Athens. The Etruscan style which developed was in fact slightly different from that used by the Greeks. The highly complex designs and symbols used by the Greek potters meant little or nothing to the Etruscans who tended merely to copy the decoration they saw on the Greek pots rather than attempt to understand its significance, so that the results were often crude and sometimes hilarious, even if they reached a high technical level. It was left to the Roman potters to develop fully the skills of the Greeks.

Oinochoe of black ware, bucchero. Etruscan, c 550 BC. (Fitzwilliam Museum, Cambridge)

The Roman Empire

According to legend Rome was founded in 753 BC, but it was not until the fifth century BC that the Romans freed themselves from the Etruscans and the beginning of an Empire greater than any that had gone before appeared. By 275 BC Rome ruled the whole of the Italian peninsula. Greece had earlier colonized parts of Italy, mainly by the establishment of trade, while to the north of Rome the Etruscans had developed a Greek-inspired culture. Gradually Rome grew in size and strength and, in conquering neighbouring

countries, absorbed a wider range of influence than had been absorbed by the Greeks.

Roman pottery is often compared unfavourably with that produced by the Greeks, but this comparison does not do justice to the skills of the Romans, who produced pots for a very different sort of society with different requirements. The Romans were interested in engineering and building and wanted to spread technical knowledge and ordered government throughout their Empire. They encouraged the growth of industries which could produce the type and quality of goods they needed. Part of Roman ideology was that conquered lands, should, as far as attainable, be as like the homeland as possible, and that such countries or settlements should be able to produce goods and buildings which could reinforce this view. Production methods tended to be quick, efficient and effective to cope with increased quantities and to be worked out so that the method of production could be used in different countries. Also it was much easier to make pots on site than to transport fragile objects. This led to the development by the Romans of the manufacture of a range of pots with a shiny red surface called red-gloss wares, usually made to carefully worked out designs. Some were left plain, others were decorated. Other styles were also made, as well as the 'coarse' wares for general use.

Red-gloss ware

Various pottery-making centres were established, at different times, throughout the Roman Empire, usually near the camps of the Legions or on a good trade route; for example at La Graufesenque in southern Gaul, and later at Lezoux in central Gaul. As each new pottery centre was established little or no account was taken of indigenous work but local styles did often affect the decoration. Roman making and firing techniques were spread over the whole of Europe.

From the Greeks the Romans learnt how to prepare fine clay by adding an alkali, and so a slip of fine particles of clay was obtained. Suitable clay fired in an oxidizing kiln atmosphere gave a bright red sealing-wax colour and texture. The ware which resulted from the use of this clay is known by several names. 'Samian' was one name given to it as the style was believed to have been developed on the island of Samos, but this is not now thought to be so. 'Terra sigillata' is another of its names; again this is slightly misleading as it means pottery with stamped figures or patterns for decoration, though in reality the term is also used to include much undecorated work made in this red clay. In general the pots can all be included under the more general heading 'red-gloss ware'.

Using carefully prepared red clay the pots were made in intricately carved moulds, a technique which had been developed in late Hellenistic Greece and adapted by the Romans. Briefly, the method was to make a hollow mould in clay, known as a pitcher mould, sometimes from a thrown pot with thick walls, which, while it was still soft would have a design, often based on contemporary metal-work impressed or incised on the inside of it. Probably a more common method was to make a solid model of the finished pot in clay and carve and model the decoration on this; when it had been dried and fired moulds could be made from it. After being fired the mould was put on to the wheel-head and the inside smeared with clay which was smoothed as the wheel was rotated. A foot, and sometimes a rim, was often added to the moulded basic bowl shape. The decoration appeared in relief on the surface of the bowl. Early bowls were decorated with patterns of flowers and foliage used in a simple way. These designs were often copied directly from Greek metalware. The pots were finished by being covered in a slip of fine clay which fired bright coral red in a clean oxidizing fire or black in a reduced kiln atmosphere, a technique explained earlier in the chapter.

Arretine ware

Arretium, modern Arezzo, gave its name to Arretine ware which was the most famous, most technically skilled and finest of the Roman red-gloss wares. The beauty and accuracy of the finish on the pots reveal excellent craftsmanship. Around 30 BC the industry developed very rapidly and lasted for about 100 years. Early Arretine pottery seems to indicate that Greek potters were employed,

as the pots were fired black using the Greek reducing technique. Later the pots were fired red either because the process was easier or because the demand was for red rather than black ware. Early Arretine decoration was well balanced with sensitive groupings of figures of Hellenistic origin such as maenads, satyrs and fauns. Wreaths, masks, scrolls, swathes of fruit and flowers, birds, cupids and butterflies were all used. Often raised decoration on metal objects was copied directly by the potters, especially from the work of the silversmith. The fineness of the incised technique on the moulds allowed clear detail which perhaps encouraged the notable naturalistic decoration.

Undecorated red-gloss ware

Plain, undecorated wheel-thrown pots were also made in red-gloss ware. Shapes were simple and undoubtedly influenced by contemporary metal shapes, having the clean, precise beauty associated with industrially produced rather than hand-thrown pottery. The most valued tableware at that time was made from metal, and the undecorated pottery set out to rival it in fineness and finish. Flat dishes of various sizes were common as well as cups with slanting sides, bowls and other domestic pottery. The centre of manufacture was often stamped on the pot, sometimes falsely; 'Genuine Arretine' has been found on pots made elsewhere. Potters also stamped their names on the pots; for example, Cerialis, a potter working at Lezoux in central Gaul during the reigns of Trajan and Hadrian, stamped his on the base of a red-gloss vessel.

As the Roman Legions moved farther west, the main production centre of the pottery industry moved first to southern Gaul and later to central Gaul. During the second century AD the central Gaulish factories were the

Bell-shaped krater with added foot. Arretine, Roman. Fine coral-red colour with relief decoration showing the seasons. 'Winter' is shown here. Rows of beads, wreaths and rosettes are included in the design. c 10 BC. Height 7½ inches. (British Museum)

Cup with relief-decoration in slip covered with purplish-black slip; probably made at Castor. c 250 AD. Height 4 inches. (Victoria & Albert Museum, London)

chief suppliers of red-gloss ware to the British markets. Centres were also established in Britain at such places as Castor, Aldgate and the New Forest, but these were small industries in comparison with the potteries in Gaul.

Other wares

Pots made in centres away from Italy seemed to encourage experiments with different styles, which were often produced alongside the more standard wares. Decoration often became livelier and more varied and potters looked to materials other than metal for ideas.

Red-gloss cup with incised decoration. North Italian or Rhenish ware, first century AD. (Richborough Museum, Ministry of Works)

Glass and leather forms for instance were imitated. The cutting of leather-hard pottery with a V-shaped instrument similar to a modern lino-cutting tool, gave a design which closely imitated that of cut glass.

Barbotine wares were also made; thrown pottery was decorated with applied ornament made by painting or trailing thick liquid clay slip on to the surface of the damp pot. The result is known as 'barbotine ware', after the French word for slip. The Romans developed the technique to a high degree of control and early designs imitated those made in relief from moulds. Hunting scenes were a common favourite. White slip was often used over a dark-firing clay; because the technique required speed and dexterity rather than precision the results were often lively and pleasant.

The introduction of alternative and often very fast methods of decoration, including rouletting made by a metal tool 'chattering' on the side of the pot as it turned on the wheel, as well as patterns made with a tool with a revolving toothed wheel, saw a decline in the artistic and technical standard of moulded ware.

Coarse pottery

Not all Roman pots were as refined as the red-gloss wares; a large number of pots had to be made for use in the kitchen as well as for the less well-to-do members of the population. Roman coarse pottery was made from local clay fired without a coat of vitreous slip. It was made on the efficient and fast potter's wheel in a variety of forms, for it was the ordinary, everyday pottery for the majority of people; it was produced at many different centres, mainly for local markets. The Romans, however, still managed, even in locally made pottery, to impose a Roman influence on form throughout the whole of the Empire. Such wares constitute a lively and often neglected range of Roman pots.

Lead-glazed ware

The final group of wares the Romans made, and those with which potters have a direct connection today, are the lead-glazed wares. Lead glazing had been discovered and used

Ewer with frieze of leaves and grapes. Green lead glaze has deteriorated to silvery iridescence. Roman, Asia Minor, first century BC/AD. Height 5 inches. (Hastings Museum)

which often had handles very like those made out of metal. The technique travelled through Italy, where it was very little used, to the Allier district of Gaul, at St. Remy-en-Rollat, Vichy. Subsequently it spread into Germany and was established at Cologne by about AD 100. When the Roman Empire collapsed, much of the technology the Romans had introduced lapsed, except for the lead glazing of pottery in Byzantium where it continued to be used and

Amphora found in Sardinia. Green and yellow lead glaze, fired upside down. Roman, seventh century AD. Height 6⅞ inches. (British Museum)

Two-handled rich yellow/green glazed cup. Form, handles and moulded relief decoration recall contemporary silver forms, undoubtedly a contemporary luxury ware. From Soloi, Cyprus, mid-first century AD. Height 2¾ inches. (Fitzwilliam Museum)

earlier by the Egyptians and Mesopotamians, though its use had never been widespread. Technically it was complicated to prepare and fire; it probably resulted in too many failures and did not seem so necessary to the Roman way of life or current taste. The red-gloss wares were prepared by dipping the pot into a slip and similar methods of production were used for the glazed wares. A green lead glaze was often used on pots made by various methods. Some were made in moulds with impressed designs or applied figures. Others were thrown on the wheel and glazed. Such pots were made by the potters of the 12th legion at Holt, Denbighshire. By 100 BC the technique was practised in Asia Minor at Tarsus and at Alexandria in Egypt on pots

Earthenware pot with red gloss surface and applied decoration of overlapping scales. Roman, made in France. Height 4⅜ inches. (Victoria & Albert Museum, London)

formed the basis of later developments in Europe. Whether or not lead glaze continued to be used in Germany or was reintroduced at a later date is not known for certain.

Faience, developed much earlier by the Egyptians and Mesopotamians, continued to be made in Egypt during the Roman occupation on more elaborate shapes. Brilliant blues were obtained from the addition of small percentages of copper; later the colours were extended to include black, red, green, purple, yellow and white. Because the paste had to be carefully prepared and the raw material was difficult to work faience wares were very expensive to produce. A stronger and more workable body was later introduced by the Islamic potters, who developed the technique fully.

Under the Roman Empire pottery production was well organized and technical knowledge was introduced to all parts of the Empire. To produce pottery in the quantity required by growing cities and large armies mass-production techniques were developed which foretold many of the production methods used by present-day industrial firms.

Roman mortarium in pale grey earthenware. (British Museum)

Roman inkpot with pigment decoration, incised IVCVNDI NDI. (British Museum)

Roman thrown red earthenware bowl with slip-trailed decoration under a pale honey-coloured transparent glaze. (British Museum)

3 THE FAR EAST

THE FAR EAST
showing the main pottery making centres of China and Japan

RUSSIA

MONGOLIA

Peking
HOPEI
(CHIHLI)
T'ing chou

SHANSI
oT'z'u Chou
An-yang

KANSU

SHANTUNG

Yellow Sea

KOREA

Chien Chou
Ju Chou
Chun Chou

K'ia-feng

JAPAN

SHENSI

HONAN

Nanking
ANHUI

Yi-hsing

SZECHUAN

HUPEI

KIANGSU

Hangchou
Chin-yen
Yuen chou

Ching-te Chen
Nanchang

CHEKIANG

HUNAN
KIANGSI
Chien-yang

Lung-ch'uan

KUEICHOU

FUKIEN
Te-hua

KUANGSI

KWANG TUNG
Canton

Swatow

TAIWAN

Hong Kong

JAPAN

Sawankhalok

THAILAND

South China
Sea

Echizen
Bizen
Seto
Tokyo
Kyoto
Arita

HAINAN

CAMBODIA

Satsuma

The art of the Far East differs greatly from that produced in the West: a completely different philosophy encouraged the growth of a unique and, in many ways, fantastic art. During the period of classical Greece, the Greek ideas were based on the idealization of the human form and the development of human history through myths, fables and stories. These ideas were accurately reflected in the decoration on pots. In contrast the Chinese were more contemplative and found enjoyment in the spiritual rather than the physical and this quality is evident in much of their pottery. Equally, technical skills developed much earlier in the Far East than in Europe or the Middle East, and this too affected the pots that were made and the designs used to decorate them.

At various times the expanding countries of the West and the settled and prosperous Chinese dynasties came into contact, each making an impact on the other. Perhaps the most important example of this is the effect of the fine ninth-century AD porcelain wares imported into the Arab world. They encouraged the development there of earthenware made in imitation of porcelain as well as instigating research into its manufacture. From the West the Chinese potters of the Han and T'ang dynasties got lead, with which to make low-temperature glazes, and later blue pigment, often called Mohammedan blue, which is a purified form of cobalt oxide unobtainable at that time in China. The lead was in the form of a frit, which is a manufactured material made by mixing lead with another material such as sand, heating it until it melts and then grinding up the glass so formed. Later the activities of the Dutch East India Company brought vast quantities of decorated Chinese porcelain to Europe which stimulated and influenced the work of the Delft potters; the Chinese themselves adapted many of their designs to the demands of the European market.

Just as decoration on Greek pots seems merely decorative today, but was in fact carefully and precisely worked out so that its meaning was clear, so it is with Chinese pots. To us the decoration on Chinese pottery may appear random and arbitrary, yet to the Chinese each object and its arrangement had a meaning. In a country where the written language had developed from pictorial symbols this is hardly surprising. The lion, horse and elephant were used to symbolize Buddha,

Earthenware urn. Neolithic, from Pan-shan, Kansu. Height 14½ inches. (Museum of Far Eastern Antiquities, Stockholm)

while the dragon represented the Emperor and the phoenix the Empress. The pomegranate stood for fertility, a pair of fish or mandarin ducks for wedded bliss; the pine tree, peach and gourd were emblems of long life; while the cassia bough and salmon leaping from the waves stood for literary success. Only when European decorative themes were introduced did the meaning become lost.

Pots were highly regarded from early times by both religious and secular leaders in China. The Imperial court commissioned work and later established an Imperial pottery factory at Ching-te Chen. Pots played an important part in the Buddhist ceremony, and altar vases, for example, received great care in their manufacture. Long and often lyrical descriptions of the different types of ware provide much literary evidence to assist in classifying pots, though sometimes such glamorous accounts confuse an already large and complicated picture.

China

A country as large and a civilization as long lasting as China has a complex history. For the sake of simplicity the development of Chinese pottery is dealt with in chronological order. China has one of the world's oldest continuous civilizations, despite invasions and foreign rulers, and each dynasty or period of hereditary rule had its own characteristics. Some dynasties were very short and only the main ones will be dealt with here.

Early period

Neolithic Chinese pottery, produced on the plains near the Yellow River, was made in the period 3000–1500 BC. Pots from Kansu province were made in reddish clay with boldly drawn geometric patterns in red, black or purplish-brown pigment painted onto the fired pots. They are related stylistically to those made in western Asia, southern Persia, Baluchistan and southern Russia, which suggests close communication at that time. Such examples of the ware as remain today are mainly burial urns or cooking utensils. The high quality of the painted decoration on the full swelling forms, and the vigour and life of these pots give them a quality which is pleasing, fresh, and lively. It is curious that later Chinese pottery seems to bear no relation to this early work.

Cooking vessels of various sorts were made, of which the most interesting were produced out of grey clay and were built with three hollow feet. This was a highly functional design, for the hollow legs provided the liquid contents with a greater surface area from which to absorb heat and this shape could sit securely in the fire. The surface of these vessels was decorated with incised textured patterns.

During the Chinese Bronze Age the working of bronze and jade was brought to a high degree of refinement. Vessels made out of these precious materials, and often intended for religious use, had a great influence on pottery forms. Many pots were made in almost exact imitations of bronze and jade vessels, and it was many hundreds of years before pottery began to be made once again with real regard for the qualities of clay.

Chou dynasty (1155–255 BC)

Major changes occurred during the Chou dynasty which included the setting up of basic government and organized religion. Confucius (about 550–480 BC) introduced a religion based on filial piety and reverence for tradition, and great emphasis was put on moderation and harmony. At much the same time Taoism, following the teachings of Lao Tzu that impersonal nature permeates everything, propounded a high and compassionate morality; later cults developed the mystical element of Taoism.

Excavated graves, many discovered during the construction of railways in the nineteenth century, are the richest source of pottery as well as other treasures of this period. It was the custom to inter with the eminent dead items which they might need in the after-life. Food in metal and bronze containers, as well as pots, were buried with the bodies of important rulers in specially constructed graves. Wives, servants and retainers were often immolated; Confucius condemned this human sacrifice. Later this barbarian practice was stopped and clay or wooden models were substituted. The majority of the pottery which has been recovered was fired to earthenware temperature and unglazed. Shapes often seem to be derived from those made by bronze

Pottery cooking pot with three hollow legs for standing in fire. Chou dynasty, c 1122–249 BC. Height about 7 inches. (British Museum)

Pots in the shape of owls. Chou dynasty. Height 5 inches. (Collection of H.M. the King of Sweden)

casting, though occasionally decorated with painted patterns.

Two significant developments were made during this period which, though not widespread in their application until later dynasties, were of great importance to Chinese pottery. The first was the use of a carefully prepared fine white clay decorated in relief in the style of contemporary bronzes. It is these wares which were the precursors of later porcelains. The second was the improved design of kilns which allowed more control and retention of heat. These kilns enabled clay to be fired to a higher temperature which gave a harder and more fused body and formed the earliest stoneware pots known. Around this time it was discovered that a simple glaze could be made by dusting a mineral like feldspar or wood ash on to the shoulder of the pots. At temperatures around 1200°C (2192°F), it will combine with the surface of the pot to form a mottled and attractive glaze. This technique seems to have continued intermittently until its use became more widespread in the Han dynasty.

Han dynasty (206 BC–AD 220)

During the Han dynasty the state became more unified and powerful, and heralded a period of consolidation and expansion under an efficient centralized administration. Confucian philosophy had a profound effect on all the art that was produced while Taoism with its mythical and mystical beliefs also had many followers. Buddhism, introduced from India in the first century AD, did not have great influence until much later.

Trade was far-ranging and extensive and brought stylistic and technical influences from other countries. Silk was exported by the

Pottery censer imitating bronze. Han dynasty. The cup-shaped body is supported on a slender stem on saucer-shaped stand. Cover is of the 'Hill vase' type moulded with mountains, leaves and animals. c 206 BC – AD 220. Height 9 inches. (Anthropological Museum, University of Aberdeen)

Wine jar. Wheel-made in shape imitating that of bronze even to the point of modelling imitation handles. Lead glaze, now iridescent. Han dynasty, c 206 BC – AD 220. Height 12 inches. (Hastings Museum)

overland route via Turkestan to the East Roman Empire and by sea to India and Persia. Glass and the substance known as liu-li, thought to have been some sort of prepared glass mixture which included lead, were imported. Lead glazing was practised at Alexandria around this time and it is probably from here that the Chinese learnt the art of glazing earthenware.

Pots were no longer made simply by hand but with the help of efficient wheels and in some cases with the use of moulds, again reflecting the influence of bronze-casting. Bronze was still the greatest influence and pottery forms and glazes followed those of bronze as closely as possible. For instance the green lead glazes enabled the colour of bronze to be copied. Over the years this glaze has become iridescent and today appears more bronze-like than it did originally. Some vases, meant for use in religious ceremonies, even had rings modelled on the outside in imitation of their bronze equivalents.

Both stonewares and earthenwares were made at this time. The so-called 'hill-censers' and 'hill-jars' form one of the largest groups of earthenwares. These jars, some 8–10 inches tall, were made for religious or mortuary use, and had a lid, on top of which was modelled a stylized mountain, hill or island representing the Taoist mythological Island or Mountain of the Blest. A reddish-grey clay was used and the lead silicate glaze was tinted green, probably with copper oxide. Other ornament usually took the form of a frieze round the side and hunting scenes often included horses, dogs, tigers, deer and birds. These designs were often made in a mould and subsequently applied to the side of the pots. Miniature wellheads and miniature cooking ranges were also made.

Braziers, cooking vessels, ladles, various bowls and dishes, tripod kettles, candlesticks and cups have all been found, as well as such pottery objects as miniature tables.

The making of stoneware, which had begun during the Chou dynasty, was extended and improved during this time; it was made by firing the clay to the much higher temperature of around 1200°C (2192°F) and was to play a vital and fundamental part in the future development of Chinese pottery. These developments were associated with the Yueh district of south-east China where some very fine pots were made. Further improvements were achieved in kiln design and enabled stonewares to be made more easily. The kilns were built into the side of a hill and the heat rose up the kiln, with the result that higher temperatures were achieved near the fire-box at the bottom of the kiln and lower ones further up the kiln. With pots made out of clay able to withstand the high stoneware temperature without collapsing, kilns could be fired in which the hot areas were used for stoneware and the cooler areas for the lead-glazed earthenware. Simple glazes of the mineral feldspar and wood ash produced thin olive-green glazes which enhanced the form, though were unnecessary from a practical point of view as stoneware is impervious to liquid.

Many of the stoneware forms are clearly based on bronze originals, having a stiffness and tightness of decoration associated with

Thrown vase from Yang-chou. Fine stoneware with thin, greenish yellow glaze. Han dynasty, c 206 BC – AD 220. (British Museum)

metal-working. However, when the forms did break away from the bronze originals and loosened up, they displayed the basic dignity and strength associated with the best Chinese art. Decoration was similar to that used on bronze. It was cut in relief and was usually limited to applied horizontal bands round the centre or shoulder of the pot; and incised combing was sometimes also used.

Invasions by central Asian tribesmen brought about the dark ages of China in which the art of lead-glazing was lost, but stoneware continued to develop. Buddhism flourished in these troubled times and strongly influenced the work which followed.

T'ang dynasty (AD 618–906)

The widespread adoption of Buddhism, with its doctrine of denial and renunciation, was consolidated during the T'ang dynasty. This was a peaceful, tolerant, prosperous and creative period which must be rated one of the richest and finest in Chinese history. Trade with other countries and religious toleration brought many foreign influences which produced rich and artistic work. The northern capital, Ch'ang-an, was the focus of Asia

attracting visitors and trade from a wide area. To the west the Roman Empire had greatly diminished and the Mohammedans had not yet achieved their success. Trade spread by land to Iran and Mesopotamia and by sea to India, the Pacific islands and Japan.

Religious toleration encouraged the influx of Nestorian Christians, the Manichaeans from central Asia and the Zoroastrians and Mohammedans from Persia and India. From AD 638 a stream of western Asiatic refugees brought Persian Sassanian material culture to China and the metal-work in particular had a strong influence on T'ang pottery forms. In the ninth century, trade through the ports of south China with the Arabs was well established.

Lead glazing was reintroduced when trade with the west was resumed. During the troubled times between the Han and T'ang dynasties, trade had lapsed and so the lead frit necessary for the earthenware glaze was not imported. With the expansion of trade a much improved lead frit was brought, enabling brighter, clearer colours to be obtained which have not lost their brilliance over the years. Hellenistic influences can be seen in some of the pots, for instance the shape of the flat pilgrim flasks as well as in ewers with handles and lips very similar to those made in Greece.

T'ang forms generally are characterized by a full, swelling, almost bursting body, contrasted with a light, fairly narrow neck. Each part of the pot relates to the other in a way suggesting movement and articulation, in contrast to the later Sung wares which have smoother, more continuous curves, suggesting stillness and peace. Decoration was bold and assertive, and was modelled, incised, stamped or painted. Necks on jugs often had five lobes which were probably derived from foliage. Bases were often casually finished with no turned foot.

Earthenware, made from a light buff-coloured body and covered with a clear lead-silicate glaze, could be coloured yellow, amber and brown with iron oxide, green with copper oxide, and sometimes, but rarely, dark blue with cobalt oxide. Decoration was often simple but very effective. Geometric patterns were painted in contrasting colours on to the body employing such motifs as chevrons, dots and stripes. The fluidity of the glaze as it melted and ran down the pot softened the edges of the colours and dappled effects were common. Glaze was often applied to the top half of the pot, leaving a bare area at the bottom, enabling the pot to be glazed quickly as well as preventing the glaze running down the pot on to the kiln shelf.

In an attempt to prevent the colours running together, flat offering dishes were made

Lidded earthenware jar. T'ang dynasty. Buff clay with white slip, green glaze inset with white and blue plum blossoms between ribbons of yellow blue and white. Lead glaze. *c* AD 618–906. Height 10 inches. (British Museum)

Earthenware headrest, with incised decoration and lead glaze. T'ang Dynasty.

with the design impressed into the surface so that the design lines acted as miniature ditches. On these flat dishes, again the designs were very simple, based on foliage, flowers and birds, and were usually painted in three colours: amber yellow, green and blue, usually on a white background. Much of this work imitates Sassanian chased metalwork.

Stoneware was made during this period at various sites in China, and continual effort seems to have been made to perfect a white body. White, the Chinese colour for mourning, was important at the elaborate ceremonial burials and this no doubt influenced the search for a white body.

Porcelain as used by the Chinese, was a term given to any ware emitting a clear, ringing note when struck; it did not have to be either white or translucent. For the sake of clarity it is simplest to refer to white translucent ware as porcelain and other high-fired ware as stoneware. The term 'proto-porcelain' is often used for white stoneware which is not translucent, though it is both misleading and vague.

The exact origins of porcelain are unknown, but it is thought to have been developed in the south at Kiangsi. Suitable materials were available for its manufacture and it was in this area, at Ching-te Chen, that the famous Imperial porcelain factory was established under the Ming dynasty.

True porcelain is made by firing a mixture of white china clay (kaolin) and china stone (petuntze) to a temperature between 1250° and 1300°C (2280°F–2370°F). With the correct mixture and with sufficient temperature fusion of the particles takes place giving a much more glassy mixture than stoneware and very much stronger. This enables thin walls to be made without loss of strength. Though this technique was probably mastered by the T'ang potters, it was not exploited by them; it was left to the Sung and Ming potters to develop it fully.

In different parts of the country various whitewares were made. In the northern province of Chihli a fine whiteware with a transparent glaze was produced. White slip was sometimes used over the grey body to achieve this. In Honan fine grey-bodied stoneware pots were produced and finished with dark glazes sometimes splashed with a creamy-grey glaze. Such wares are now thought to pre-date the so-called Chun wares of the Sung period.

Yueh ware is a general term covering pots made at Chekiang province in east China. Various sites have been found dating back to AD 250, though the best work was made in the T'ang period and later. It was here that the use of a pale green glaze, sometimes opaque, sometimes transparent, was developed. Generally they are referred to as greenwares, though the glaze was later called celadon and reached a peak of perfection during the Sung dynasty.

The Chiu-yen type of ware was made from a light grey clay with a thin creamy-white glaze. Jars had looped handles, the vases had collar rims, and chicken-head spouts were often used on ewers. Decoration consisted of incised bands of diaper or star patterns.

A wide variety of pots were produced during the T'ang dynasty which included lidded jars, bowls, bottles, vases, ewers, offering dishes, cups, rhytons, spittoons and cosmetic boxes. It is also worth mentioning the fine and delicate tomb figures produced at this time. Originally made from wood, the

ters to develop their skills and produce some of their finest and most delicate work. Materials were carefully prepared and special mixtures enabled a wide variety of techniques to be practised. Highly sophisticated cross-draught kilns allowed high temperatures and rich glaze effects to be obtained. Re-established in the south, the potters soon produced pots equal to those made by their predecessors in the north, and much of the work attained new technical and aesthetic heights. Markets were established both in China and overseas for these wares. It is difficult to believe that in those troubled times the arts of peace flourished so successfully. On the whole the court tended to patronize art which looked backwards, imitating the ever-popular bronze and jade, but this did not prevent the production of much more lively and inventive work.

Shapes tended to be less simple, and form was considered to be more important than decoration. Contours were smoother than those made by the T'ang potters and a wonderful serenity and stillness pervades the best work. Stoneware pots were collected and savoured by the court and were as valued as objects made out of more precious materials. Imperial patronage tended to encourage the study of the archaic with the result that many potters believed that the imitation of jade was the ideal in pottery glaze. Glaze descriptions such as 'mutton fat', 'congealed lard', 'rich and unctuous' equally describe the best qualities of jade. Unfortunately, on some wares made for the court the search for glaze quality as opposed to form often resulted in fantastically beautiful glazes over less interesting forms.

Northern Sung wares

For the sake of simplicity, the pots can be divided into those produced in the north until 1127 and those subsequently produced in the south.

Ting ware was particularly favoured by the court and is undoubtedly one of the great Sung products. Made at Ting-chou in Hopei province in the north, this fine white porcelain has a coolness and simplicity which is technically excellent and visually enchanting. Bowls, plates, saucers, vases and lidded pots were all thinly coated with a dense ivory-coloured glaze. Three different colours were made: pai-ting was brilliant and white, fen-ting had the colour of ground rice, while t'u-ting had a coarser body and a yellower glaze. Foot rims were finely turned on the wheel and the pots were fired on their rims, which were unglazed and subsequently banded with metal. The best decoration was incised directly into the soft clay, and foliage designs

figures retained a simplicity of form yet captured all the grace and movement the human figure could achieve. Horses and camels, too, were modelled with great sensitivity. Coloured lead glazes were used with great effect on some of the models, helping to heighten the sense of unreality of the models. Other pieces were coloured with pigments which have now disappeared.

Sung dynasty (AD 960–1279)

In contrast to the preceding T'ang period, the art of the Sung potters is peaceful and poised even though the times were often troubled and uncertain with invaders making frequent attempts to take over the country. The dynasty was not firmly established and the continual invasions by the Ch'in Tartars eventually caused the court to move, in 1127, from the northern capital of K'ai-feng in Honan province to the southern capital of Hangchou. The period was, however, enormously active artistically. Court patronage encouraged pot-

Ting bowl with lid. The well integrated fluted decoration and the strong form are typical of the best pieces of Sung pottery. Dated AD 1162. (British Museum)

were often used with great freedom. Moulded decoration was also used, though it lacked the clarity of incised work. Bowls foliated in six lobes and decorated with lotus sprays were particularly beautiful.

Chun wares, taking their name from Chun-chou in Honan province, date back to before the Sung period and continued to be made long after, but reached a peak of achievement during this time. Shapes were, for the most part, plain, with great emphasis placed on the thick opalescent lavender-coloured glaze which flowed from the rim, leaving it darker in colour. Often thick rolls of glaze formed near the base of the pot. Splashes of purple on some wares gave a startling and not altogether subtle effect, though technically it is generally admired. The court tended to patronize forms imitating bronze, such as the rectangular bulb bowls with startling and rare purple glazes, rather than the less flamboyant globular jars, bottles, bowls, dishes and vases with rich and luminous pale blue glazes.

Celadon is the name given to green glazes obtained from iron-bearing glazes fired in a reduction kiln. The name derives from Celadon, a character in a seventeenth-century French play, who always wore green clothes. Various sites produced different shades of green which ranged from dark olive transparent to opaque pale blue-green, though the basic firing technique was the same. The main group of celadons, made in the north, and known as northern celadon, is characterized by a transparent dark shiny olive-green glaze, often used over finely carved floral designs which were picked out and heightened by the glaze. The pots have a depth of colour and vigour of design distinguishing them from the

more refined celadons made for the sole use of the northern court. Conical bowls, spouted ewers, circular boxes and high-shouldered vases were made.

Ju ware, from Ju-chou, was the most highly prized and rarest group of celadon wares; made from about 1107 to 1127, it was for the use of the court. Known specimens are few, and when sold today command a price of many thousands of pounds. The forms are simple and well proportioned, but lack the vigour of other wares; their great beauty lies in the glaze, which is smooth, opaque and deep bluish-green.

By far the largest group of stonewares from the north were those taking their name from Tz'u-chou in Hopei province. Made from light grey-coloured clay and covered with white slip, these wares possess all the life and vigour lacking in some of the highly refined contemporary court wares. Painted decoration characterizes them and distinguishes them from any other contemporary group. With a dark brown or black clay pigment, flowers and foliage were freely painted in a direct and vigorous manner, having the clarity of calligraphy and the spontaneity of a rapid sketch. Sometimes the slip was scratched, revealing the grey body; peony designs combined with

Tzu-chou ware, stoneware with white slip and dark brown painted decoration. (British Museum)

meanders, and diaper patterns were popular. Colourless or cream-coloured glazes were most common. Later, red and green enamels were used with great effect, as were green glazes. Vases, wine jars, brush pots, pillows, bowls and boxes were among the range of objects, all produced for ordinary as opposed to court use.

Southern Sung wares

The invasion of the north by the Ch'in Tartars caused the Sung Emperor to move the court to the south. Potters moved with the court, taking their techniques with them, and southern potters were not slow to react to this new stimulus. Celadon wares, formerly made at Yuen-chou, were now produced at Lung-ch'uan in the western part of Chekiang. A thick, dense, hazy, pale green glaze with a wide-meshed crackle covered pots made from a light grey clay which flashed red when exposed to flame, as, for example, on the foot ring.

Some celadons had, as decoration, dots of iron pigments which turned a rich, dark, iridescent brown against the pale green glaze in the kiln. Lung-ch'uan celadons formed the largest and most productive group of wares at this time and were exported to Japan, central Asia, Persia, India, the East Indies, the Persian Gulf, Egypt and Africa. Much of the ware was mass-produced and was graded according to quality, with low grades going to export, and the better wares kept for the home market. Conical bowls, flat dishes, incense burners, vases and dishes or basins with pairs of fish or dragons in unglazed relief were made. Plastic modelling of dragons and other animals was often done on funeral vases.

Kuan, meaning Imperial, ware was produced in or near Hangchou for the use of the court. The thick bluish-green or grey-green glaze was applied in many layers, giving it a rare depth and luminosity. A crackled effect was deliberately sought to give the ware the look of jade.

Ch'ing pai wares originated at different sites in Kiangsi province. They are true por-

Vase with cover, green glaze stoneware with incised decoration. Height 16½ inches. Yu Yao, Chekiang. tenth century AD. (Ashmolean Museum, Oxford)

Right: Porcelain pot with thick 'fat' pale green celadon glaze, Lung-ch'uan ware. Twelfth or thirteenth century. (Victoria & Albert Museum, London)

Stoneware bowl with rich brown oil-spot glaze. Height 4 inches. Northern Chinese. Sung dynasty. (Victoria & Albert Museum, London)

Thrown bowl with brown mottled glaze from Honan. Bowl diameter 5 inches. Sung dynasty. (Hastings Museum)

celain and are the southern counterpart of the Ting wares. The pots were fired to a high temperature to achieve translucence and the pale blue or pale green glaze, sometimes called Ying ch'ing, was fired to a lower temperature. Shapes were fine and delicately potted and showed little or no influence of bronze shapes. The thin fluid glaze tended to run and settle in hollows, enhancing any finely carved decoration. One Chinese description of pots seems to fit this ware rather well: 'Blue as the sky after rain, clear as a mirror, thin as paper, resonant as a musical stone of jade'.

Porcelain, however, was only a small part of the total output; most pots were made in stoneware, the largest group of which was Chien ware, made in Fukien province in southern China. This was made out of a dense stoneware body which was used mainly for, among other pots, the production of tea bowls covered in dark brown glaze. Various different types of glaze were given appropriate names, especially by the Japanese, by whom they were greatly admired. Thick lustrous dark brown glazes which broke lighter brown on the rim or over relief decoration were given the general name 'tenmoku'. 'Hare's fur' was a term used to describe a streaked glaze, while an 'oil spot glaze' appeared to have spots of oil on the surface. Other wares with dark glazes were made at,

among other sites, Honan and Kiangsi.

During the short-lived Yuan dynasty (1280–1367) a new ware was made called Shu-fu which continued the development of fine white porcelains. Shu-fu porcelain was produced near Ching-te Chen, and glazed an opaque pale bluish-green colour; it was one of the forerunners of the fine Ming porcelains. Decoration was often in low relief and motifs included flowers and phoenix.

Ming dynasty (AD 1368–1644)

The breakdown of the Mongol domination of the East saw the return of a new liberal Chinese dynasty and a subsequent renaissance of the arts. Movement was away from the quiet and austere ideals of the Sung period to colour and ornament. Great energy was put into building and most of China's ancient architecture dates from this period. This enormous creative activity was reflected in the various sorts of pot which lost their formal contours and became much less constrained. Shapes became more diverse, with a continuously changing profile. Pots produced for Imperial use were highly finished and no expense was spared in their production; Imperial kilns, for example, were, if necessary, fired half-empty and any pots considered imperfect were broken. This was to ensure that no inferior work left the pottery.

Three major developments in the production of pottery were made in the Ming dynasty. Pure white porcelain was manufactured at the Imperial factory established under government control; colour was introduced in the form of underglaze painting or enamelling and so superseded monochrome glazes. A large proportion of the pots were made at the large centre of Ching-te Chen in the province of Kiangsi. Ching-te Chen on the river Ch'ang was geographically well placed for the development of the industry. Both china clay (kaolin) and china stone (petuntze) were

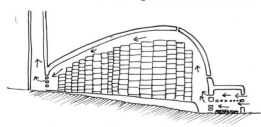

Chinese cross-draught kiln, showing the firebox with embers on the right; used at Ching-te Chen

Porcelain stem cup with underglaze blue painted decoration. Ming dynasty, c AD 1368–1644. Height $4\frac{1}{4}$ inches. (Victoria & Albert Museum, London)

Blossom vase (Mei-ping) for holding branches of prunus blossom, with blue painted decoration. c AD 1450. (Victoria & Albert Museum, London)

apparent under certain lighting conditions. During the reign of Yung Loo (1403–24) this decoration reached its peak in such pots as small delicate cups and bowls resembling lotus pods made for holding in the hand.

It is, however, the famous blue and white ware of this period which must claim first attention. Cobalt in various forms had been imported at different times from the Middle East. With the re-establishment and expansion of trade during the Ming Dynasty, cobalt was brought in the fourteenth century from Persia where it had been used much earlier to decorate pots. The fresh and pleasing combination of a fine white glazed body and blue painted decoration had been much admired by the Chinese who wanted to produce the decoration for themselves. The imported cobalt was expensive and eventually a less pure supply was obtained from within China. Cobalt was simple to use; it was mixed with water and painted either on to the unglazed pot or on to the unfired glaze and made good use of the traditional skills of Chinese calligraphers and artists. Indigenous Chinese cobalt was an impure ore of cobalt and manganese which produced a grey pigment rather than a blue one. Mixed in the proportion of three parts imported ore with two parts of Chinese ore, a rich blue was obtained, called at various times Sumatran blue and Mohammedan blue.

Decoration on early blue and white ware was outlined in dark blue and thin washes filled in the enclosed spaces. Much use was made of flower and plant designs arranged in geometric divisions of borders and panels. Perhaps the best of this ware was made early in the fifteenth century during the reign of Hsuan-te (1426–35), when the designs became more orderly and the style as a whole became less cramped. During the sixteenth century the human figure was more freely drawn and often set in landscapes. Later, Arabic or Persian inscriptions were incorporated into the designs. In Chia Ching's reign (1522–66) the blue became purplish and the designs broadened to include emblems and less formal subjects such as, for instance, children at play.

A further discovery of this time was that a thin wash of copper oxide on the glaze, when fired in a reducing atmosphere, will produce reds which range from salmon to dark pink-purple. The skill of obtaining these copper-red colours was developed during the reign of Hsuan-te (1426–35) but there was no method of using this technique to produce intricate designs so simple shapes were used. A rich tomato-red colour could be obtained which was often used with great effect on delicate stem cups. Because control over the

available locally, as was kiln fuel, while the river provided a quick and cheap method of transport. Many different production sites were established in and around Ching-te Chen though not all have yet been identified.

White wares in porcelain or fine stoneware were produced throughout the period; most were decorated with a variety of techniques which included incised, moulded or etched decoration. 'An hua' or 'secret' decoration was a specialist method in which the design was lightly carved into the body or painted in white slip. The pot was then covered with white glaze and the design only became

colour was difficult these red designs were limited to fish or fruit.

Painting in coloured enamels, which are low-temperature glazes applied to the fired glaze and refired in a low-temperature muffle kiln, was developed during the reign of Ch'eng Hua (1465–87). The so-called 'tou-ts'ai' style of decoration, meaning 'contrasting colours', employed washes of apple green, red, aubergine and lemon over a lightly drawn design in underglaze blue. Small pieces such as wine and stem cups were decorated with chickens, fruit and so on. The 'chicken-cups', as they have come to be known, possess the delicate refined qualities associated with the reign and have never been surpassed in either skill or sensitivity.

Another technique to produce richly coloured and decorated pots involved applying different coloured glazes, separated by raised ribs of clay, directly on to the biscuited pot. The boldness of the technique encouraged simple bold patterns which often favoured floral designs richly coloured in turquoise, yellow, aubergine and dark blue.

The 'five-colour' or 'wu-ts'ai' style is the general term covering all polychrome wares. Designs were outlined in dull red or black and the colours were thickly applied. A palette of tomato red, turquoise blue, yellow, green, aubergine and black was used.

Yellow, the Imperial colour, was developed especially successfully during the reigns of Hung Chih and Cheng-te (1488–1521).

Towards the end of the sixteenth century the china clay deposits which existed near Ching-te Chen were almost exhausted and the other fine materials necessary for the production of porcelain were difficult to obtain. At the same time, while no technical problem seemed too difficult, the general standard of design varied widely. European trade demands were beginning to have an effect both on the form and on the decoration, and export wares were of a generally inferior quality.

Ch'ing dynasty (AD 1644–1912)

During the Ch'ing Dynasty great emphasis was put on technical ingenuity and perfection rather than aesthetic considerations, with the result that some work seems cold and unfeeling, however well it is made. From 1680 the Emperor took a personal interest in the arts and sponsored the development of twenty-seven different handcrafts in the palace at Peking. The Imperial pottery factory was rebuilt and working conditions improved. During the two following reigns competent supervisors at the factory re-established and maintained a high standard of manufacture and the quality and finish on pots were

Porcelain teapot with design of buds, flowers and bird painted in 'famille verte' enamel K'ang Hsi, Ch'ing dynasty, c AD 1700. Height 5 inches. (Hastings Museum)

carefully sustained. A wide range of brightly coloured monochrome glazes was introduced, though on forms which tended to be formal and dull.

The Dutch East India Company, established in 1602, was soon conducting a large and thriving export trade with China, and Spain, Portugal, Holland, England, France, Denmark and Sweden were represented at Canton. The Europeans favoured some shapes and designs more than others and eventually the Chinese adapted their production accordingly. This had no noticeable effect on pots made for internal use in China, but around the early part of the eighteenth century such items as salt-cellars, cruets, and tea and coffee cups with saucers were made for export. European motifs were incorporated into the Chinese designs, which as a result became crowded and their meaning either obscured or lost.

Decorated porcelain ware, which was produced in fairly large quantities in the reign of K'ang Hsi (1622–1773), employed the traditional Chinese designs of prunus, peony, lotus and chrysanthemum as well as historical scenes. The main style of decoration was that employing families of enamel colours such as 'famille verte', in which large areas were painted in different greens. Yellow, red, aubergine and black were also used in this way. Clear, fresh colours and adventurous subject matter gave these wares charm and elegance. The colours, often painted directly on to the pot and known as on-biscuit, were covered with glaze which gave a design with a soft and subdued quality.

The reign of Ch'ien Lung (1736–95) saw the last great period of Chinese ceramic activity. Clay was used to imitate, very successfully, bronze, jade, shells, wood and lacquer. Western trade was at its height and much ware was taken to Canton and decorated before they were exported. Lacework decoration, in which pressed or deeply incised holes were filled with glaze, sometimes known as 'rice-bowls' after the rice-

Fine red stoneware teapot based on bamboo design. Yi-hsing ware. These wares were widely exported to Europe where they proved to be very popular, especially the teapots, which were copied almost exactly by the Elers brothers in England, among others. c AD 1700. Height 4 inches. (Hastings Museum)

Artisan paintings showing the various processes involved in the making of porcelain. Chinese. late eighteenth or early nineteenth century. (British Museum)

Obtaining the clay from the mountains

The potter's wheel

Decorating the unglazed ware

Applying the glaze and drying in the sun.

Firing the ware

shaped translucent holes, was very popular.

Ching-te Chen was not the only production centre. Peasant wares were made in many areas using local materials and intended for local use. In one area low-fired stonewares were produced which could be used directly on the naked flame. Three major groups of ware, Swatow, Yi-hsing and Blanc de Chine were, apart from their technical excellence and beauty, highly influential in the West.

Swatow ware was a provincially produced porcelain made during the seventeenth century and later which was decorated with great verve in green and red enamel. Much of this was exported to Japan where it was greatly admired as well as to Europe where it influenced the designs used on porcelain. Boats, mariners' compasses, crabs and crayfish were often used as decoration, as well as the more conventional designs. Made for everyday use, the designs have a freshness and spirit partly derived from their rapid method of production.

In the late seventeenth and eighteenth centuries, Yi-hsing ware and Blanc-de-Chine wares were made and exported to Europe in large quantities. Yi-hsing wares from Kiangsu province formed the largest group of unglazed wares. Made from finely prepared red-brown clays, they acquired a slight gloss at high temperature. The pots were either thrown and turned or made by pressing clay into clay moulds. Teapots in a wide range of shapes were a principal product. Some were smooth and round, others were square or hexagonal in shape. Later wares imitated materials such as bamboo or metal. They were exported to Europe in large quantities where they stimulated Bottger, Elers and Dwight in their researches into the making of porcelain. These pots, often known as buccaro wares, had a pleasing simplicity of form and colour.

Blanc-de-Chine, produced at Te-hua in Fukien province, was also exported in large quantities to Europe. It was a very different product, a low-temperature porcelain paste which was highly vitrified and translucent milky-white in colour. Plastic modelling of dragons and the like was sometimes carried out on the necks of bottles, but the chief product consisted of statuettes of the Buddhist goddess of mercy, Kuan-yin.

Korea

Geographically situated north-east of China and forming a natural link with the southernmost island of Japan, it was inevitable that Korean pots should both reflect Chinese culture and be one of the means of conveying Chinese influence to Japan. Yet though many wares were closely related to those made in China, potters in Korea did develop techniques and styles which became distinctively Korean, and reflected native culture. Early Korean wares showed great similarity with the burial pottery of China. Jars, libation cups and food bowls were made and mounted, rather elegantly, on hollow stems which were often split and carved.

Silla period (c 50 BC–AD 935)

During the period known as Old Silla (AD 400–600) high-fired wares with a hard vitrified body were made and many were decorated with mottled ash glazes. When the kingdom became united under one ruler in the period known as Unified Silla (AD 600–925),

Grey earthenware chafing dish with incised decoration. Korean, Silla Dynasty, c 50 BC – AD 935. Height 7½ inches. (Victoria & Albert Museum, London)

Korean bowl. Silla dynasty, c AD 57–918. Height 3 inches. (Victoria & Albert Museum, London)

Korean porcelain bowl, celadon glaze. Twelfth century. (Victoria & Albert Museum, London)

Pre-Korai box with cover. Height 3½ inches. (Victoria & Albert Museum, London)

the Buddhist doctrine of cremation was followed. Many burial urns from this period have survived which were made in the form of ovoid covered jars, cylindrical boxes and long-necked bottles often decorated with floral and geometric designs. Stoneware at this time was often glazed an olive-brown and some white wares were produced. During this period green lead-glazed earthenware was also made, probably using lead imported from China.

Koryo dynasty (AD 918–1392)

During the Koryo dynasty Korean potters began to develop their own styles subtly

White porcelain bowl with cream coloured glaze. Early Koryo dynasty. Height $2\frac{1}{2}$ inches. (Victoria & Albert Museum, London)

Octagonal Korean pigment box. Height $1\frac{3}{4}$ inches. (Victoria & Albert Museum, London)

Porcelain lidded wine ewer with sensitive and lively underglaze decoration. Korean. Yi dynasty, seventeeth or eighteenth century. (British Museum)

different from those of China. Influenced to a large extent by the techniques and styles of the Sung dynasty, after a transitional period lasting about 100 years, the finest pots were made. The best ware was undoubtedly the various celadon glazed pots. They were related to the northern celadons of China but the glaze often had a bluish tint. Decoration was incised, carved or moulded with great vigour. Floral scrolls, boys holding branches, and the Buddhist motifs of ducks, water and lotus petals were all used. Porcelain similar to the Ting wares as well as the finer Ch'ing pai wares of China were also made.

One of the most distinctive methods of decoration which was developed was that in which incised patterns were filled with white or black slip under the celadon glaze. Lace-like in effect, the technique was sometimes fine and delicate; at other times, fussy and over-ornate.

Yi dynasty (AD 1392–1910)

The Yi dynasty saw the first native rulers of Korea who ruled until the dynasty ended in 1910, when the country was annexed by Japan. Koryo celadons continued to be made, as did the white porcelain, and few technical

developments took place. The Japanese invasion during the sixteenth century weakened the country and afterwards the wares, generally, are of a rougher and less refined nature though often possessing great charm. Pots for daily use, such as bean pots, jars, wine flasks and bowls, were decorated with a remarkably direct iron brushwork, giving them strength and vigour rarely found in the more sophisticated Korean wares.

Japan

While the Korean potters developed their own subtle styles closely akin to those of China, the Japanese pots, though still influenced by China, were much softer and more 'naturalistic' in feel. Where Chinese pots had precision and severity of style, and were intellectually conceived, the Japanese forms were gentler and more intimate, reflecting perhaps the

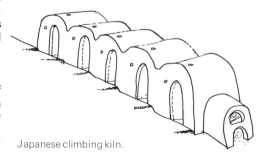

Japanese climbing kiln.

influence of the lower temperature and moister climate of the country.

Neolithic Japanese pottery made for a period of about 3000 years was made entirely by hand-built methods and fired to earthenware temperature. Known collectively as Jomon ware, it was made by coiling clay strips one above the other and the sides were then beaten into shape. Some of the ware was decorated by impressing cord or plaited rope into the surface. Open-topped bowls tapering towards the base seem to have been a popular form. Immigrants from the Chinese mainland brought more sophisticated making and firing techniques. The use of the wheel led to smoother-shaped forms. Later, other tech-

niques such as more elaborate kilns enabled T'ang lead-glazed, splashed wares and the olive-glazed stoneware to be made.

When trade broke down, Chinese influence was reduced and Japanese potters made quieter, softer ash-glazed wares, such as bottles with incised floral designs.

Medieval period

There is a story that Toshiro, a Japanese potter, returned in AD 1227 from a visit to China, bringing back more sophisticated stoneware production methods, and, finding suitable clay, established a pottery at Seto in the province of Owari. True story or not, the thirteenth century saw the production of

Pottery figures, warriors. Northern Wei dynasty (AD 386–535). (British Museum)

High-shouldered stoneware vase with a narrow neck. Decorated with incised whorls under a transparent green ash glaze. Japan. Ko-zeto ware. Kamakura period. c AD 1300. Height 10 inches. (British Museum)

Stoneware jar for containing rice, showing the patchy glaze caused by the high firing in a wood-burning kiln. Japan, Shigaraki ware. c AD 1338–1573. Height 13⅞ inches. (British Museum)

Japanese stoneware pottery on a significant scale.

Other pottery centres were established, often by Koreans or under their influence. During the fourteenth century several recognized production centres were set up, each with its own characteristics. Six old centres are known: Seto, Tokoname, Shigaraki, Tamba, Bizen and Echizen.

It is at the end of the sixteenth century, when Hideyoshi's conquest of Korea caused the immigration of Korean potters with their potting techniques and knowledge, that the industry became most productive. Social changes at that time caused the priests and aristocracy to be supplanted as patrons by the more numerous groups of feudal lords and wealthy commoners.

Tea ceremony

Tea was beginning to be drunk ceremonially and demands were made for suitable vessels. The tea ceremony spread from the Zen buddhist monasteries to the wealthier classes. Tea masters took a personal interest in the vessels required and often worked with the potter, who gained an elevated position in society. The ceremony employed the use of a small jar

Above: Stoneware teabowl with painted decoration in brown, black and white over grey glaze by Kenzan, Kyoto. Eighteenth century. Height 2½ inches. (Victoria & Albert Museum, London)

Below: Raku teabowl, for use in the Tea Ceremony. The Old Pine. Attributed to Sonyneah. Eighteenth century. (British Museum)

for the powdered tea, a drinking bowl, a washing bowl, a cake dish and, occasionally, a water-holder, incense box, incense burner, fire-holder and a vase to hold a single spray of flowers. Samurai would often choose a highly valued tea utensil as a reward for service, so highly regarded had the vessels for the tea ceremony become.

Each centre produced its characteristic ware. Seto was perhaps the most important of these, and here pots were produced under the direction of various tea masters, the most well known of whom is Furuta Oribe (c AD 1580–1615). Thick opaque glazes containing feldspar were decorated with painted houses, flowers and geometric patterns in green and blue for characteristic Oribe ware. Seto black glaze had a lustrous and lacquer-like quality.

Bizen ware was heavier and rougher and many vessels for daily use were produced here. The fine reddish clay was often left unglazed and dark grey or black 'straw marks' caused by firing the pots in straw are characteristic. Tokoname wares stand out with a strong, powerful quality and large water jars are still produced there.

As part of the tea ceremony the decorating and firing of pots in the process, which is now known as raku, was started by the Raku family. Raku was a method of producing pottery by firing it quickly to a comparatively low temperature. Much of the pottery was made with coarse-grained rough clay to enable it to withstand the firing process, but the forms were carefully considered and the glazes were often austere and simple. Raku tea bowls were greatly liked by the tea masters for use in the tea ceremony.

The late seventeenth century saw a period of sophistication in pots made for the tea ceremony. Studied roughness and asymmetrical effects on the raku pots eventually led to the debasement of the forms. Functional qualities of the pots became unimportant, and aesthetic and sensual qualities were the chief consideration; bases were often untrimmed and rough, and glazes thick and treacle-like.

Porcelain

Porcelain was not made in Japan until after 1600, when suitable white clay was found at Arita. The style matured rapidly under early Korean guidance and bold enamel designs in red, yellow, green and blue were used in the mid-seventeenth century. Japanese designs tended to change the colours of nature, and water was liable to flow red, flowers to bear green blossoms and trees indigo fruit.

The so-called Imari wares, made at Arita, were elaborately decorated and stimulated by the establishment of the Dutch East India Companys' trading post, it was produced in

Stoneware bowl with dull brown snakeskin glaze and gold lacquer at tip. Satsuma ware, sixteenth century. Height 3¼ inches. (British Museum)

large quantities, mainly for export. Imari underglaze blue porcelain had a soft restrained quality. The technique of decorating with overglaze enamels was used sensitively on Kakiemon wares. Soft reds, yellows and blues were used on symmetrical designs on blue and white porcelain. Exquisite porcelains were made during the eighteenth century and a transfer technique was developed to enable the duplication of designs for place settings. Many of these wares were copied by factories at Derby and Worcester in Britain.

The city of Kyoto expanded rapidly in the late seventeenth century and the so-called Kyoto wares became important, especially for the production of earthenware. Nonomura

Narrow-necked porcelain vases with painted decoration of flowering sprays and dragons. Kutani ware, c 1720. Height 5 inches. (Hastings Museum)

Two-tier box with a lid, porcelain with underglaze-blue and enamel painted decoration, Nabeshima-style. Arita. (Victoria & Albert Museum, London)

Ninsei was a potter associated with Kyoto who developed painted enamel decoration and influenced, among others, the great decorator Ogata Kenzan (1664–1743). Trained originally as a calligrapher, Kenzan developed an economical, near-abstract style of spontaneous and powerful brushwork. Soft browns, blacks and blues were his favourite colours. Other individual potters, Mokubei and Dohachi, followed him and the contemporary Japanese potter Shoji Hamada continued this tradition until his death in 1978.

Kyushu, the Japanese island nearest Korea, was the most sensitive to Asian and Korean influence which was reflected in the wares made there. Jugs, large water jars, lipped pouring vessels, bowls and plates were made in fine, dark coloured clay covered with a thick, buff glaze, with a coarse crackle. During the seventeenth century they were decorated in iron-brown pigment designs as well as black and white slip inlays.

The long tradition of local potteries and great master-potters continues today, as does the feeling of the use of 'natural' clay qualities in the pots. Studied 'accidental' decoration on asymmetrical forms are often highly valued. Japanese pottery, though owing much to Chinese influence, developed a studied freedom which is completely indigenous to Japan and today exerts a strong influence on studio potters, especially in Britain and the USA.

4 ISLAMIC COUNTRIES

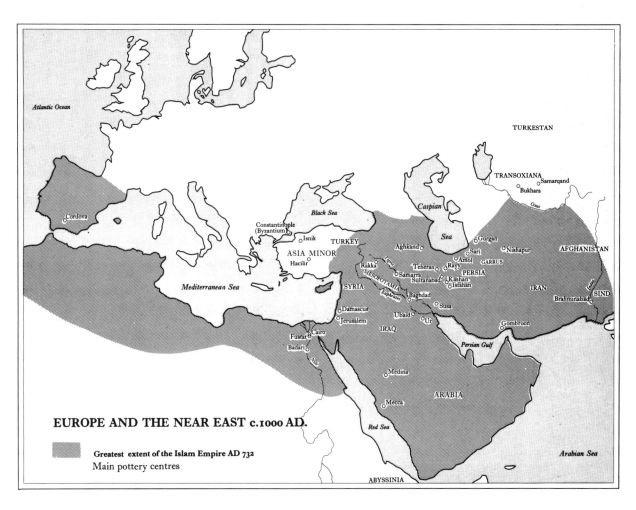

EUROPE AND THE NEAR EAST c.1000 AD.

Greatest extent of the Islam Empire AD 732
Main pottery centres

At the end of the seventh century AD, the countries of Islam formed a huge Empire which extended from the borders of India in the east, through Persia, Mesopotamia and north Africa into Spain. In a matter of three generations the Islamic faith had spread rapidly unifying many races, countries and people.

By the first century AD the ancient civilizations of Mesopotamia and Egypt had greatly declined politically and socially with a corresponding fall in the quantity and quality of arts and crafts. Persia, having fought Byzantium for so long, had exhausted itself. The

Two-handled bowl with blue alkaline glaze. Syria, fourth century AD, Height $4\frac{3}{4}$ inches. (Fitzwilliam Museum, Cambridge)

fourth and fifth centuries saw a further decline throughout the Arab world in settled life and an increase in nomadism which did little to stimulate the production of pots. The Arab tribes, which made up a considerable though largely nomadic and pastoral population, acknowledged no authority but that of their own tribal rulers. No major unifying force existed in the area until, in AD 622, the inhabitants of Medina, a prosperous trading city, welcomed Mohammed and his religious teachings which formed the basis of the Islamic or Muslim faith. Mohammed quickly attracted a strong following and in due course the religious faith gave the Arabs their unity. The eventual result was a completely new and cohesive spirit, in which religious, political and social organizations were established.

Mohammed declared that the Koran was not only the word of God but a guide to the way of life and forbade its use in translation; thus a single language was introduced which could be read throughout Islam and this had the effect also of unifying diverse peoples.

Muslims believe that the revelation of god is twofold, coming firstly from the writings of the Prophet, known as the Koran, and secondly from the relation of the manner of life of the Prophet. Traditionally the account of what the Prophet said or did was passed on by word of mouth, but in the ninth century a complete record of these accounts was made. This record was known as the Hadith or Traditions of the Prophet and it stated, for example, that idolatry in the form of human or animal representation was forbidden, as was the use of precious metal for tableware. Wine, too, was not allowed. These commands had some influence on the design and decoration of pottery. For example, geometric and abstract patterns were often used in preference to those depicting figures, though there are plenty of exceptions. The technique of lustre-painting, originally developed on glass, was adapted for use on pottery, probably because it imitated gold and silver. Much attention was given to the manufacture of fine decorated pottery, which was highly valued in the absence of vessels of precious metals. There is at least one record of verses dedicated to the beautiful bowls adorning the table of some wealthy man. The prohibition of wine meant the absence of wine jars, which in Greece, for example, had provided many decorative containers for the export trade and, as a result, had been sent throughout the Mediterranean area. Water containers, often made with long tapering spouts, were made.

Pottery was not used in Islam for religious purposes until the thirteenth or fourteenth century when the production of tiles to decorate mosques became widespread. The tiles were often decorated with Arabic script; the angular kufic or the cursive neskhi was used, though these often developed into mere patterns rather than inscriptions.

The establishment of an ordered government over a large area and the growth of towns and industries favoured the development of extensive internal and international trade. The route to China through central Asia brought the Arabs into contact with the Chinese and this had a major influence on Islamic pottery during three successive periods. The whitewares and richly painted earthenwares of the T'ang dynasty (AD 618–906) inspired the Muslim potters in the ninth century; the fine Sung porcelains of the eleventh and twelfth centuries were a second influence and, finally, the blue-and-white wares of Ming China produced further changes and developments.

A comparison of the backgrounds and approach to pottery making in China and Islam, however, reveals important differences. No royal patronage or court pottery existed in Arabia nor was the craft ever practised from a purely aesthetic point of view as it often was in China. All pots made by the Islamic potters had a use, mostly in the daily life of a Muslim, and qualities in the pots were rarely made just for their beauty. But when finely made Chinese pots, especially the porcelains, were imported into Islam, they were admired by the Arab potters, who imitated and copied them, often slavishly, using completely different pottery techniques, before adding ideas of their own.

All the pottery made by the Muslim potters was fired to earthenware temperatures which are lower than those required for stoneware and porcelain. The necessary knowledge and raw materials did not exist for firing pots to a higher temperature and many experiments were made in an attempt to imitate the whiteness of Chinese porcelain at earthenware temperatures.

The results of these developments were not limited in application to Islam but were, in time, to affect the whole of western pottery. The use of white opaque tin glaze with coloured painted decoration, as well as lead glaze over coloured slips, were processes which spread across Europe; the former technique into Spain, Italy and then to the rest of western Europe, and the latter into Europe through Byzantium and Italy.

Much of the beauty of Islamic pottery lies in its decoration rather than its form. The long tradition of painted and decorated wares of Mesopotamia and the Near East was continued and developed by the Islamic potters. Whether the designs were painted, carved, moulded, or built up in relief, they were always well thought out and carefully arranged on the pot.

Potters made almost all the utensils for day-to-day living. Form related to the function of the pot was always a primary consideration, though Islamic pottery is thought of as one of the most richly decorative styles. The range of vessels made was extensive and included water containers, water pots with long tapering spouts for ablution rituals, cups, beakers, braziers and spittoons, though it is the numerous bowls, often richly decorated, which receive most attention today.

Pre-Islamic period until AD 632

Before the growth of Islam there had been a long tradition of painted pottery throughout the Near East which is fully described in Chapter One. Goblets, painted with zig-zag patterns and tigers, have been excavated at Susa and date back some 3700 years. By 1700 BC the dead were buried in cemeteries, and pottery, weapons and jewellery were buried with them. A variety of well preserved pots have been found in these graves, many with a long spout imitating both in form and decoration the beak of a bird, for use probably in religious ceremonies. Geometric decoration was also used on the pots.

The use of glaze had been developed in Mesopotamia around 1500 BC and had come into fairly widespread use around 500 BC. Beads made from soapstone and glazed a turquoise colour had been made at, among other places, Badari in Egypt. Later a lead glaze was discovered in Babylon during the time of the Kassites (1750–1170 BC) and the technique was eventually brought to Persia. Tin oxide was added to opacify the lead glaze as early as the eighth century BC and was used to glaze building bricks used in Nimrud in Assyria. The most famous example of the use of this technique is the Ishtar Gate, built by Nebuchadnezzar (604–562 BC). Iron, copper and antimonate of lead were used to colour the tin glaze. Lead glazes allowed a wide colour range that was functional at a fairly low temperature of 1000°C (1832°F) and made possible the production of some brilliant colour effects. The use of tin oxide in a glaze died out until the ninth century AD when it was used by the Mesopotamian potters to imitate the whiteness of Chines porcelain.

The Empire of the Sassanian Kings (AD 224–650) in Persia saw little development in

Earthenware jar, applied clay decoration, turquoise blue glaze. Syrian, fourth century AD. Height 19 inches. (Fitzwilliam Museum, Cambridge)

Amphora-shaped vase with two handles and moulded decoration. Sassanian, c 300 AD. Height 12 inches. (British Museum)

the art of the potter, apart from the manufacture of large liquid storage vessels. These were wheel-thrown with moulded designs and decorated in a blue glaze. Similar pots are still made in remote parts of the country today.

Early Islamic wares (AD 632–c 1150)

Pottery production was slow to respond to the Islamic expansion, mainly because the movement was primarily concerned with establishing political and economic control rather than patronizing the arts. The Umayyad dynasty (AD 661–750), with its capital at Damascus in Syria, was, for example, largely engaged in physical and spiritual conquest. In time the faith spread throughout the Near East, where the Islamic army was welcomed as a great liberator. Through conquest the Greco-Roman art of Syria and Egypt and the Sassanian art of Persia and Mesopotamia were all absorbed into the Arab culture. Syria had been a Roman province and had been under strong western influence which included Greco-Roman type ornament with strong naturalistic foliage, animals and figures. From the West, however, came also the influence of Assyria and Babylon, with emphasis on formal designs of repeating symmetrical patterns with a strong abstract tendency. These two styles merged into what has come to be known as the arabesque style. The new Muslim decorators indulged in all-over patterns infinitely repeated. While many of their patterns retained the abstract quality, naturalistic renderings of flowers and foliage were often used in largely symmetrical compositions.

In AD 750 the Persian house of Abbasid took over power and the capital was moved east from Damascus and established at Baghdad on the Tigris, moving the centre of artistic influence back from Syria with its strong western background to Mesopotamia. A beautiful and exotic city was built which rivalled Constantinople, the capital of the Byzantine Empire, in both splendour and commercial success. Arts and scholarship were pursued in a rich and colourful oriental atmosphere.

Most of the pottery of this period was made in and around the new capital of Baghdad. At Samarra, north of Baghdad, the Abbasid Caliphs built, occupied and left a large and rich palace during the ninth century. From the ruins of the palace it has been possible to identify the four main groups of pottery of the period: unglazed ware, lead-glazed ware imitating the Chinese T'ang splashed ware, white tin-glazed ware with painted decoration and lustreware.

Unglazed ware

Until the influence of Chinese pottery stimulated new processes and encouraged the search for different techniques, Muslim potters continued to work much as their predecessors had done. Unglazed water pots, made in buff clay, had been made for centuries throughout the whole area of the Near East and even today the industry continues. Because the unglazed clay was slightly porous, water continually seeped through the walls of the pot to the outside where it evaporated. This caused loss of heat which helped to keep the water inside cool and fresh. Such pots were often made up in quite complex clay moulds fired to a low temperature which were filled by pressing in clay. Intricate designs were carved or stamped into the clay mould, before it was fired, in a way similar to that used by the Romans for the production of their red-gloss wares.

Lead-glazed splashed wares

T'ang polychrome splashed wares from China were imported in the ninth century and at first inspired almost exact copies by Islamic potters. Red clay was used for the body covered with white slip. This was splashed with various colouring oxides onto a transparent lead glaze. This resulted in the yellow and brown colours running down the pot as lead glazes are very fluid. Later, purple aubergine and black extended the colour range on the pots. Islamic potters soon improvised their own methods of decoration. Sgraffito decoration,

Tin-glazed earthenware bowl with blue painted decoration. Mesopotamia, ninth century. Diameter 8 inches. (Fitzwilliam Museum, Cambridge)

for example, which was the technique of scratching a pattern through a clay slip of contrasting colour, usually white, to show the dark body beneath became common. Traditional patterns of palmettes and rosettes were used. This was the main difference, in appearance, between the Chinese and Arabic splashed pots. Inspection of the clay body of these pots also helps to make the distinction clear as the Chinese wares were fired to a higher temperature. Sgraffito technique was also used widely on other types of Islamic pottery, of which the most important is the group of wares that were covered with single colour lead glazes over relief decoration. Rich green and yellow runny lead glazes had been in limited use during the Roman occupation of Egypt; the relief decoration had often been of the Greco-Roman naturalistic style. In the ninth century the Egyptian potters brought their skill to Mesopotamia where the style of decoration changed; the use of kufic script, for example, became more popular.

White tin-glazed wares

White pots which resembled the white porcelain wares from China, were still one of the ideals of the Islamic potters. They found that the nearest they could achieve was to use an opaque white glaze with the use of tin oxide. The discovery that the addition of tin oxide to the glaze rendered it white opaque had been discovered some 1000 years earlier by the Babylonians who had used the glaze with great success on bricks and tiles though, as far as is known, not on pots. The technique was now rediscovered in Mesopotamia. A good, reliable, even white surface was achieved. The white tin glaze was simple to apply to the pot as it did not need to go over a white slip and it was more stable in the firing than transparent lead glaze.

It is unlikely that the Islamic potters realized what a fantastic and far-reaching discovery tin-glaze would prove to be. Not only was the white surface relatively simple to achieve but its clean good looks and even quality made it

Earthenware plate, tin-glaze, with blue and green painted decoration which has run on the raw glaze to give the characteristic blotting-paper effect. Eighth or ninth century. Diameter 15 inches. (Victoria & Albert Museum, London)

ideal for painted decoration of all sorts. As the materials were more carefully prepared the whiteness and regularity of the surface was improved. In time the art of tin-glazing spread through north Africa, eventually being taken by the Arabs into Spain where it formed the basis of Hispano-Moresque ware. From there it spread into Italy and formed the basis of Italian maiolica. In due course it spread throughout Europe to France, Delft in Holland, and Bristol and Lambeth in England.

The Arabs themselves were not content to leave the dishes and bowls plain. They recognized the possibilities presented by the pure white surface and almost immediately started decorating the unfired glaze with painted designs. Various colouring pigments were used but the most popular was cobalt oxide, deposits of which were found in Arabia. This oxide gives blue when used on or in a glaze. Early dishes decorated with cobalt blue tended to have simple, rather naïve designs. Occasionally green obtained from copper was used and later a purple-brown from manganese was developed. Early tin-glazed dishes can be recognized by the fuzzy quality of the decoration, as the pigment, when applied to the raw tin-glaze, tended to spread and lose definition. Later, cobalt ore was exported to China where it encouraged the blue and white porcelain of the Ming period.

Lustrewares

The fourth major technique used by the Muslim potters at this time was that of lustre. To achieve the effect of lustre, the potter must have detailed knowledge and great skill, for the difference between success and failure is very slight. Too much heat and the lustre will burn away, too little and it will not shine. Lustre is said to have been inspired by the famous gold dishes made by Sassanian goldsmiths and was in widespread use towards the end of the ninth century. It is one of the few techniques used in Islamic pottery which can truly be said to be entirely indigenous to the Near East rather than to China. The technique is thought to have been invented in Egypt for use on glass around AD 700–800 and was brought by craft workers to Mesopotamia. Briefly, the technique involves preparing a special mixture of the sulphates of gold, silver or copper, and red or yellow ochre to act as a painting medium. This mixture is painted on to the fired glaze and the pot is fired a third time in a smoky (reducing) atmosphere at a low temperature. The metal oxide, reduced to metal, is suspended on the glaze and appears as a dull metallic film at this stage. Burnishing removes the ochre and reveals the lustre in all its brilliance. Unfortunately, the lustre does not retain its brilliance and over the years often changes colour and becomes dull.

Early lustrework tended to be more colourful and was often used in combination with other types of colouring pigment. On some pots plain gold lustre was used on a white tin-glaze, on others ruby lustre was used on a white background either alone or in combination with other colours, and lustre-work in gold and silver was also carried out. When the lustre coating was very thin it appeared as yellow-brown or olive. Because the technique was so difficult, some centres, for example Nishapur in Persia, failed to produce it successfully and here the technique of underglaze painting was to be developed, as will be explained later.

By the end of the ninth century the use of yellow-brown lustrework predominated. Early centres were mainly in Mesopotamia. The decoration on lustrework made at Samarra was characterized by an absence of the human figure in preference for floral and geometric motifs. Other lustrework centres included representations of humans and animals in their designs, though often in very stylized arrangements.

Highly acclaimed, the lustrewares of Baghdad were widely exported, reaching such places as Samarqand, Brahminabad in Sind, Egypt and Medina Azahra near Cordova in southern Spain. By the end of the tenth

Earthenware bowl with tin-glaze decorated with brown monochrome lustre. Floral decoration. Mesopotamia, ninth century. Diameter 12 inches. (British Museum)

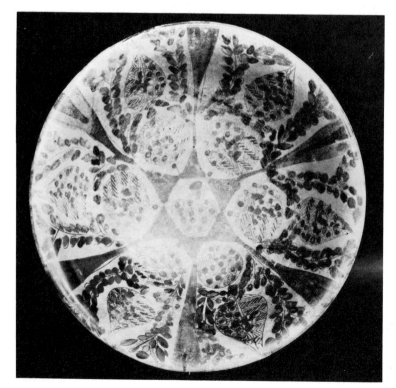

century, however, the industry was greatly reduced in size, the majority of lustreware potters having moved to work for the newly established Fatimid Court in Cairo.

Regional pottery

In different areas various sorts of wares were produced which, while following the teaching of Islam, also reflected local traditions. In East Persia, painted pottery, sometimes known as Samarqand ware, was made at

centres such as Samarqand, Nishapur and Sari. It demonstrated a unique quality long before pottery of great interest was made in the rest of Persia. The eastern provinces of Persia and the lands beyond the river Oxus, often known as Transoxian, were united under the Samanids, a Persian dynasty from AD 874 to 999: Bukhara was their capital city, Samarqand the chief city. The trade routes to the East lay through Samarqand and this had an indirect effect on the pottery in the province.

The ninth and tenth centuries saw what, in many ways, was one of the highest and purest interpretations of Islamic ideas in pottery. The potters of east Persia were unable to make lustreware, and so turned their attention to other ways of decorating the white ground of the pots. They were particularly keen to find ways of using colour decoration which did not run under the lead glaze. It was discovered that colouring pigments first mixed with fine white clay remained stable under a transparent glaze. The resulting pigments

Bowl with painted decoration, East Persia, tenth century. (Arts Council)

Below: Earthenware dish with black design in kufic script on white slip. East Persian, Nishapur, ninth or tenth century. Diameter 14½ inches. (Victoria & Albert Museum)

Earthenware bowl with bird design painted in coloured slips over white slip. East Persian, Sari, tenth or eleventh century. Diameter 7½ inches. (Victoria & Albert Museum)

Earthenware bowl, design painted in coloured slips on white background with sgraffito detail. Persian, Samarqand, tenth century. Diameter 7¾ inches. (British Museum)

Earthenware bowl with colourless glaze over design painted in white slip over black ground. Persia, Nishapur, ninth or tenth century. Diameter 10¾ inches. (Victoria & Albert Museum, London)

were less fluid to apply and encouraged simple, formal designs. White slip, over a red body, was decorated with a black or purplish underglaze pigment as well as dark brown, dark red and aubergine. Using the basic colours of the calligrapher, simple bands of designs in kufic script were painted on to the white pot, often round the rim. Large areas of the bowls were left white which gave them their most striking characteristic, in contrast to the later decorative techniques which developed in Persia, where most of the surface was covered with patterns. Such phrases as 'Generosity is (one) of the qualities of the blessed', 'Peace and blessing', 'Good fortune', 'Blessing' or 'Good fortune and perpetuity' were used. Simple patterns were developed from the kufic script, decorative dots were used and occasionally very stylized animals and birds can be found. No examples of human figures have been discovered, reflecting a strong religious influence.

At Sari, in Persia, a pottery centre on the Caspian Sea pots were decorated by similar methods but a wider range of colour was used and a particularly beautiful green was added to the palette. Stylized birds moving across bowls, and radiating stalks and flowers, are typical. The pigments used have retained a brightness of colour and the almost modern conception of the designs makes the bowls very attractive.

Persian sgraffito wares

Influenced by the Sassanian engraved metalwork the sgraffito technique was further developed in Persia in the tenth century. Mesopotamian potters had used the technique on their lead-glazed bowls under splashed

Bowl with sgraffito decoration through white slip showing dark body, recalling Sassanian engraved metalwork. Green-coloured rim. Twelfth or thirteenth century. Diameter 9 inches. (Fitzwilliam Museum, Cambridge)

Earthenware bowl with painted decoration of a cheetah on a chain. Persia, Nishapur, *c* 900 AD. Diameter 8¾ inches. (Victoria & Albert Museum, London)

colour decoration, but the Persian potters developed the technique much more fully. The so-called 'champlevé' or carved style of the Garrus district, lying south-east of the Caspian Sea, is characterized by large areas of white slip left on a dark ground and was an extremely successful use of the technique brought to perfection around the late twelfth and thirteenth centuries. Sometimes the transparent glaze was colourless, sometimes tinted green. Fine lines scratched through the slip in simple geometric designs produced an effect very much like that of chased metalwork. In the Amol and Aghkand district green, brown and purple colouring oxides were painted on to the carved slip and animals and birds were incorporated into the designs.

Egyptian fatimid dynasty (AD 969–1171)

The Fatimid dynasty in Egypt established their independence of Baghdad in AD 969 and became the new cultural centre of the Islamic world. Immigrant artists and craftworkers continued the artistic traditions of Baghdad in Egypt but new styles did develop. While failing to surpass the potters of Mesopotamia in the shape of the pots, they produced technically excellent and beautiful lustreware, with colours ranging from rich, deep copper-red to pale lemon-yellow. The designs combined the classical naturalistic style and the formality of oriental patterns with a strong Christian influence. Fantastic birds, animals and human figures were shown, as were priests and incense burners. Nasir-i-Khuaran, who visited Egypt from 1046 to 1050, wrote: 'At Misr [the Arabic name for Egypt] pottery of all kinds is made. . . . They make colours for them like those of the stuff called bugalimun.

The colours change according to the ways in which the vessel is held.' Bugalimun was a sort of shot silk which describes exactly the changing colour of lustreware.

With the fall of the Fatimids in 1171 there came a decline in the production of pottery in Egypt; many potters moved east again into Mesopotamia and Persia, and some may have moved as far as southern Spain.

Middle Islamic period
(*c* AD 1150–1350)

Major changes were brought about in the Islamic Empire by the invasion of a number of Turkish tribes from central Asia. The Seljuqs entered Persia and Syria, accepted the Muslim faith and gradually gained control of the Empire, entering and conquering Baghdad in 1055. In 1171 the Ottoman Turks overthrew the Fatimid house of Egypt and in the thirteenth century captured Asia Minor from the Byzantine Empire. Unlike the early Islamic period, no permanent court was established and the centre of culture moved from place to place absorbing and expressing new techniques and stylistic influences. This period, lasting some 200 years, is considered to be the great classical period of Islamic arts. New techniques were employed in architecture and many new ideas were forthcoming in both science and arts. Ceramics were not excluded from this flowering of the arts. Pottery centres which had been established at Baghdad, Cairo and Samarqand earlier were now supplemented by new centres in northern Persia, most notably at Kashan. Potters tended to set up workshops where their wares would be most easily available, and so many potteries were found on trade routes.

The fine white porcelain wares imported from Sung China (AD 960–1279) encouraged the Islamic potters to experiment further to produce similar wares for themselves. Unlike the potters of the early period who only copied the surface colour and, to some extent, the shape of the Chinese wares, the Islamic potters now experimented in the mixing up of a vitrified body by the addition of ground glass to the clay body.

Centres of production

Kashan, 125 miles south of Teheran, is the most famous centre set up in Persia where work of a high technical and artistic standard was produced well into the fourteenth century. Complete genealogies of potter families, some dating from the tenth century and continuing for 400 years, are known. Kashan was never a seat of government, but developed as a peaceful industrial centre. Vases made in Kashan were given special mention in

Earthenware bowl, design carved through white slip to show dark body. Monochrome glaze. Persian, Rayy, Garrus type, thirteenth century. Diameter about 7 inches. (Fitzwilliam Museum, Cambridge)

Earthenware jar with incised decoration under green glaze. Persian, c 1200. Height 17 inches. (Victoria & Albert Museum)

lists prepared after the capture of Baghdad by Hulagu Khan in 1258. Also produced in large quantities were tiles used to decorate the walls of mosques and tombs. As well as having finely painted designs these tiles were also made in complicated shapes in the form of crosses or stars which interlocked to form complex patterns.

Lying on the main route across north Persia, Rayy (Rages) was, along with Kashan, one of the major centres of production of a wide variety of pottery. It was the main centre for the production of the monochrome carved ware often known as the Seljuq ware.

Rakka was an ancient caravan city on the Euphrates in north Mesopotamia and was a major production centre, very much associated in style with pots made at Cairo.

Gurgan, to the south-east of the Caspian Sea, was a production centre for lustreware and other types of pottery. In 1942 a discovery of treasure in Gurgan, buried in the

Earthenware bowl with carved and moulded decoration under a monochrome turquoise blue glaze. Persian, Rayy, twelfth or thirteenth century. Diameter 7½ inches. (Fitzwilliam Museum, Cambridge)

early thirteenth century, proved to be of extraordinary beauty. In 1221 the town was destroyed by invading Mongols and the inhabitants buried their possessions. Vessels were packed in earthenware jars which were carefully buried in sand. Much of the work is attributed to the Kashan and Rayy potteries, but archaeological evidence suggests that some pots were also made at Gurgan. All the pots can be dated between 1200 and 1220.

Three major developments in the pottery of this period enable convenient divisions of the type of ware produced. Firstly, a fine white, semi-vitrified body similar to porcelain was artificially made for the production of white and coloured wares which formed a large part of the so-called Seljuq wares; secondly, richly coloured and finely painted decoration was developed; and thirdly, alkaline glaze was introduced on a large scale for the production of the famous rich turquoise-blue wares.

Fine Seljuq monochrome wares

Ting ware and Ch'ing pai wares of the Chinese Sung Dynasty (AD 906–1179) were imported into Persia towards the end of the tenth and beginning of the eleventh centuries. Both were fine white wares with either an ivory-white or a bluish-white glaze. These wares with their hard-vitrified body stimulated the Islamic potters, who invented a new artificial body with which to try and make similar pots. An artificial clay body had been used much earlier by the Mesopotamians and Egyptians for the production of faience wares, but whether or not there is a direct connection is not known.

A long treatise on the technique of the Seljuq potters, written in AD 1301, explains how the body was made. Quartz pebbles, crushed and powdered, plus an alkaline frit of potash and borax were added to the clay. The result was a low-temperature, translucent soft-paste body, similar to that produced later in eighteenth-century Europe, and quite a good imitation of genuine porcelain. As a clay body it would have been difficult to work due to a lack of plasticity, but it was quite strong when fired and allowed pots with thin walls to be made. The result was a whiter, finer and harder body than that of previous wares. Further translucent effects were achieved by piercing the walls with small holes which were subsequently covered with glaze. This heightened the whole transparent effect to one of great delicacy. Many of these bowls were decorated with carved designs. The powdered quartz and alkaline frit, when mixed with water, served as an excellent glaze. Because the glaze and body matched so closely and fused so well they fitted together with no danger of the glaze flaking. Sometimes these glazes were coloured by the addition of the metal oxides of copper or cobalt which, in the alkaline-based glaze, produced rich, deep colours of blue and

turquoise. Other colours, including soft purple, yellow, green and brown, were also made.

White-wares dating from the middle of the twelfth century are rare and as skills improved greater quantities were made. The refined nature of these pots made in the thirteenth century can hardly be overpraised and their delicate quality has rarely been matched.

Later, moulds were used for the production of faceted bowls which closely imitated metal-work. The definition of the moulded ornament lacks the clarity of carved decoration, but their appearance is pleasant and rich. Moulds were also in common use for the production of tiles.

Decoration on the Seljuq wares was often carved in bands round the bowls or, on faceted bowls, in panels. Subject matter was dealt with in a rhythmic style and neskhi inscriptions were often interwoven with foliage.

Painted and decorated wares

One of the problems confronting the Persian potters was the production of colourful decorated ware. Various different methods were used to produce this, the second major group of wares of this period. It had been found earlier that colouring oxides run under lead glazes because they were too fluid, and attempts by the east Persian potters to make the pigments stable by the addition of white clay had resulted in pigment which had lost its fluidity altogether and which restricted the designs that could be produced.

Various solutions were tried. One technique, known as laqabi, meaning painted, was developed, in which the artificial clay body was carved with raised lines which would act to prevent the pigments running together. An almost jewel-like effect, of a coloured carved design, set on a white background, was achieved. Flat dishes with formal designs of animals, birds and figures coloured with rich blue, yellow, purple and green worked well. Kashan seems to have been the main production centre.

In time this painting technique led, in Persia, to the production of a highly sophisticated and technically complex ware using coloured enamels in what is now known as Minai decoration. It was used to produce work which looked like contemporary illuminated manuscripts. The 'haft-rang' technique was developed and was often used to complement Minai decoration. Haft-rang was a method of underglaze decoration in which pigment was painted directly on to the biscuit-fired pot which was then dipped into a clear glaze. Unlike enamels, underglaze colours only developed their brilliance during the

Seljuq white earthenware bowl. Incised floral decoration under purple glaze. Persia, probably Rayy, c AD 1150. Diameter $7\frac{3}{4}$ inches. (Victoria & Albert Museum)

Earthenware bowl with blue and black painted decoration under a clear glaze. Persian, Khan, thirteenth century. (Victoria & Albert Museum)

Dish with carved and painted decoration under colourless glaze, laqabi ware. Persian, c 1150 AD. (British Museum)

Earthenware cup on tall stem with Minai, i.e. enamel decoration over underglaze painted decoration. Persia, thirteenth century. Height $4\frac{5}{8}$ inches. (Victoria & Albert Museum)

subsequent firing. Pale blue, purple and green underglaze colours were used and acted as a background to the enamel decoration which was added later.

Minai decoration was more complicated and required several firings to produce the final piece; first the pot was biscuit-fired, then glaze-fired; then followed the third much lower-temperature enamel firing. Glazes were usually white but on occasions a pale blue was used.

Enamels are low-temperature glazes prepared in frit form by melting the ingredients in a crucible and grinding them before applying them to the pot. Mixed with a suitable oil medium they can be made to stick to the shiny glaze surface. Rich and varied colours can be obtained at the low temperature and the enamel technique allows detailed designs to be painted as the colours do not run and lose definition. Since the enamels have already been carefully prepared as frits, which reveal their colours, the subsequent firing only changes these slightly. This gives the enamel artist a truer palette from which to work. This is comparatively rare in pottery as most raw materials only reveal their colour after being fired. Black, chestnut brown, red, white and leaf gilding were used. Many of the designs were outlined in black. Early Minai decoration, reflecting Mongol influence, depicted large figures, formally arranged. Later, the figures got smaller, a fact related to the contemporary interest in illuminated manuscripts and miniature painting generally.

Lajvardina ware used an enamelling technique in which a limited range of colours, usually black, red and white and sometimes gold, were painted on to a cobalt-blue or a rich turquoise glaze.

The greater control over colours and the fineness of the enamel technique encouraged artists who had worked on illuminated manuscripts to decorate bowls. Many designs show contemporary scenes in great detail and serve as an accurate social record of the time.

Narrative scenes are also fairly common, as are ornamental arrangements of horsemen, hunters and court scenes.

Underglaze painting with alkaline glaze

It had been found that coloured pigments were less likely to run under a glaze which was made of alkaline material such as potash or soda rather than one made of lead, and pots decorated with this technique form the third major group of wares. The so-called 'silhouette' wares, made in Persia in the twelfth century, had solid designs painted under the glaze. Thick black pigment was applied direct to the pot with designs made either by painting or carving through the pigment. Foliage and figures, often used in combination, were favourite themes. The designs were covered with either an ivory-white glaze or a rich turquoise glaze.

Gradually the colour range was extended and painted decoration in which colouring oxides were painted on to the pot or on to the unfired glaze was developed. At Rakka in north Mesopotamia hunting scenes in black, blue and red-brown were painted under clear or turquoise-coloured glaze. Production at Rakka was brought to a halt in AD 1259 when the city was invaded by the Mongols, though the technique was further developed and practised in other parts of Syria until the fifteenth century.

In Persia the painting technique was used at Kashan from the beginning of the thirteenth century and from about fifty years later in the Sultanabad region in west Persia. Here decorative schemes usually involved scroll work, geometric patterns and leaves. Animal figures were rare and human figures and inscriptions were entirely absent. Painted ware is usually attributed to the Sultanabad region in the late thirteenth or fourteenth centuries. The range was further extended to include pierced ware, with painting under a turquoise glaze. Later, more naturalistically painted decoration was developed. It is probable that skilled potters travelled widely and settled wherever and whenever their products were most valued.

Lustreware

The production of lustreware in Egypt was greatly reduced with the overthrow of the Fatimid court in AD 1171 and their subsequent loss of power caused many artisans to emigrate. Many lustre potters moved back to Mesopotamia and Persia.

At Rakka, in Mesopotamia, lustreware was produced similar to that made earlier in Egypt, though the style of decoration changed later and the more miniature style of the Persian decorators was copied. Following the style of

the contemporary production of Minai wares, the designs became generally smaller and more complex. Figures were often set in formal foliage designs, sometimes on horseback; animals and birds were common and, later, panels were used to divide the designs.

The earliest known Persian lustreware was made at Rayy, near Teheran, with decoration very much like that produced in Egypt, though painted with a broader style, and is dated 1179. Generally, the wares lacked the refinement of those made earlier in Egypt or those which were made later in Persia. Designs were often used in combination with blue painted under a greenish glaze. Occasionally

White earthenware jug painted in overglaze enamels. Persian, Kashan, early thirteenth century. (Victoria & Albert Museum)

Hollow earthenware cat painted with lustre decoration on an opaque white glaze. Rayy, Persian, thirteenth century. (British Museum)

the pots were carved in high relief with arabesque ornament combined with neskhi inscriptions.

Lustreware made at Kashan, the other main centre of production in Persia, was distinctive because of the density of detail which was scratched through the painted lustre before it was fired. The spread of the Mongol Empire, which at one time linked China, Russia, India and Persia, brought with it much Chinese influence, evident in the dress and ornament subsequently depicted on pots. Kashan was one of the few cities to survive the invasion, though one report suggests that the gunpowder-equipped Mongols often spared the craftworkers, allowing them to continue working, and the production of lustreware continued well into the fourteenth century.

Mameluke wares of Egypt and Syria

The Ayyubids, who succeeded the house of the Fatimids in Egypt in AD 1171, were

Earthenware bowl, white tin-glaze with yellow lustre decoration. Persian, Rayy, c 1200. Diameter 7½ inches. (Victoria & Albert Museum)

Tile decorated in lustre on an opaque white glaze. Persia, Kashan, thirteenth century. (Arts Council)

themselves overthrown in 1250 by the Mamelukes, who ruled over Egypt and Syria until 1517, when they in turn were defeated by the Ottoman Turks. The Mamelukes checked and defeated the Mongols and gave refuge to artists fleeing from Mesopotamia and Persia. Centres of pottery production were re-established at Damascus and Cairo. The main products seem to have been pots made for containing strong oriental spices and medicine which were exported to Europe. Designs in relief were painted in blue and black.

Late Islamic period (*c* AD 1350–1900)

Tamerlane or Timur the Lame (AD 1336–1405) was one of the most ruthless and merciless of the Turkish leaders. In 1369 he established a new Mongol Empire in India,

Russia and the Levant, making Samarqand his capital and himself sovereign over conquered Islam. A brief revival of the arts took place as Tamerlane had a great love and respect for art and architecture and surrounded himself with the most skilled craftworkers of the time. However, it was not until the third great period of Islamic history, which began with the conquest of Constantinople in 1453 by Mohammed II and the establishment of the Ottoman Empire, stretching into Egypt and Syria as well as into Europe, that the arts had their next major revival. Much of the Empire remained intact until the nineteenth century.

Isnik ware

Ottoman pottery overshadowed many contemporary Islamic wares and, with its main manufacturing centre at Isnik near the west coast of Asia Minor in Western Anatolia, it became known as Isnik ware, of which three main types have been identified. Often known as 'Rhodian' or 'Damascus' ware, the pots were characterized by a bright and richly painted decorative style painted on to a fine white clay slip and finished with a clear shiny transparent glaze. Large dishes, standing-bowls, jars, ewers, lamps, pen-boxes and wall tiles were made in a sandy, whitish clay body. Miletus ware was made out of red clay covered with a layer of white slip.

Decoration, usually painted, included deep cobalt blue, turquoise, green and purple. Later a rich brown-red colour was added, known as Armenian bole. This had to be applied thickly and is consequently raised above the other decoration. Patterns and designs were based on naturalistic renderings of such flowers as carnations, roses, tulips and hyacinths, while borders were often filled with arabesques and scrolls. The style, starting in the late fifteenth century, deteriorated and finally ceased towards the end of the seventeenth century.

Bowl, with richly painted design of plants and foliage on white slip under clear glaze. Turkish, Isnik ware, sixteenth century. Diameter about 11 inches. (British Museum)

Earthenware bowl, design painted in blue on white body under transparent glaze. Turkish, Isnik ware, early sixteenth century. Diameter 17 inches. (Victoria & Albert Museum)

Blue and white wares

Ming blue and white wares were imported from China in the late fourteenth century and once again the Islamic potters were stimulated by the skill and invention of the Chinese pots. The earliest of these wares were small bowls made in Persia which had blue decoration painted on to the unfired clear transparent glaze over a white ground. Foliage, often delicately interlaced with flying birds, is typical of early designs. Breakdown of Chinese trade in the seventeenth century at the end of the Ming dynasty prompted European traders to place orders for blue and white ware with Islamic potters. This further encouraged the copying of Chinese designs with subjects such as dragons, peonies and cloud patterns and these were often outlined in black. Some blue and white wares were made in Syria but most were made in Persia at Meshhed and Kirman where production continued until the nineteenth century.

Safavid period and later
(AD 1499–1736)

After 850 years of foreign rule Persia again became an influential, well-administered nation under the Safavid Dynasty, 1499–1736. Two hundred years of stable government encouraged the arts, the peak of which was achieved under Shah Abbas the Great (AD 1587–1620). His capital, at Isfahan, was filled with and surrounded by many skilled craftworkers. He himself was a collector of fine pottery and his collection still exists in the shrine of the Safavid family at Ardabil in Azarbaijan. Interest in all types of pottery brought about a major revival of the craft.

Kashan again flourished as a pottery centre and the technique of producing a soft paste type of porcelain was revived. Famous Chinese green-glazed ware, known as celadon ware, was also emulated using a smooth grey-green glaze. Gombroon ware, so called because it was shipped through the port of Gombroon (modern Bender Abbas) on the Persian Gulf, was also made. It was exported to India and Europe where, in the seventeenth century, it became very fashionable, especially in England. The pots were characterized by a fine, white, slightly translucent body sometimes with pierced or incised decoration covered with a shiny glaze. Jars, bowls, plates and ewers with tapering spouts were made.

Earthenware stem bowl, painted in blue and green in a design of foliage and roses under a clear glaze. An example of the ware known as 'Golden Horn'. Turkish, Isnik, about AD 1635. Height about 12 inches. (Victoria & Albert Museum)

Above: Fine white earthenware stem bowl, pierced design filled with clear glaze and painted with blue and black pattern. This pottery was known as Gombroon ware, because it was shipped through the port of Gombroon. It was extremely popular in Europe. Diameter $8\frac{1}{2}$ inches. (Victoria & Albert Museum)

Lustrewares, which had ceased to be made during the fourteenth century, were reintroduced in the late seventeenth century. Designs were painted in ruby or yellow-brown on a white or deep blue glaze. Sometimes the body was fine and white and much of the decoration consisted of stylized flowers showing little or no evidence of foreign influence.

The so-called 'Kubachi' wares were made in northern Persia and used the technique of underglaze painting. Large plates and dishes were painted in brown, green, yellow, dull red, black and white under a clear colourless crackled glaze. Early designs included animals, figures and even portraits but, later, plant and foliage designs predominated.

The general standard of most crafts declined in Persia during the nineteenth century, though traditional pottery of a high standard is still made there. Recently it was possible, for example, to replace old tile-work on mosques and tombs with contemporary work of a

Earthenware dish, polychrome enamel painting recalling the early Minai wares. Persia, Kubachi type, early sixteenth century. Diameter $12\frac{1}{2}$ inches. (Victoria & Albert Museum)

Bottle, earthenware with painted decoration under clear glaze. Persian, Narghiti, *c* 1700. (British Museum)

quality equal to that produced 500 or 600 years ago.

Islamic art is an amalgam of Byzantine, Persian and Chinese influences but, no matter how strong the foreign influence, the Muslim potters soon adapted what they saw for their own use. Islamic pottery cannot be regarded merely as an inferior sort of Chinese ware, for the two approaches to pottery were completely different. One of the strengths of Islamic pottery was that it was practical and well designed; and few people can fail to admire the vigorous Samarqand wares of the ninth and tenth centuries or the fine white Seljuq bowls from Kashan.

5 EUROPE (c AD 500-1850)

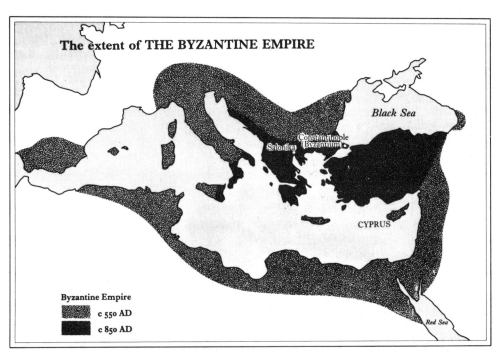

The extent of THE BYZANTINE EMPIRE

Black Sea

Salonika Constantinople Byzantium

CYPRUS

Red Sea

Byzantine Empire
c 550 AD
c 850 AD

Below left: Earthenware dish with sgraffito design of bird scratched through white slip, Touches of brown and green under a pale yellow glaze. Byzantine, fourteenth century. Diameter $9\frac{1}{4}$ inches. (Victoria & Albert Museum, London)

Below right: Two white earthenware bowls, largely reconstructed. Examples of Byzantine white-glazed wares with painted decoration. From Athlit, Palestine, thirteenth or fourteenth century. Widest bowl, diameter $5\frac{1}{2}$ inches. (Victoria & Albert Museum, London)

As techniques and skills developed and the demand for smooth-surfaced pots increased, four major groups of ware evolved. From the Islamic world the use of the white opaque glaze spread throughout the whole of Europe to give tin-glaze ware, much of which was decorated with painted designs. The second group was the lead-glazed wares which had been developed by the Romans and were continued by potters in Byzantium and later in

Western Europe. The use of salt-glazing by German potters produced a third group, which was first made in the fifteenth century; the fourth group was the fine porcelains made in the eighteenth century.

Lead-glazed wares
Byzantium

In AD 330 Constantine declared the ancient Greek city of Byzantium the new capital city of the old Roman Empire and the Byzantine Empire was founded. The city became thought of as the 'new Rome' and its name was changed to Constantinople in honour of the Emperor. For a further 1000 years many aspects of the old Roman Empire continued with a government centred on Byzantium, though gradually a new civilization developed. Only in 1453, when the Turkish armies over-ran Constantinople, did the last vestige of the Roman Empire disappear. Geographically, Constantinople had a powerful and commanding position: situated at the meeting point of Europe and the Orient, on a waterway connecting the Mediterranean with the Black Sea, well fortified and with a good harbour. Little wonder Constantinople has been described as the cross-roads of the world. It was attacked at different times by Christians, Muslims and pagans, and absorbed many aspects of the different cultures. When trade was at its height Constantinople must have been an incredible warehouse, with goods and people from many countries moving through it.

Early influences may have come mainly from the West, but the collapse of Rome as the centre of the Empire brought significant changes. The oriental influence in art soon showed itself with an emphasis on formal style, vivid colouring and rich ornament. In most of the art that remains today this change can be seen quite clearly, though the development in pottery is difficult to trace because of the relatively small number of pots found.

Unlike Islam, Byzantium placed no ban on

Earthenware bowl, sgraffito design of two figures carved through white slip under yellow transparent glaze. Byzantine, fourteenth century. Diameter $6\frac{1}{2}$ inches. (Victoria & Albert Museum, London)

the use of gold and silver vessels for domestic purposes; pottery was not as highly valued and the craft, as a result, was not so well developed. There is no evidence, for instance, that lustreware was made.

The red-gloss wares which had been widely produced throughout the Roman Empire continued to be made in parts of the Byzantine Empire for some time after AD 300, though the pots lacked the precision of those produced under the Romans. The art of lead glazing practised by the Romans was retained and during the eighth and ninth centuries was employed on a wide range of thrown forms. Green and pale yellow lead glazes were used, as were other more colourless glazes. During the Isaurian Period (AD 717–876) green glazes were often used on some of the most pleasing Byzantine ware.

Theophilus, a monk writing about the arts and crafts in the eleventh century, speaks of the crafts of glass-making and gilding which are closely related to pottery, but only makes a passing reference to ceramics, indicating that the craft was not highly regarded at that time. Only during the period of the Palaeologans (AD 1261–1391), when the country became impoverished by constant wars and religious and social upheaval, and the gold and silver vessels on the royal table were changed for ones made out of clay, did the craft gain in stature.

Much excavation has still to be carried out to identify all the sites where pottery was made, but the chief ones were probably at Constantinople, Salonika, the Caucasus in south Russia, Corinth and Cyprus.

Byzantine art did not begin to develop as a distinctive style until the eighth and ninth centuries. It was, primarily, a style based on religious belief but was derived artistically from two sources. One was the classical Greco-Roman style and the other was the oriental style from the East. Byzantine art, unlike the Greek style, was not naturalistic but ritualistic, shown, for example, in the treatment of Greco-Roman themes in a stylized formal way.

The wide origins of many of the designs used on Byzantine pottery is indicated by the animals they depict; the dove, a common Christian symbol, is shown, as are ducks which were commonly used in Egypt as decorative motifs of symbolic or pictorial importance. Fish, too, shown with open mouths, recall those used by the Egyptians. Lions and leopards of a heraldic type with long waving tails reflect western influence. Hares and the human-headed lion are very Persian in character. The griffin and centaur were mythological rather than representational of nature. Deer, dogs and gazelles

Earthenware dish with sgraffito design of a stork carved through white slip and splashes of brown in the glaze. Byzantine. (British Museum)

were among other animals shown, but the favourite animal, however, appears to have been the eagle, symbolizing goodness, alertness and power. The human figure, usually in grotesque or formal poses, was sometimes represented; it was very rarely shown naturalistically, reflecting perhaps the attitude of the Byzantine Church that forbade the representation of the human form as being idolatrous.

Byzantine pottery can be divided roughly into two main types: the first is that made in a whitish body, glazed and often decorated with underglaze painted designs, and the second is pottery made out of red clay covered with a white slip, often with sgraffito decoration.

White-bodied wares were the largest and the most impressive group of Byzantine wares and were developed around the ninth century AD under the Macedonian Dynasty. Plates, dishes, bowls, cups, goblets and fruit bowls with long hollow stems were among the pots made. Colour in the form of an underglaze was painted directly on to the whitish biscuit pot and the whole covered with a transparent glaze. Various shades of brown were used as were yellow, green. blue and occasionally bright red in the form of small dots and outlines. Crosses and rosettes, as well as animals, figures and birds were incorporated into the designs. Tiles for use as architectural decoration were also made from white clay and decorated with underglaze colours.

Undecorated ware covered in a yellowish glaze was both cheap and quick to produce and was made in large quantities for domestic use. Liquid containers in the shape of jugs and beakers were the most common forms, while dishes, plates, strainers, cups and cooking vessels were also made.

One group of white-bodied ware was decorated with applied clay and is often known as petal ware. Flattened balls of clay were applied to the pot while it was still soft and one side of the pellet was smoothed into the side of the pot. The result looks like fish scales or petals. Impressions of stamps made from clay or wood were often used to decorate the insides of bowls. Real or imaginary animals were popular decorative subjects.

Red-bodied slipware

The use of fine white slip over red clay was developed around the tenth century and was used to great effect on the inside of bowls. Many were decorated with sgraffito patterns and covered with clear or coloured trans-parent glaze. Early sgraffito ware had a linear decoration in which the design was scratched with a fine point. Geometric patterns of scrolls, dots and zig-zags were used. Spatial decoration was achieved by using a flat chisel-like tool to take away large areas of the slip, thus leaving the darker body to show up the white design in slight relief. Circles, wavy lines, formal trees, chequered patterns, crosses, rosettes, five-pointed stars, animals, fish and birds were common designs. The human figure appeared only occasionally. Slipwares were sometimes painted with green and brown underglaze colours. Marbled ware, produced by using different coloured slips which were swilled round the inside of bowls, was made around the middle of the fourteenth century.

On the evidence of present excavations Byzantium would appear to be essentially a repository of techniques and processes. It was here that the Greek language and learning were preserved, the Roman Imperial system continued and Roman law codified. Much

Red earthenware plate with incised decoration through white slip and yellowish lead glaze; painted in red slip with touches of green and purple. Diameter 16¼ inches. From the German region of Crefield. Dated 1746. (Victoria & Albert Museum)

early technology was retained and developed during the expansion of Europe in the Middle Ages. Potters continued to use lead glaze which was improved technically to give smoother results. In the ninth century its use spread to Germany, the Low Countries and Britain. However, the later birth of a new Greco-Oriental art dedicated to the glorification of the Christian religion is evidence of a rich and thoughtful civilization. Further excavation will undoubtedly bring to light further pottery and then perhaps the Byzantine pottery style will become more fully known.

Other wares

Lead-glazed wares were by far the most popular ranges of pots made throughout the whole of Europe, with each area developing distinctive styles. The pots were relatively easy to make and fire, and no expensive processes were required. Most were made from local clays and were covered with a white or cream slip and a clear lead glaze often splashed with colouring oxides. Designs often reflected local flowers and foliage or commemorated special events.

Shapes, basically, were designed to be strong and practical and were meant for home or farm use. Influences were, however, absorbed from other sorts of pots; for example the albarello-shaped jars made in Beauvais in France were based on tin-glazed Italianate and Islamic forms. The decoration, incised through a white slip and picked out in runny coloured oxides, was a local adaptation.

In central Europe red wares often with lively slip-trailed decoration were made, in which floral and animal motifs were carried out with simplicity and vigour. The shapes and styles of decoration were quite distinctive to the area. In Northern Germany the lead-glazed slip-decorated wares were superbly made with formal designs based on tulips either incised through the slip or painted underneath the clear glaze. It was from this area that many potters emigrated to Pennsylvania in America during the eighteenth century and set up workshops which made wares with decoration based on the German styles, though the shapes changed to fit in with the new style of life.

Spain

The most distinguished pottery made in Spain before the Roman conquest (218 BC) was that made in the east of the peninsula by the Iberians. Celtic invaders had settled there by the sixth century BC and established the Iberian culture. Trade with Mediterranean countries brought, among other goods, Greek decorated wares which the Iberians attempted to copy. This eventually led to the development around 500 BC of a painted style indigenous to the Iberians. Light-coloured clays, firing yellow or pink, were used to make thin-walled, wheel-made pots. Goblets, flat-based jugs, low-footed bowls and urns were produced. Their most distinguishing feature was the decoration painted on to smooth, slip-covered pots. Iron and manganese oxides were used which fired a wine-red

SPAIN c. 1550 AD.
showing tin-glazed earthenware centres

Urn made from red clay painted with stylized floral pattern. Iberian from cemetery of Oliva, Valencia, Spain, c 500 BC. Height 22 inches. (Museo Arqueologico, Barcelona)

Moorish Spain

It was the Moorish invasion of Spain and the establishment in AD 756 of the Caliphate of Cordova under the Umayyads that a new and completely different culture was introduced. This Muslim culture led in time to the development of a new pottery style, the influence of which was felt throughout Europe.

Cordova became the intellectual centre of the western world during the Umayyad period (AD 756–1031); Christian scholars from France and Italy studied Arabic and ideas were exchanged. Trade, especially with Islamic countries, was extensive. Excavations indicate that considerable quantities of pottery were imported from Mesopotamia. Lustreware fragments, for example, of Mesopotamian origin dating to the latter part of the tenth century have been excavated at Medina Azahra on the outskirts of Cordova. Such fragments have only been found on the sites of palaces, which indicates that lustreware was a luxury item, much admired and expensive to acquire, and certainly not produced in Spain at that time.

Hispano-Moresque wares
(c AD 1200–1800)

It was not until the thirteenth century that the potters of Spain, using techniques developed in Islam, began to produce a new and exciting style of their own. They used a white tin-glaze applied to biscuit fired pots and fired the glaze in a second firing. The surface was then decorated with designs in rich lustre and fired a third time. On many pots colours were painted on to the glaze before it was fired. It is possible that potters capable of making lustreware emigrated from Egypt during the twelfth century to Spain and eventually established their own potteries.

Ibn Said (AD 1214–86), writing around the middle of the thirteenth century, refers to glazed and gilded earthenware made at Muravia, Almeria and Malaga in southern Spain. It was in this region, known as Andalusia, that the first Spanish lustreware was made in any quantity at this time. This came about for two reasons. Invading Christian armies had conquered much of Muslim Spain and by 1248 only a small area in the south was left under Muslim control and so manufacture was restricted to this area. The other reason was that Iranian potters, fleeing from the Mongol invasion of Arabia, settled in fairly large numbers in Malaga in the thirteenth century, bringing with them their detailed knowledge of the production of lustreware and underglaze techniques. They also introduced cobalt blue, the use of which was hitherto unknown in Spain. So the necessary knowledge and skill were available and formed here the basis of an

colour. Designs were rich and varied, employing geometric shapes as well as stylized birds, fish, plants and the human figure.

During the Roman occupation of the country, they introduced their own pottery style and methods of manufacture but with the Roman withdrawal in the fifth century AD many of the technological improvements lapsed.

Visigoths (c AD 500–756)

The Visigoths, invading from the north at the beginning of the sixth century AD, established a kingdom which lasted until the Moorish invasion in AD 756. They made Toledo in central Spain their capital. Little is known about the pottery made by the Visigoths, but two groups, which reflect two major influences, have been identified. The first group was the low-fired, red earthenwares decorated with impressed and moulded designs, and generally left unglazed. This reflected, perhaps, a continuation of the methods of decoration used by the Romans. The second group of wares was decorated with simple yellowish or greenish glazes. Trade and contact with the Byzantine Empire during the seventh and eighth centuries may have been the means by which the glaze was introduced into Spain.

industry which was to thrive so successfully for nearly 300 years.

The Hispano-Moresque wares can be divided into three main groups each roughly following the other in time and divided on a stylistic basis. The first group, employing predominantly Moorish designs, was made at Malaga in Andalusia and later at Valencia. The second group, made around the end of the fifteenth century, continued until *c* AD 1700 at Manises, a suburb of Valencia; this combined some Gothic motifs into what were primarily

Muslim designs in what came to be known as the 'mudejar' style. The last group of wares was made in the eighteenth century and showed a strong French influence.

Early wares (*c* AD 1200–1450)

Though they were made over a considerable length of time comparatively little is known about the early wares. Bowls, dishes and pitchers as well as storage jars were produced and exported to Sicily and Egypt as well as to England. The forms and designs on the pots

Earthenware dish, decorated in the 'cuerda seca' technique in which unglazed lines pick out the design painted in blue, green, yellow and brown enamel on a white tin-glaze. Seville, fifteenth century. Diameter 14¾ inches. (Victoria & Albert Museum, London)

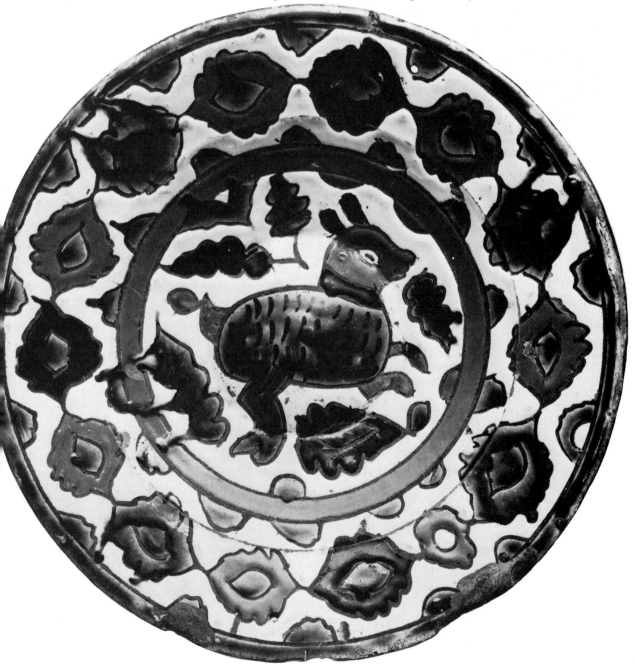

Earthenware bowl with bryony decoration in blue underglaze and lustre. Valencia, *c* 1460. (British Museum)

A medieval woman potter using a cut stick to make a pattern on a pot, while kicking the wheel round with her foot.

clearly owed much to Islamic influence and especially to the Islamic centres at Rayy, Kashan and Rakka. Designs were usually carried out in two shades of blue on a white ground painted onto the raw glaze, and finished with copper-golden lustre. The kufic script was used as decoration as were foliage designs of great complexity. Geometric designs were also popular.

Large decorative vessels, made in sections, probably in a mould, are perhaps the most famous products of Malaga. The Alhambra vase, named after the Alhambra palace in which one was found, is an example of these. Special niches were built in the Castle of Alhambra, Granada, to accommodate the magnificent pieces. The vases, standing nearly four feet high, are remarkable technical achievements. High, flat, wing handles immediately mark them as decorative objects. Painted decoration often consisted of bands of kufic script and some had panels depicting animals such as deer. That it was considered worthwhile to produce such ornaments in pottery decorated with lustre is a measure of the wealth of the country at that time and its high regard for lustreware.

Hispano-Moresque ware also sometimes exhibited the so-called 'cuerda-seca' (meaning 'dry cord') technique. Areas of dry pigment, usually black, separated different coloured glazes and prevented them running into each other. The technique was developed mainly for use on flat dishes during the eleventh and twelfth centuries in Valencia, probably because of the failure at the time to produce lustre. However, 'cuerda-seca' technique became popular again in the fifteenth century when formal designs were carried out on vases as well as dishes.

Other areas such as Aragon, Valencia and Catalonia continued to produce pots very much in the Muslim style, and styles varied from region to region. Much of the vitality of the pottery industry seemed to be lost with the Catholic re-conquest of Andalusia in 1487 and virtually no lustreware was produced in this area after the beginning of the sixteenth century. Muslim potters fled from Murcia and Granada to re-conquered Valencia, and it was here that lustreware of a different style and brilliance thrived in the fifteenth century.

Mudejar style (AD 1450–1700)

Manises, near Valencia, became the main centre of production in the fifteenth century and there are at least two references to Manises potters travelling to France at the request of local officials, which is an indication of the success of the Spanish pottery industry. Valencia had earlier been taken from the Moors and had come under the influence of the Catholic Church and a strong Gothic influence with the result that decoration on

Earthenware dish with 'mudejar' style of decoration. Imitation bands of Arabic script lead into the centre shield of the Arms of Castile and Leon, probably arms of John II of Castile, 1407–1454. Blue underglaze and gold lustre. Valencia, fifteenth century. (Wallace Collection, London)

Valencian pottery became distinguished by the merging of the two major influences in Spanish culture of the time. From the north it took the Gothic emblems and from the south the Muslim, resulting in the 'mudejar' style. Originally the Valencian potters had made pots in imitation of their Andalusian predecessors, but gradually they developed a style of their own in which the blue and white and lustred wares show a more European character. Brilliant gold as well as iridescent blues, reds and yellows were combined with deep cobalt underglaze paintings.

European Gothic influence was characterized in general by more naturalistically rendered ornament, the use of heraldic devices and shields, and inscriptions of a Christian nature in Gothic script. Muslim influence was evident in the treatment of ornament, and intricate designs continued to be made. Kufic script, used as stylized decoration, was often combined in the same design as Gothic.

Plants and foliage shown in the designs included berries, flowers, bryony leaves as well as golden and blue vine leaves. Animals

Drug-jar or albarello with bands of bryony and vine leaves painted in lustre and enamel on a white tin-glaze. This was a standard pattern popular with the Manises potters. Valencia. Early fifteenth century. Height about 12 inches. (British Museum)

such as songbirds, falcons, cocks and long-legged waterbirds, bulls, goats, pigs and hunting dogs were popular design motifs – the human figure rare.

Heraldic devices included the eagle as well as the lion and dragon. Armorial motifs were popular and designs were carried out for many of the royal families of Spain as well as other parts of Europe. Gothic inscriptions included such expressions as 'Ave Maria gratia plena' and 'Senora Santa Catarina guarda nos'.

The designs were still stylized, though they were painted with more naturalism than hitherto. The combination of arabesque ornament and animal motifs encouraged a free decorative treatment which often produced beautiful results. In one example a naturalistically painted deer sits happily under a beautiful arabic 'Tree of Life' design. Around the middle of the fifteenth century Manises ware became very popular in Italy and for this market the ware was decorated with the coats-of-arms of famous Italian families. Such pottery, exported in Majorcan ships, became known in Italy as maiolica.

In the late fifteenth and early sixteenth centuries came the influence of the Renaissance style from Italy. Shapes imitated more closely those of precious-metal-work and the designs those of painting, though classical motifs of leafy garlands and swathes of fruit and flowers, grotesques, masks and acanthus scrolls never became really popular. Dishes became more elaborate with petals, scallops and raised repoussé work incorporated into the designs; and woven brocade velvets seem to have influenced some of the more ornate work. While the magnificence of the painted dishes can be admired for their technical skill and richly patterned decoration, the underside of the dishes often carried a simpler and more attractive design.

Lustreware was highly regarded and valued, and most of the magnificent decorated dishes were made for special occasions. Tables were not laid with individual place settings; instead each person took their portions of food from central dishes which encouraged potters to make these as ornate as possible since they were large and static.

Shapes, other than dishes, were generally few and simple. Following the oriental tradition, cylindrical jars with concave sides, known as albarellos, were widely made for the use of the apothecary. Gallipots, used for storing dry foodstuffs, bowls, drinking mugs and round platters were also produced.

With the unification of Catholic Spain, the growth of strong trade and the absence of Muslim law forbidding the use of precious metals, lustreware lost its exotic quality and was replaced by imported Venetian glass, Chinese porcelain and fine metal-work.

Eighteenth-Century French style

Hispano-Moresque ware was revived in the eighteenth century at Alcora in Valencia. Artists were brought from France to teach the contemporary popular styles of form and decoration found there. Little or no lustreware seems to have been made and instead painted decoration was carried out in blue or in a combination of blue, yellow, green and brown on a bright white background. Arabesque designs of great delicacy were popular, as were subjects copied from engravings and rococo floral motifs. The work produced was chiefly remarkable for its extravagant,

Earthenware wall plaque with white tin-glaze or painted maiolica decoration. Baroque form was popular with the Spanish Alcora potters and ornate shapes were made in the form of busts, chandeliers and basins. Around 1750. Height 9¾ inches. (Victoria & Albert Museum, London)

ambitious and grandiose forms, consisting of busts, elaborate chandeliers, large wall-cisterns, basins and similar objects. Production ceased around AD 1800 in the face of competition from English cream-coloured ware and European soft-paste porcelain.

Talavera de la Reina

Pottery made at Talavera de la Reina in central Spain forms a separate group of wares. It was not decorated with lustre but with underglaze colours painted on to or under the glaze. It is first referred to in 1484 and the characteristic milky-white glaze painted with blue, emerald green, yellow and orange was produced in a great variety of shapes. Talavera pottery, it was said, stimulated the appetite because it enhanced the savour of food with its shining

purity. In 1575 the pottery received royal patronage and it was successfully traded throughout Spain. A group of potters was also sent to establish a pottery at Puebla de los Angeles in the then recently acquired colony of Mexico.

The individual character of Talavera pottery is noticeable in its coarsely made large white dishes which were vigorously painted with dark blue figures of songbirds, deer, rabbits and heron, enclosed in borders of rough foliage and tendrils. Other colours such as manganese purple and reddish-orange were added later. Many of the pots were very large, consisting of dishes, two-handled jars, basins for lemonade, jugs, barrels and cisterns. Candlesticks and inkstands were made in fanciful human or animal shapes. Attempts were made in the sixteenth century to fall in with the fashion from Antwerp which had a decorative style based on pierced ironwork and strapwork, interwoven with caryatids and stylized floral motifs.

During the seventeenth century the palette was extended to include intense copper greens, yellows and purples. A monochrome blue and white style was developed which was strongly influenced by contemporary engravings depicting, for example, landscapes, wild beasts or children at play. A writer in the seventeenth century favourably compares Talavera plates with those from China, and the pottery was generally highly regarded. The quality of the work deteriorated during the eighteenth century, but pottery with vivid green decoration still appears from this area to this day.

Italy
Early wares (c AD 500–1200)

During the period AD 500–1000, the earlier Roman pottery tradition continued in various forms, but the breakdown of central government and the consequent decline in the arts meant that few new developments were made during this time. Contact with the Byzantine Empire, through Venice and Ravenna in the north, was probably responsible for the wider use of lead glazes. Recent excavations have brought to light a range of domestic pottery produced around the seventh and eighth centuries glazed in a dark green or yellow lead glaze. Vessels have also been found at Ostia, the port of Rome, and also in Rome itself, dating to the ninth century, on which decoration for the most part was limited to combed lines or applied pellets of clay in the shape of rosettes.

During the eleventh and twelfth centuries decorated bowls were imported from the Muslim countries. These were often set into outside walls of churches, such as those at Pisa, for use as decoration. Special niches were often left in the walls to hold the bowls. The bowls, though greatly admired, were never put inside churches, probably because they came from a pagan country. It was not long before this decorated ware was being imitated in Italy by the Italian potters.

It is interesting that Italy, a country with a long tradition of painting, should adapt the technique of painting on pottery and develop it as a branch of the arts of the Renaissance. Decoration on much of the pottery, especially in wares made in the sixteenth century, is

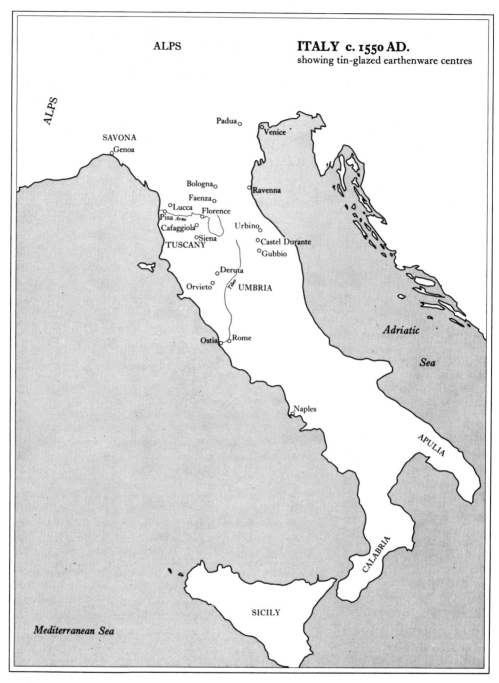

ALPS

ALPS

ITALY c. 1550 AD.
showing tin-glazed earthenware centres

SAVONA
○Genoa

Padua○

○Venice

Bologna○
Faenza○
○Lucca
Pisa *Arno*　Florence
Cafaggiola○
○Siena
TUSCANY

○Ravenna

Urbino○
○Castel Durante
○Gubbio

○Deruta
Orvieto○　UMBRIA
Tiber

Ostia○　○Rome

Adriatic

Sea

Naples

APULIA

CALABRIA

SICILY

Mediterranean Sea

often superior to the form, and it is the painting which is most highly valued. In some ways this contradicts one of the basic principles of pottery, that form should dominate over surface decoration, and goes against the usual criterion for evaluating the work of the potter. Italian pottery must be looked at from a different point of view if it is to be enjoyed, though the decorative processes developed in Italy were essentially those used by the potter. A limited colour range imposed by the colour-

ing oxides and a method of painting directly on to the unfired, absorbent glaze surface, which eliminated rubbing out or over-painting, led to the development of a bold and fresh style of decoration which can only be thought of as a branch of ceramic art.

Tin-glazed earthenware only became known as maiolica in the fifteenth century. The name was derived from tin-glazed ware imported from Spain on boats from Majorca. Italian maiolica ware can be divided into three distinct groups based for the most part on decorative treatment.

Archaic or early period (*c* AD 1200–1400)

In Italy the use of white tin-glaze on light red bodied pots began around AD 1200. At first it was used only on small areas or confined to the inside of bowls, the remainder having a clear glaze. The use of the glaze seems to have spread slowly, appearing first in Sicily and later in northern Italy. Colouring oxides were painted directly on to the raw glaze and colours were limited to copper green painted in broad areas and often outlined in manganese brown or purple. Blue was not introduced until later. Early painted designs often reflected the Romanesque style of decoration in which natural forms were freely translated into linear patterns which were, at their best, calm and severe. For example, birds or beasts supporting a coat-of-arms were shown, but decorative themes echoing those of the Islamic potters were also used. Vegetables,

Earthenware drug vase or albarello. White tin-glaze with maiolica decoration painted in purple and green. Simple geometric or floral designs in a limited range of colours are characteristic of early maiolica wares. Italian, late fourteenth century. Height 7½ inches. (Victoria & Albert Museum, London)

foliage, animals, abstract patterns and geometric forms are found in the decoration though the human figure was rarely included. Little or no attempt was made to create an illusion of depth, volume or movement and the designs tended instead to be static and peaceful. Occasionally the design was enriched by modelling details in low relief. Trailing vines, bunches of grapes and coats-of-arms were, for example, modelled on pots in Orvieto.

Forms were mainly those used in medicine or on the table. Albarellos, based on the bamboo shape, were widely made to hold medicine, as were ovoid jars and water pots with stirrup handles. Globular jugs, derived from the Greek vases, and very tall elegant jugs, which seem to have a more Gothic appearance, were produced for the table.

Severe or formal style (*c* AD 1400–1500)

Fifteenth-century Italian tin-glazed ware developed more formal designs due to two major foreign influences. From northern Europe came the Gothic style and from Spain came the Oriental style.

Shapes generally tended to be those which had been made during the early archaic period, though in general they became more elaborate, and designs and form were purposefully related in a way which was later to be ignored. The undersides of bowls and the insides of pots were glazed white and were often decorated. Different regions produced distinctive ware, much of which was local in character. The palette became larger and richer and included a range of primary colours as well as green, purple and brown.

Extensive trade in the fifteenth century between Florence, Pisa and Lucca in Italy and Barcelona and Valencia in Spain brought the rich Hispano-Moresque wares of Valencia to

Two-handled maiolica jar with design on white tin-glaze painted in manganese purple and blue. Florence, early fifteenth century. (British Museum)

Italy. Around 1420 the green and purple Valencian wares inspired a novel Italian style painted with foliage and from this developed a decorative style of great distinction known as the 'Florentine green family'. The pattern consisted of formal repeating designs recalling peacock feathers, painted mainly in green on a white background. In Tuscany, in particular at Faenza, a series of two-handled globular jugs was made, using a rich ultramarine blue or, more rarely, green, in slight relief. Oak leaves, derived from a Valencian design, formed the main decorative motif.

Fifteenth-century Italian potters were unable to make lustreware and imitated its effects in yellow and purple colours painted on to the raw glaze. From these imitations several superb types of decoration developed with thoroughly Italian figure painting added to the original Spanish ground motifs.

Gothic ideas on decoration were reflected in the more formal designs on pottery. The motifs used appear as types or symbols and

Above: Drug jar, maiolica, with twisted rope handles. Design, painted in blue and orange, showing the Arms of Ranieriof, Perugia. Florence, 1475. Height 6 inches. (Hastings Museum)

Earthenware bowl with white tin-glaze and painted maiolica decoration. An example of the 'severe' or 'formal' style of decoration. The pattern of formal repeating designs recalling peacock feathers, painted in green on a white background, was probably derived from the designs on imported Valencian wares. Florence, Italy, c 1450. Diameter 11½ inches. (Victoria & Albert Museum, London)

not as pictorial images. Foliage, radiating beams of light, initials, sacred monograms, heraldic emblems, religious figures and animals all appeared in designs during this time.

A period of more settled government during the second half of the century saw the beginning of a new style of decoration related more to the Renaissance. The palette acquired warmth, and orange was often used instead of lime yellow.

Renaissance style (*c* AD 1500–1600)

By 1500 the technique of maiolica was well established throughout much of northern Italy. Individual centres were clearly established with their own recognizable characteristics. The whole nature of pottery decoration had departed from that based primarily on Spanish and Gothic influence to one which reflected the attitude of the Renaissance and a completely indigenous style developed. Favourite local meeting spots at that time were the pharmacies, which were lavishly decorated with ornately painted maiolica drug-vases. This fashion, together with the contemporary style for displaying large decorative dishes on sideboards and tables, reached its height in this period. This encouraged potters to produce richly decorated ware. Individual ceramic artists, too, began to emerge, largely due to the patronage of the wealthy nobility. The work of these artists was often as highly valued as that of the fine artists and had, besides, the advantage of an imperishable medium. Local schools of painting influenced pottery decoration and many designs were copied directly from drawings by famous artists.

While forms generally became more complex and ornate they were often overshadowed by the decoration. A plate or bowl would often have quite intricate shapes, reflecting the influence of metalwork, and would be used to provide the background for a detailed painted composition. Nevertheless, the painting was still related to that achieved by maiolica painting rather than oil painting, though in the new pictorial style, often known as 'istoriato' because it usually illustrated a story, elaborate scenes were depicted in great detail. Mythological subjects began to replace religious ones, and cupids, satyrs and dolphins were introduced. However, in Umbria, the home of St Francis, religious subjects remained most popular.

Pottery centres in different areas developed distinctive independent styles and techniques. At Castel Durante in the Duchy of Urbino the height of the 'istoriato' style was reached in the work of Nicola Pellipario. His work was often stimulated by engravings by

contemporary artists though these were never merely copied but interpreted for the ceramic technique. His drawings of animals had a supple liveliness as if they were poised for easy movement, and they often appeared in idyllic landscapes. Colours in his designs were delicately graded.

Lustreware was made for the first time in Italy at Deruta, near Perugia, using skills learnt from the Moorish potters fleeing from the Christian conquest of Spain. From about 1501 onwards a golden mother-of-pearl and a ruby lustre were made at Deruta. Because lustre decoration allows no tonal changes, and has to rely for its interest on surface reflections designs tended to be simple and bold. In the early pieces simple combinations of lustre and one other colour on a white background were used; later, surfaces were made in relief to enhance the effect of lustre. Scales, bosses and gadroons were introduced, in imitation of precious metals, which caught and reflected the light. Early Deruta ware was fairly conventional with the rim used as a border around the central motif of a bust or heraldic arms.

Cafaggiola potteries enjoyed the patronage of the Medici family and produced their best work from 1500 to 1525. Jacopo Fattorini was a famous pottery painter whose work often had a characteristic dark-blue background. It is probable that he studied in the workshop of Botticelli or Donatello. At

An Italian potter, *c* 1560, after Cipriano Piccolpasso's *The Three Books of the Potter's Art.*

Dish, maiolica with lustre decoration. Gubbio, Umbria. Here lustre decoration was brought to perfection. Rich ruby and gold lustre are used in this scene, 'The Judgement of Paris', with Cupid shooting from the clouds. An inscription on the back reads 'Lalto Gin dizio di'l Trojan Pastore'. First half sixteenth century. (Wallace Collection, London)

Dish, maiolica, painted in Baroque style. Faenza. Moulded externally with palmettes in relief, the inside carries a light and swift sketch of a female head in blue and yellow. *c* 1570. Diameter 10 inches. (Museum of the Decorative Arts in Prague)

A page showing potters at work, from Arte Del Vasaro, The Three Books of the Potter's Art. *Cipriano Piccolpasso*, 1524–79. (Victoria & Albert Museum, London)

Gubbio, in Umbria, lustre decoration was brought to perfection by Maestro Giorgio Andreoli who developed particularly successful iridescent golds, ruby-reds and silver. Designs were often painted by Nicola Pellipario and lustred by Giorgio Andreoli. Tinted backgrounds were used about the middle of the century, grey and pale blue being the most common colours. White was often added for highlights. At Faenza, work on coloured backgrounds was highly developed.

Cipriano Piccolpasso wrote a three-volume treatise around 1556–57 in which he describes and illustrates in detail the techniques used by the maiolica and lustreware potters. Shapes, colours, glaze recipes, and decoration are all detailed and the books give a fascinating account of contemporary workshop practice.

Baroque style (*c* AD 1570–1650)

The counter-reformation around the middle of the century led to a movement against the 'istoriato' style of pictorial representation. The development of a fine, smooth white glaze at Faenza encouraged the reduction and restriction of decoration to small areas, often painted entirely in blues or yellows. Here the roots of the baroque style of decoration which developed at the beginning of the seventeenth century can be seen. In this style shapes were not limited to those traditionally produced but based on the forms of objects made in precious metal. Table services of many pieces, plates, dishes, ewers, wine coolers, candelabra, drug pots, flasks, inkstands, busts and obelisks were all produced, often in complex forms. Decoration, at its

Plate, maiolica. Decoration, painted lightly and quickly, is based on the work of the followers of Raphael and is typical of the Baroque style. Urbino, *c* 1590. (Wallace Collection, London)

Small-footed bowl painted in cobalt blue, yellow and orange on white. The restricted style of decoration is typical of this period. *c* 1560. (Victoria & Albert Museum, London)

Above Small flat bottle, probably for holding precious liquids, Egyptian faience. From around 2000 BC small votive objects and cosmetic containers had been made in the artificial body known as faience. During the Roman occupation of Egypt the technique was developed to enable larger forms to be made and the colour range widened to include yellow, white and purple. *c* 800 BC. Height 3 inches. *(Petrie Collection, University College, London)*

Above right Small jar with side lug handles, handbuilt and painted with a bold, abstract geometrical design in red and white pigments. From Hacilar, Turkey, *c* 7000-6000 BC. About 3½ inches tall. *(British Museum)*

Right Round bowl with painted decoration. From Baluchistan, *c* 3000 BC. *(British Museum)*

Clay animal on wheels, possibly a children's toy. Egypt, *c* 2500 BC. Fired clay. *(British Museum)*

Above Survey tablets listing the areas and dimensions of five fields. Not fired. Egypt, *c* 1980 BC. About 5 inches in diameter. *(British Museum)*

Red-gloss ware, Roman, finely made in a decorated hollow mould. Finished with a shiny red slip glaze.

Porcelain pot painted in tou-ts'ai enamel decoration which gives brilliant colours. Chinese, Ch'eng hua (1465-87). Diameter 5 inches. *(Percival David Foundation of Chinese Art)*

Left Dish with underglaze red and cobalt blue painted decoration. Chinese. Dated 1671. Diameter 14 inches. *(Percival David Foundation of Chinese Art)*

Right Earthenware bowl with decoration painted in coloured slips. Iran, Nishapur, tenth or eleventh century.

Below Earthenware plate with clear glaze over a white slip-covered ground. The naturalistic design is painted in rich, bright colours, typical of this period. Turkey, c AD 1500.

Right 'Cross' by Peter Voulkos. Stoneware with low-temperature glazes. 1959. Height 30 inches.

Far right Flat-sided stoneware bottle with trailed decoration by the famous Japanese potter Shoji Hamada, c 1960. Height 7 inches.
(Ian Bennett)

Below left Bowl on foot, painted and poured colour decoration, stoneware, about 12 inches tall. Sandy Brown, 1986.

Below right Soft neck vessel, handthrown and assembled, saltglazed, 13 inches tall. Robert Winokur, 1982.

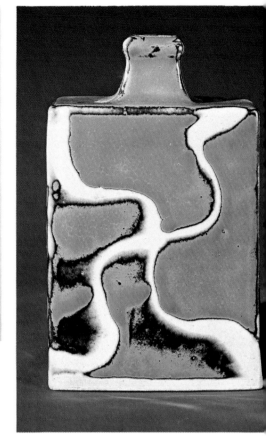

Earthenware plate, modelled with relief decoration and glazed brown and white. The decoration shows the Virgin adoring the Child. Northern Italian, *c* 1575. (Wallace Collection, London)

Inside view of earthenware stemmed bowl showing ornate sgraffito decoration carved through white slip: colour is used under the clear glaze. Northern Italy, *c* 1450. Diameter 13 inches. (Victoria & Albert Museum, London)

best, was delicate and limited to a palette of dark and light blue, yellow and orange. Drawing was often lively, having the freshness of a sketch, and avoided the elaborate and colourful detail of the 'istoriato' style.

Ware exported to France became known as faience after Faenza, one of the production centres, and potters travelled from Italy throughout Europe to teach the technique. Industries were established by Italian potters at Rouen and Nîmes in France and Antwerp in Belgium.

The seventeenth century saw the return of religious subjects in decoration and a general dislike of unpainted areas. New colours were introduced, such as pea-green, but the palette was generally restricted. Baroque shapes were often complicated and largely based on gold, silver, copper and bronze objects. Applied plastic ornament in the shapes of monsters, sphinxes, mermaids and so on, and internal divisions in vessels, are evidence of the declining value of pottery and the general feeling that it must be made to imitate metal.

Lead-glazed Sgraffito wares

Venice and Ravenna in the north were subject to intensive influence from Byzantium, as were Sicily, Apulia and Calabria in the south. It was here that the lead-glazing tradition was continued and developed, and around AD 1300, in imitation of and in competition to the white opaque glaze being used in other parts of Italy, white slip was used to give a white ground. The design was scratched through this to reveal the dark body underneath and subsequently glazed in a clear lead glaze. Some fine plates with modelled border pat-

terns of leaves were made. Later green and brown colouring oxides were painted on to the glaze but these ran on the lead glaze and the rich mottled effect produced was quite unlike maiolica. The designs, too, were different, being related to Gothic influences rather than Renaissance ones. The work reached its height in the sixteenth century when complicated shapes with modelled ornament were made.

French, German and Netherlands tin-glazed wares
France

Though records exist that show the Duc de Berry took Valencian potters from Spain to central France around 1332 to produce tin-glazed earthenware, little is known of the wares they made there. There is evidence, too, that Muslim potters fled from Catholic Spain to southern France where they made tin-glazed wares. Some of the earliest French maiolica, known to the French as faience, was decorated with geometric painted designs in copper green and manganese purple and is similar in style to early Italian wares. Regular production, however, seems to have started in the sixteenth century and again the work produced shows a strong Italian influence. Immigrant Italian potters settled and worked at Nîmes in Provence and at Rouen near the

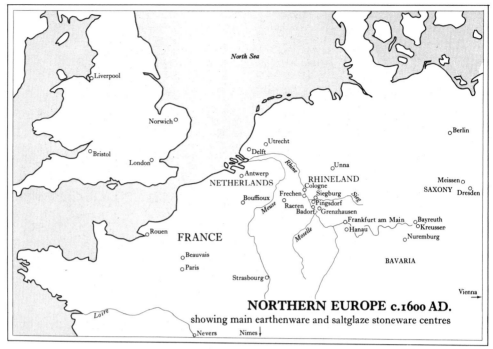

NORTHERN EUROPE c.1600 AD.
showing main earthenware and saltglaze stoneware centres

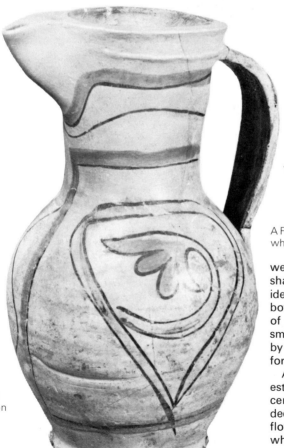

Earthenware jug with polychrome decoration on white tin-glaze. Bordeaux region, France, thirteenth century. (Museum of London)

A French potter of the thirteenth century working the wheel with a stick.

west coast, and made pots which in their shape, decoration and general style are almost identical to contemporary Italian wares. At both centres the wares showed the influence of the work of the Royal gold- and silver-smiths. Large, decorative dishes, surrounded by ornate borders, and vases of elaborate forms were made.

At Nevers in central France, an industry was established towards the end of the sixteenth century and developed a naturalistic style of decoration in which birds and sprays of flowers were painted in blue and white on a white or a pale yellow ground. Painted designs on imported Chinese blue and white porcelain wares were also imitated.

Oval dish modelled in relief with water snakes, river fish and shells on dark blue background, by Bernard Palissy. French, 'pièce rustiquè'. Late sixteenth century. (Wallace Collection, London)

Albarello-shaped vase with white tin-glaze and painted decoration. French, Rouen, c 1540. Height 10¾ inches. (Victoria & Albert Museum, London)

Towards the end of the seventeenth century the expanded industry at Rouen flourished and developed a unique, decorative style known as 'style rayonnant'. It was based on the work of ornamental engravers and silversmiths and the designs were painted mainly in blue on a white ground. Drapery, foliage and other Renaissance motifs were incorporated into the designs which were painted on finely moulded shapes.

During the eighteenth century the industry again expanded and the Italian influence was largely superseded by the imported Chinese porcelains and the Dutch Delft wares. Ruinous French wars resulted in edicts, in 1689 and 1709, which said all gold and silver vessels should be melted down, and the French faience industry was accordingly stimulated by the demand for replacement wares. At Rouen the 'style rayonnant' was enriched by the use of further colours such as red and yellow, and the range of vessels extended to include many more accessories for the table such as fashionable ice-pails, dredgers for powdered sugar, boxes for precious spices and stuffs, salt cellars and basins.

The middle of the century saw the adaptation of the rococo style of decoration which reflected the influence of contemporary painters such as Watteau and Boucher. Garlands of naturalistically painted flowers and shells framed finely drawn pictures with amorous or pastoral subjects.

Earthenware dish, tin-glaze with painted decoration. French, Rouen, late seventeenth century. Diameter $14\frac{7}{8}$ inches. (Victoria & Albert Museum)

At Strasbourg, near the German border, technical changes were introduced in the second half of the century. Hitherto, colours had been painted directly on to the raw tin-glaze in the process sometimes known as in-glaze decoration. The new technique, copied from the porcelain factories, was that of using enamels in which the specially prepared coloured enamel glazes were painted on to the fired glaze and fixed by a third low-temperature firing. The main advantage of enamels was the wide range of bright colours which could be obtained.

Porcelain painters from Germany brought with them the necessary knowledge and skill and adapted the style of naturalistically painted flowers and finely modelled figures which had been used on porcelain to that of maiolica. Tureens modelled in the shape of vegetables or animals – a popular shape was a boar's head – were also made for sideboards or banqueting tables.

Germany

Some of the earliest German maiolica wares were made at Nuremberg in the sixteenth century, though maiolica tiles, often for stoves, had been made much earlier. Dishes and drug jars were produced and, in their designs and shape, showed a strong Italian influence. The maiolica industry at Kreussen, however, while imitating Italian designs, often made shapes similar to those of the local stoneware industry.

Two important German factories were established in the second half of the seventeenth century, the first of which was in 1661 by Dutch religious refugees at Hanau. At first the style was predominantly that of the Dutch

Porringer, earthenware, white tin-glaze with blue and yellow decoration. Hamburg, 1631. Height $7\frac{1}{8}$ inches. (Victoria & Albert Museum, London)

Delft wares made in the Chinese style, but gradually European designs were developed. In these, patterns of scattered flowers interspersed with small exotic birds and groups of dots were painted on typical jugs which had tall, narrow necks and handles in the form of 'twisted rope'. By the 1750s designs were painted with the traditional in-glaze maiolica decoration and also enamel over-glaze.

The second major factory was established, in 1666, by a French potter at Frankfurt-am-Main. Here German maiolica flourished into a rich, highly decorative and ornamental ware which contrasted favourably with the more mundane products of nearby Hanau. Decoration, usually painted in blue, was covered in the clear glaze known as 'kwaart' to give added depth and shine. Plates and dishes with smooth, ribbed or nine-lobed rims, vases, jugs and basins were made. Typical Frankfurt designs were of strong Chinese influence and showed, for example, a scene in which 'Chinamen' were set in a stylized landscape with rocks, shrubs, birds, butterflies and insects. Naturalistic designs, more European in character, such as were made at Hanau, were also painted.

Maiolica factories contined to be established in Germany in increasing numbers during the early eighteenth century. Changes in drinking habits resulted in the widespread manufacture of tea, coffee and chocolate services and this, combined with the discovery of porcelain by Bottger in 1709 and its subsequent commercial production, affected the design and decoration of maiolica in general. For example, the fine naturalistic painting known as 'German flowers' first employed on Meissen porcelain was adapted to the use of the tin-glaze potter at Strasbourg in France, where the style of decoration became known as 'Strasbourg flowers'. This in turn affected the German products. Influence, too, was felt from the Du Paquier porcelain factory at Vienna which existed at that time.

Maiolica factories throughout Europe adapted themselves to and even expanded under the changed conditions of eighteenth-century Europe. Their products existed by the side of fine porcelain wares which fulfilled the need that existed for luxurious goods while maiolica provided a cheaper but acceptable

Earthenware tankard with maiolica decoration of birds and foliage. German, 1775. Height 6 inches. (Hastings Museum)

Earthenware jug, white tin glaze with painted decoration. Austrian, Gmunden. c 1725. Height 8¾ inches. (Victoria & Albert Museum, London)

Six-sided dish, maiolica. This painted and gilded design imitated that of the Japanese Arita wares in both form and style. Delft, Holland, early eighteenth century. Diameter 13½ inches. (British Museum)

Drug vase, earthenware with white tin-glaze and broadly painted decoration. Antwerp, sixteenth century. Height 8½ inches. (Victoria & Albert Museum, London)

Earthenware jug with relief decoration: 'The Adoration of the Magi', and 'The Massacre of the Innocents'. Nuremberg, the workshops of Paul Prenning, c 1550. (Victoria & Albert Museum, London)

alternative. It was, however, the large-scale introduction into Europe of English cream-coloured wares with their high quality and fantastically low prices which finally brought about the collapse of the industry throughout Europe around 1800.

Netherlands

The earliest maiolica made in the Netherlands was at Antwerp when production started at the beginning of the sixteenth century in a pottery established by a friend of Piccolpasso from Castel Durante in Italy. Maiolica was painted in the Italian style of decoration. The industry centred itself almost exclusively at

Delft near Rotterdam in the second quarter of the seventeenth century and the ware became known as Delft. The founding in 1609 of the Dutch East India Company resulted in large amounts of blue and white Chinese porcelain being imported into Europe and this was imitated by the Delft potters. It is significant that the Guild of St Luke admitted potters to

Barber's bowl, tin-glazed earthenware with Chinese-style decoration painted in blue. Dutch, late seventeenth century. Diameter $13\frac{1}{4}$ inches. (Victoria & Albert Museum, London)

Dutch earthenware punch bowl, white tin-glaze painted with blue, green and yellow design commemorating the Peace of Ryswick, 1697. Diameter $12\frac{1}{8}$ inches. (Victoria & Albert Museum, London)

its ranks for their skill at painting and decorating rather than potting.

Around the middle of the seventeenth century the pottery industry in Delft expanded rapidly, due to two events. One was the fall of the Ming dynasty in China which disrupted trade and so caused a drastic fall in the number of Chinese pots arriving in Europe, and the second reason was the availability of suitable pottery premises due to the lapse in the brewing industry in Holland. The Dutch potters used finely prepared clays and

Chinese designs painted in blue. They also used a transparent lead glaze over the decoration, known to the Dutch as 'kwaart', which gave the pots an even gloss, and the colours greater depth; this resulted in wares almost identical in appearance to the blue and white wares of China. Later, decoration was influenced by the work of contemporary oil painters. European landscapes, portraits and figure subjects were interpreted by the Delft potters. In the eighteenth century green, red and yellow were added to the earlier palette of blue and purple. Polychrome wares, imitating the enamelled porcelain wares made during the reign of K'ang Hsi (AD 1662–1772) in China and the rival Arita Japanese porcelain, known in Europe as Imari ware, were also produced.

German stonewares and saltglaze
Early period (c AD 400–1000)

Despite the disappearance of most of the technology introduced by the Romans throughout most of the Empire, some skills remained in modified form. In Germany coarse pottery, some of it reflecting Roman forms, continued to be made for domestic use. Technical developments were slow until economic and social changes stimulated industry. During the ninth century improved

firing methods enabled higher temperatures to be reached in the kiln, and a harder, tougher ware was made. A productive industry developed in the Rhine valley around the seventh century AD when pots for domestic use, elaborated with simple painted decoration in red clay, were made. Forms were simple and sometimes incised decoration was included. Pots made in the Rhine Valley at Pingsdorf and Badorf were imported into England around the tenth century. Higher firing temperatures and more carefully prepared clay resulted in a harder and more vitrified body which in time became known as stoneware or 'steinzeug'.

Early high-fired ware (c AD 1000–1200)

The development of high-fired ware, produced for the first time in the West, was the culmination of a long pottery tradition in the Rhine Valley where abundant supplies of workable clay encouraged the industry. Unlike the red coloured earthenware this grey clay, with its high sand content, was able to withstand top temperatures without collapsing. A plentiful supply of wood and, later, good-quality coal as well as the Rhine which made it possible for the wares to be transported easily ensured the continuing success of the industry.

Stoneware is characterized by a hard, dense, impervious body which emits a clear ringing sound when struck. In some ways stoneware is similar to porcelain in that both are vitrified and non-porous, but stoneware is not usually white or translucent. Glazes capable of being fired to a high temperature were unknown to the early German stoneware potters and relatively unimportant as stoneware is impervious to liquids. This no doubt encouraged the use of salt-glazing when it was discovered. Early stoneware forms changed from being squat to a more slender and Gothic character. Jugs, cooking pots and cooking utensils seem to have been most common. Washes of a fusible red clay were used both as decoration and to improve the surface texture of the pot by making it more smooth.

Saltglazing technique

Saltglazing was used for the first time around the late fourteenth or early fifteenth century and is, after the discovery of hard-paste porcelain, Germany's most important contribution to the art of pottery. Suitable clay which lay in vast quantities in easily accessible beds in the Rhineland was very high in silica, and reacted well with common salt thrown into the kiln towards the culmination of the firing. It was discovered that at a high temperature (1200°C, 2192°F) salt (sodium

Jug with short tubular spout, wheel-made. Traces of red painted decoration. This ware was imported into England where it was copied by the English potters. Eighth or ninth century. Excavated Burstow Castle, Sussex. Height 7 inches. (Hastings Museum)

White saltglaze jug. Found in the City of London. Throwing rings, the splayed foot and the tall elegant shape are typical of the early white wares of this area. Siegburg, Germany, fifteenth century. Height 10 inches. (Victoria and Albert Museum, London)

also necessary which could reach the high temperatures required. Potters were able to draw on the resources and skills of the metal smelters who had developed suitable refractory materials and had learnt how to obtain high temperatures.

Other factors also influenced the development of the industry. As well as supplying much technical information the metal-working industry which had been well established in Germany for over 200 years, were producing finely worked metal objects. This stimulated potters who wanted to copy the crispness of the metal forms as well as the fine engraved designs; because the saltglaze formed from vapour is very thin and tends not to obscure fine detail but to heighten and pick it out, the fine designs used on precious metal-work were used with equal success on the saltglazed pottery. At Raeren, the centre which specialized in brown-ware, a glaze almost identical to bronze was developed and, though its resemblance to metal may have been fortuitous, the popularity of the ware was possibly due to this resemblance.

The other main factor which stimulated the making of saltglaze was the increased consumption of ales and wines throughout Europe. Around AD 1500 a coarse, malt liquor drink was greatly improved by the addition of a new ingredient, hops; the result was a widespread increase in the drinking of ale. Inns and taverns became popular and the new saltglaze pottery drinking vessels were in great demand. England, too, enjoyed this new drink and a large trade was established to provide the country with the necessary drinking vessels. Wine, too, was exported, throughout Europe, including England, in stoneware wine bottles. The demand for drinking vessels of all sorts, especially the 'canette', a pint pot, and the tall tapering 'schnelle', encouraged the production of saltglaze stoneware which was preferred to earthenware or metal tankards.

Saltglaze wares fall into four groups, each one having a main manufacturing centre and each having its distinct characteristics.

Saltglaze brown-ware

Raeren, near Aix-la-Chapelle, was the main centre for the production of brown-coloured saltglaze. Here the art of saltglazing was fully developed and the rich, bronze-like colour was very popular. Ware was specially made for, and exported to, France, Sweden, Norway, Spain, Poland, Hungary, Denmark and England and it was often decorated with royal coats-of-arms. The best pots were made in the second half of the sixteenth century.

The vessels most commonly made were the pint drinking mug or 'canette'. Round-bellied

chloride) volatilizes into sodium and chlorine and the sodium combines with the surface of the clay to produce a chemically simple but extremely tough and resistant glaze. Occasionally the glaze so formed was smooth and brown, at other times it had a surface like orange peel, and sometimes it was mottled brown and cream. Its colour and texture depended to a large extent on the clay body on to which it went, different sorts of clay slips giving different colours, but the glaze coating was always thin. Salt for the process was imported up the Rhine or came from the salt-mines of Unna in Westphalia.

Apart from suitable clay and salt, kilns were

mugs of fine clay with little or no decoration other than a band of pattern in relief round the neck were produced with a rich, brown glaze. Large jugs, turned on the wheel to remove throwing marks and perfect the profile, were made in three separate pieces – neck, body and foot – and joined together before the clay had fully dried out. Other popular forms were the three-handled Kaiser jugs, nearly a foot high, pilgrim flasks for holding spring water, pocket flagons in the shape of prayer books, puzzle jugs and jugs in the shape of cannons.

Friezes of relief decoration were a popular form of decoration, and were designed with great originality by Jan Emens (Jan Emens Mennicken), the leading potter at Raeren, from about 1566 to 1594. Motifs depicted classical scenes, and included naked figures of male and female gods. Some were based on engravings specially produced by German artists and included religious scenes and scenes recording social events such as parties or festivities. Later Emens produced a series of huge jugs with double friezes of classical subjects.

One of the major products were the so-called Bellarmines, full, round-bodied jugs with narrow necks, often with a large capacity. These were decorated with a grotesque bearded face modelled on the neck and were perhaps the most famous of the brown-wares: they were named after Cardinal Bellarmine, a medieval priest who forbade drinking, though the grotesque face had been a popular decorative motif long before Cardinal Bellarmine made his pronouncement.

Pots made in Cologne were similar to those produced at Raeren in that they had a similar brown colour which was achieved by the use of an iron wash which gave shades that varied from chestnut to a dull yellow. The decorative motifs were different. Some white-ware was also produced in Cologne. Decoration tended to imitate precious stones in metal settings, and the influence of the Italian Renaissance can be seen in busts set under arcades. Texts, such as 'Drink and eat, do not forget God', in Gothic script were often combined with classical acanthus leaves and medallions. Early in the sixteenth century potters were banished from the city of Cologne because the poisonous chlorine fumes emitted by the kilns during the salting process were thought to be excessive, and the potters moved to the nearby city of Frechen. Here, good, plastic clay and a welcoming city saw the growth of an industry which by 1650 was to rival that at Raeren. Decoration was characterized by applied scrolls of foliage, leaves and rosettes stamped symmetrically over the full-bodied pots. Medals and acanthus leaves continued to be popular motifs.

Saltglaze wine jar or bellarmine, supposedly showing the face of Cardinal Bellarmine on the neck. Royal Coat of Arms in relief. The mottled glaze effect is the result of the salt thrown into the kiln. Dated 1591. (Museum of London)

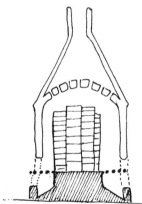

A round updraught kiln used in Germany, c 1720, to reach high stoneware temperatures.

Saltglaze white-ware (c AD 1550–1800)

White-wares were developed around 1550 at Siegburg, on the River Sieg. Accounts involving potters are first found in 1427, which indicates a well-established industry. Guilds protected both the potters and the industry,

Saltglaze jug with applied relief decoration showing the crucifixion with characteristic German austerity. The Apostles are shown in a frieze round the pot. The work of Jan Emens. Raeren, 1575. Height 8 inches. (Victoria & Albert Museum, London)

and long family traditions over hundreds of years are recorded.

Early ware, produced in this area before about 1400, was hard and vitrified and made from brown or dark grey clay. Later, jugs were made, thrown on the wheel and left with finger mouldings at the base, often known as pie-crust decoration, and embellished with simple applied rosettes and grotesque faces. Around 1400 clay was more carefully prepared and moulds of wood or metal were used to make relief decoration, known as sprigs, which were applied to the pot. Tall red jugs, 'Roit Kroichen', with clay rings in the handles, were also made until the production of white-ware became most popular and the production of red jugs ceased at Siegburg.

Around the middle of the sixteenth century the finest white-ware was developed. The white body used for the pots did not react too well with the salt, and the glaze was thinner and less shiny than that on the earlier brown-wares. The forms included tall, slender tapering drinking mugs and ewers, with long spouts imitating metal forms, for dispensing the best wine, puzzle jugs, large candle sticks and baluster jugs. Fine detailed relief decor-

ation included religious subjects such as the Garden of Eden, Temptation, Annunciation, Last Supper and Flagellation; in contrast anti-Catholic scenes showing clergy and monks in scenes of wild debauchery, mythological scenes and heraldic devices were also popular.

Larger or more complicated pots were made in moulds, but pots thrown on the wheel were often left with the throwing marks, giving them a pleasant and lively appearance. Tall thrown jugs were graceful and elegant.

Coloured wares

The district of Westerwald, sometimes known as 'Kannenbäckerland', or 'Country of Pot Makers', housed several pottery-making towns of which the most important were Grenzhausen, Grenzau and Hohr. Many potters fled to this area from the ravages of the Thirty Years War (1618–48) and with the decline of the industry at Cologne, Siegburg and Raeren, the potteries flourished. In the early seventeenth century, a long established but undistinguished pottery industry was suddenly given life and vitality. Saltglaze ware made in this area had, until then, been brown, white or cream, depending on the body used, but the new potters introduced the use of cobalt-blue and manganese-purple backgrounds to produce coloured if subdued wares. A prosperous industry developed which was to flourish for some 200 years. Saltglazing does not favour the development of bright colours and the ultramarine, navy blue and aubergine purple combined with the grey background to give a startling if sombre effect. The pots were made out of light, bluish-grey clay and were decorated with bold, relatively unskilled designs of notches, plain circles and rosettes, depending for their effect on the added colour. The ware proved very popular throughout Germany and other parts of Europe. The drinker, it seems, no longer wanted amusement from the friezes of relief decoration, or instruction from the texts, but no doubt inspired by the colourful maiolica wares, they wanted colour. Dishes, plates, tableware, figures and, later, modelled objects such as inkstands were produced.

Enamel-decorated ware

Kreussen, near Bayreuth in Bavaria, was the centre of the fourth and most costly saltglaze style. Light brownish-grey saltglaze wares as well as stoves had been made at Kreussen since the beginning of the sixteenth century; it was from these wares that the new styles were developed, stimulated by the popular maiolica wares which had been coming into Germany from Italy for some time. There was

Saltglaze tankard with enamel decoration showing the Emperor of Germany and the Electors. Kreussen, Germany, 1696. Height 7 inches. (Victoria & Albert Museum, London)

Saltglaze tankard with applied decoration. Raeren, c 1650. Height 6 inches. (Hastings Museum)

Saltglaze tankard with applied rosette decoration. Grenzhausen, c 1620. Height 6 inches. (Hastings Museum)

Saltglaze jug with moulded decoration of biblical subjects. Siegburg, sixteenth century. (Victoria & Albert Museum, London)

already a long-established glass-painting industry in Kreussen which used opaque low-temperature lead glazes, known as enamels, on the glass, much of which was used in churches and cathedrals. This technique was adapted for use on the saltglaze pots, and fused in a second, low-temperature firing. The technique came into use around 1620 and lasted some 130 years. Pots were made out of greyish-brown clay and shapes were kept fairly simple. The two most popular forms were the shallow and broad canette or drinking mug and the plain oviform jug. The bright-coloured opaque enamels were painted on to the plain background. A dark glaze was often used which provided a rich contrast to the bright enamels. The formal designs were carefully worked out and gave a pleasant effect. Glass-painters were often employed to decorate the pots, and simple bands of figures, such as 'Planets', 'Apostles', and 'Elector', were very successfully used on tankards and the like. In later work the whole body was covered with enamel decoration and the effect became crude and overbearing.

Other styles

An equally crisp, if simpler, style similar to Raeren was developed at Bouffioux in Belgium, and at other places in the Walloon country. Large pieces such as barrels, Bellarmines, chemist's jars and boxes for holding medicines, pills and powders, as well as canisters, pocket flasks, cruets, inkstands and teapots, were made. Ornament was kept to a minimum and consisted of medallions and simple raised lines and popular grotesque masks, imitating those made at Frechen.

It was from Germany that John Dwight and the Elers brother saw and probably learnt the art of high firing which they brought to England in the second half of the seventeenth

century. The technique had a profound effect on seventeenth- and eighteenth-century pottery in England; German saltglaze wares were highly regarded and were, for example, presented to Elizabeth I. Great technical skill was required to achieve the clean, sharp relief decoration and careful kiln control to obtain a good glaze. Artists who worked out relief designs became well known and their designs can be recognized; such masters as Balden Mennicken, Jon Emens and Jan Baldems became well known. The finest saltglaze pots were often mounted on stands and the rim covered with finely engraved metal; in the case of jugs, ornate metal lids were also fitted.

'The Derby Potter' from a Meissen original, modelled in Derby, showing a barefoot potter using a European kickwheel, c 1770.

Saltglaze jug with moulded and modelled decoration. Raeren, late sixteenth century. Height 10¼ inches. (Victoria & Albert Museum, London)

6 GREAT BRITAIN (UNTIL AD 1700)

GREAT BRITAIN
showing some of the pottery making centres

North Sea

Glasgow

Newcastle
Sunderland

Belfast

York

Leeds

Dublin

Irish Sea

Liverpool

Chesterfield

Trent

Lincoln

Stoke on Trent
Derby
Nottingham

Tunstall
Longport
Burslem
Cobridge
Hanley
Bradwell Wood
Shelton
Fenton
Lane End
Lane Delph
Longton

Tickenhall
Stamford
Castor

Thetford

Grand Union Canal

Worcester

St. Neots

Ipswich

Colchester

St. Albans
Harlow

London
Thames
Cheam
Wrotham

Bristol

Glastonbury

Rye

Barnstaple
Fremington
Bideford

Old Sarum
NEW FOREST

Chichester

Plymouth

St. Ives

Britain's geographical position as an island made her less susceptible to conquest, and hence skills were, on the whole, introduced slowly and developed much later than in similar societies on the Continent. Migrations of people did, in time, bring new techniques and eventually one of the largest ceramic industries in the world was formed.

Neolithic, Bronze Age and Iron Ages

It is probable that pottery had been introduced into Britain around 2000 BC, though recent excavations and improved carbon-dating methods indicate that it may have been earlier. Pots at that time were hand-built; they had distinctive rims and some had incised decoration. Vessels with a distinct shoulder developed soon afterwards which were to serve as models for later cinerary urns. Around the first part of the second millennium BC, drinking vessels in the form of beakers were made, copied from wares brought by migrations of the so-called Beaker people who probably originated in southern Spain. Simple, incised chevron designs on the sides of beakers helped to provide a better holding surface as well as being decorative and some were inlaid with white clay or paint of some sort.

Cinerary urns with a prominent shoulder and sides tapering to a narrow base began to be made around 1500–1000 BC. Larger urns were produced in the late Bronze Age.

Pottery, as a whole, became more sophisticated during the Iron Age (500 BC–AD 43). Invaders from Gaul brought knowledge of iron-working, and pottery was made thinner and with a smooth surface in imitation of the metal objects. A simple potter's wheel was introduced at this time; forms generally became more symmetrical and developed an elegance and finish hitherto lacking.

Roman occupation

The Roman invasion and conquest of Britain in AD 43 brought a superior and sophisticated technology; this included the more careful preparation of clay, an efficient potter's wheel and improved kiln design. Roman red-gloss wares, made principally in Gaul, were imported into Britain in fairly large amounts though recent excavations at various sites such as Chichester and Upchurch, in Kent, indicate that red-gloss wares were made in Britain. Coarse unglazed pottery was made in fairly substantial quantities at a number of sites in Britain and, strange to say, each site produced some pottery with its own characteristics. At one or two centres pots were glazed with a thin pale yellow lead glaze, as for example at Holt in Denbighshire, where thrown bowls with white slip decoration were covered with the lead glaze.

Castor ware

One of the largest and most important sites for the production of everyday pottery was that at Castor in Northamptonshire: its development was due partly to the proximity of the

Below left: Beaker with incised cross-hatched and triangular design. Soft grey body. Aberdeenshire, c 2000–1500 BC. Height 7 inches. (Anthropological Museum, University of Aberdeen)

Dark brown decorated pot made on a slow wheel, with incised decoration. Iron Age. (Ministry of Works)

Fine grey bowl with
spout at rim. Thetford
ware. Height 4 inches.
(British Museum)

London-York Ermine Street and also to the
excellent plastic clays which were available. A
whole range of wheel-thrown pots were
made for domestic use out of the local clay
which fired a pinkish-buff colour. Basins,
jugs, mixing bowls and beakers were among
the pots produced. Dark grey or black-coated
wares were also made.

Different coloured clay slips were used to
decorate some of these pots, especially the
beakers. Scrolls and leaping animal designs
were trailed in thick slip on to the pot, a
process known as barbotine decoration. Designs were freely carried out and the results
had a pleasant liveliness, though the decoration often resembled that produced by the
silversmiths. The decorated pot was dipped in
dark brown or black pigment to colour the
surface, though occasionally purple or red
tones were achieved.

New Forest ware

Potteries in the New Forest area produced
two sorts of ware. One was a dark-coloured,
plain ware, often deep red or purple. Many
shapes were copies of those made at Castor
but their own distinctive style developed
which included shapes with impressed sides
recalling the form of leather bottles. They also
made decorated wares. Patterns were impressed into the surface of the pots, in the
form of rosettes, stars or crescents, or painted
in slip in abstract designs built up exclusively
of straight lines and circles.

Dark Ages

The withdrawal of the Roman legions saw the
lapse of most Roman technology, and Saxon
pottery forms were based on those made
before AD 43. Cinerary urns, with high shoulders and decorated with incised designs,
applied clay and impressed patterns, seem to
represent the highest achievement.

Major technical advances, however, were
made around the seventh and eighth centuries. Trade with the Continent increased
and immigrant potters settled at sites along
the east coast. In due course the fast wheel
was brought to England as well as the use of
galena glaze. In the Low Countries and the
Rhineland the use of both the fast wheel and
lead glaze had been either maintained from
their introduction by the Romans or reintroduced from the Byzantine Empire. It is significant that the east coast of England, particularly near the Wash, was quick to import
and use the technological improvements,
leaving the remainder of the country to continue with hand-building production methods and either open firing or very simple kiln
arrangements.

Saxo-Norman wares (c AD 700–1066)

Three distinct wares have been found which
make up the so-called Saxo-Norman type of
pottery. The first, St Neots ware, was soft,
grey, soapy to touch and had substantial
amounts of powdered shell mixed with the
body. It was bright red, purple, brown or dark
purple in colour, which suggests it was open
fired. Deep bowls, shallow dishes, cooking
pots, six to eight inches high, and jugs with
rouletted decoration were made.

Secondly, Ipswich ware, made as early as
the eighth century, was the forerunner of
Thetford ware, made from the tenth to the
twelfth century. It was the first ware to show
marked European influence. The body was
hard, sandy and grey, and the forms reflect
closely those produced in the Rhineland.
Cooking pots, bowls, storage vessels, decorated with applied and impressed bands of
clay, and spouted pitchers were made. No
glaze was used.

The last and most interesting type is Stamford ware, first found at Stamford on the
borders of Northamptonshire and Lin-
colnshire and made from the local estuarine
clay. This ware was both finer and whiter than
the other two wares. However, what makes it
so exceptional is that parts of the cream-
coloured pots were glazed a pale, transparent
yellow colour and this was perhaps the first
glazed pottery to be made in England. The
glaze was made by dusting lead in the form of
galena, which is a natural sulphide of lead, on
to the shoulders of the damp pot. Glazed
bowls and spouted pitchers were made here
as well as unglazed cooking pots. The
spouted pitcher, by far the most common
form, usually had three strap handles, a tubular spout and a rounded base trimmed with
a knife round the edge. Stamford ware was
widely distributed and was sold throughout
the east Midlands.

Medieval pottery (AD 1066–1600)

The Norman conquest of AD 1066 is usually
considered to mark the beginning of the
medieval period in Britain. To some extent

Pottery ewer with convex base, tubular spout and small handles. Yellow, lead glaze. A rare example of the first group of English glazed wares, copied from imported ware from the Rhineland. East Anglia, tenth or eleventh century. Height $7\frac{1}{2}$ inches. (British Museum)

Mediaeval jug, wheel made, excavated at Pevensey Castle. It shows traces of blackening by fire and may have been used for mulling wine and been linked with the wine trade of Bordeaux. Thirteenth century. (Hastings Museum)

pottery reflected the architectural activity of the period, becoming bigger and technically better. Pottery was never highly regarded in Britain by the wealthier classes until the eighteenth century, when fine, white, industrially produced pottery, imitating the fineness of Chinese porcelain, was made. In medieval Britain most people tended to eat off wood

and drink from horn or leather containers, leaving pewter, silver and gold utensils for the use of the rich. Pots were used for storing and serving ale or wine and, mainly, for cooking or preparing food.

English medieval pottery is artistically of great interest and historically is the forerunner of the later Staffordshire wares as well as the lead-glazed wares made in many parts of the country. Jugs and pitchers form the most important group of medieval wares. They are distinguished by a rare dignity and strength of form. The introduction of the fast wheel and improved kilns and the use of lead glaze, formed the basis of its production.

These jugs were made at various sites, many as yet unidentified, and fired in comparatively simple kilns to a temperature of around 1000°C (1830°F), having been previously dusted with dry powdered galena. The clay body varied in colour from red to buff, depending on the local clay source, and usually had ground shell or sand added to improve its throwing qualities. The fast wheel was used for the manufacture of these pots, which are remarkable for their lightness and

Earthenware pitcher, with mottled green glaze decorated with incised vertical lines, standing on four pressed feet. (Museum of London)

Tall pitcher of the baluster type with splashed green glaze. Late thirteenth century. Height about 12 inches. (Museum of London)

Above centre: Jug with modelled relief decoration, Nottingham. Fourteenth century. (Ministry of Works)

Jug with decoration painted in white slip, Rye, Sussex, *c* AD 1300. Height 8 inches. (Hastings Museum)

Red earthenware tiles with contrasting inlaid designs in white clay of heraldic animals. Mainly used on the floors in churches. Keynsham Abbey, Somerset, England, Thirteenth century. (Victoria & Albert Museum, London)

thinness. A common feature of the earlier jugs is the convex or sagging base. This is thought to have been a continuation of the tradition of rounded bases which would sit firmly on uneven earth floors or, more probably, in the embers of a fire. The introduction of wooden tables and flat surfaces necessitated the thumbing of the bottom edge of the pot and this is often found on many of the later jugs. Occasionally, small tripod feet were added.

The finest jugs were made during the thirteenth century in forms which were tall and slender and preceded the development of smaller, more squat ones in the fourteenth and fifteenth centuries. Handles generally were sturdy and well placed both aesthetically and functionally. They were always firmly joined on to the pot and occasionally were splayed out to form a pattern. Both round and flat, strap-like handles were made. Decoration was simple but effective, with the forms of the jugs remaining dominant and un-cluttered. On some jugs coloured slips were trailed or painted on to the pots, sometimes combined with applied strips and pads of clay. At Cheam and Rye simple designs were painted in slip of a contrasting colour. On most pots the yellow-brown glaze, occasionally tinted green with copper, was the chief decoration.

Other pots made at this time included cooking and storing vessels, pipkins,

Two-handled tyg with glossy brown glaze. Cistercian ware, Early sixteenth century. Height 5 inches. (Hastings Museum)

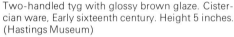

Above right: Aquamanile, in the form of a stag, with mottled brown yellow glaze, used for hand-rinsing at the table. Fourteenth century. Height 9½ inches. Victoria & Albert Museum, London)

saucepans and flat frying pans. Flasks and pilgrim bottles in many sizes and forms, some flattened, have been found at Old Sarum, Wiltshire, and were probably made locally. Aquamaniles or water holders with short spouts, some in the form of animals, were produced to hold water for washing hands during or after meals.

Tudor pottery (c AD 1500–1600)

By Tudor times the range of vessels had widened to include cisterns, stove tiles and candle brackets, mainly finished with a smooth glaze. Finely moulded relief decorations of Tudor roses and shields-of-arms imitating the decorative technique of imported German saltglaze ware were used on tiles and pots. Jug forms became much more squat and were glazed in a rich moss or speckled green cucumber glaze: both form and colour of the pots imitated contemporary metal flagons, which were very popular.

Cistercian ware

A group of finely made and well-fired pots, found on or near the sites of Benedictine monasteries, was probably made by the monks and is often known as Cistercian ware. Production seems to have been reduced by the dissolution of the monasteries in 1540, and finally ceased in the seventeenth century. The ware is hard, indicating a fairly high firing temperature, and characterized by a dark red body, glazed inside and out with a dark brown glaze stained with manganese. Occasionally, trailed white slip and applied pads of white clay were used for decoration. Drinking cups with several handles were made and preceded the much more common tyg. To a large extent this tradition of hard-fired, slip-decorated earthenware was continued from around the beginning of the seventeenth century until about 1700 at Tickenhall in Derbyshire.

Tiles

The production of medieval tiles should also be mentioned, though outside the range of this book. These were usually made in red clay with a design impressed into the soft clay which was subsequently filled with clay of a contrasting colour, usually buff or white. Simple heraldic motifs, shields-of-arms, stylized flowers and animals were common designs. The tiles were often used for the floors of cathedrals and abbeys. An early example from Halesowen Abbey is dated 1290. Examples still in their original position can be seen in the chapter houses of York Minster and Westminster Abbey. Production, at various sites, lasted until the late 1600s.

Drinking tankard ('canette'), earthenware. Cistercian ware, late sixteenth century. (Museum of London)

English earthenware (*c* 1600–1750)

Earthenware, fired only once and glazed with powdered galena dusted on to the leather-hard pots, continued to form the basis of much of the pottery made in England until the late eighteenth century. Its method of production was, with one or two exceptions, only slightly affected by the techniques introduced from the Continent either of tin-glazed earthenware in the sixteenth century or of saltglazed stoneware in the seventeenth century. Techniques were improved, kilns became more sophisticated and styles of decoration became more distinctive. The impulse towards refinement in the eighteenth century and the production of white saltglaze ware and cream-coloured ware eventually had a much greater effect. Interest in these much finer wares reduced production of this type of earthenware, until it virtually ceased at the end of the nineteenth century.

Lead-glazed earthenware was essentially produced for local markets, and the use of local materials and the development of local traditions resulted in a variety of decorative methods on a wide range of pots. Much of the

earthenware had a peasant charm which derived from the simple practical forms and the fresh vigorous slip decoration carried out in the different but limited range of clays. English lead-glazed earthenware forms one of the great achievements of English folk art.

Staffordshire slipware

Staffordshire was the largest and most important centre where slip-decorated earthenware was made. Excellent local clays and wood for firing the kilns probably accounted for the establishment of potteries in the area in the first place. The earliest known examples of Staffordshire slipware date back to the first half of the seventeenth century, though the production of lead-glazed earthenware generally seems to have been well established here before then, with a market beyond that locally available. Staffordshire butter pots, for example, used by farmers for storing and

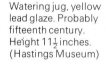

Watering jug, yellow lead glaze. Probably fifteenth century. Height 11½ inches. (Hastings Museum)

Two-handled porringer with black slip trailed on to a layer of wet white slip. Found in London. Middle seventeenth century. Height about 3 inches. (Museum of London)

Slipware dish by Thomas Toft. Trellis work border of black and tan slip on white ground. Clear lead glaze. *c* 1675. (Stoke-on-Trent Museum and Art Gallery)

distribution, were well known throughout the Midlands. Wares for farm and household use were the main products made out of red clay and glazed with the lead galena glaze.

Slipwares are so called because they are decorated with liquid clays of different colours in the form of slips either poured or trailed on to the pots. Though the technique was highly developed in Staffordshire it was used in other areas such as Wrotham, London and so on.

Staffordshire slipwares reached their peak around the end of the seventeenth century and fall into three groups: flatware, such as plates and dishes; hollow ware, comprising drinking vessels, jugs, and lidded pots; and miscellaneous ware, such as candlesticks, cradles, money boxes and chimney ornaments.

Toft wares

Though large quantities of hollow-ware forms were decorated with slip, by far the best known pieces are the flatwares, comprising dishes and shallow bowls some twelve to twenty-two inches across. The dishes were either thrown and turned on the wheel or made in a hollow clay or wooden mould, and decorated with vigour and robustness. The large dishes, usually made for special occasions such as weddings or christenings, reached their peak in the work of the Staffordshire Toft family, and much so-called Toft ware was made by other potters imitating them, so great was their fame.

Reddish buff clay was used for the body of the dishes and covered with a layer of white or cream slip which formed the background for the trailing of red, dark brown and tan slips. Designs were outlined and filled in with a wide variety of patterns. Human figures were drawn with little or no regard for anatomical detail and, like those painted on the tin-glazed blue-dash-chargers, had the naïve quality associated with talented but untrained artists. As such, the dishes have unique charm. Favourite subjects included royal scenes, such as King Charles II hiding in the oak, as well as portraits of popular figures and cavaliers. Coats-of-arms, mermaids, Adam and Eve, and the Pelican in her Piety, symbolizing the eucharistic sacrifice of Christ's death on the cross, were also popular. Designs were beautifully balanced within a rich trellis border pattern. Ralph and Thomas Toft often incorporated their name into the border as part of the pattern.

One development in the eighteenth century made by Samuel Malkin was the use of moulds with patterns incised into the surface. Clay was pressed over the mould and the pattern was left in slight relief. The pattern

was subsequently decorated with slips of different colours, and quite complicated designs could be repeated easily.

Other imitators of the Toft style of decoration included Ralph Simpson, Richard Meir, Robert Shaw and Ralph Turner.

Other centres making earthenware

Many local pottery centres existed throughout the country in the seventeenth and eighteenth centuries. All made lead-glazed earthenware, but each developed its own forms related to local needs as well as its own methods of decoration. None of the centres achieved the mastery of the Staffordshire potters in slipware decoration, though some

Slipware dish with design of owl, six little owls and another bird. c 1715. (Stoke-on-Trent Museum and Art Gallery)

Cup with trailed slipware pattern and inscription. Clear lead glaze. 1699. (Stoke-on-Trent Museum and Art Gallery)

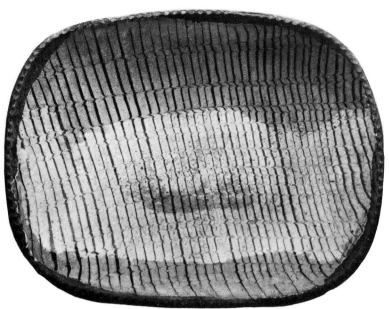

Press moulded earthenware slip-decorated baking dish, with traditional 'feathered' decoration. Made in Sussex. Length 12 inches. (Hastings Museum)

Baking dish with slip-trailed decoration, dated 1795 (Museum of London)

red clay. One of the better known products were the large harvest jugs, some of which were dipped in white slip and decorated with designs scratched through to show the red body, using the sgraffito technique. Lively decoration included coats-of-arms, lions and unicorns, ships in full sail, mariners' compasses and floral designs.

Wrotham ware, which was made as early as the beginning of the sixteenth century in Kent, continued to be made until the end of the eighteenth. It reflected the influence of imported German stoneware in both form and decoration, and sprig-moulded decoration, usually made in white clay, was applied to the red pots. Fleurs de lis, roses, crosses, stars and masks were common motifs, as well as bucolic inscriptions. The forms produced included tygs, posset-pots, two-handled mugs and candlesticks. Handles made by weaving different coloured clays together were a distinctive feature of Wrotham ware.

Printer's type was used for decorative purposes on late eighteenth-century Sussex pottery. The type was pressed into the soft clay and the impression inlaid with clay of a different colour.

At Harlow in Essex the so-called Metropolitan slipwares were made from around 1630 for the London market. The decoration tended to be more sober and to reflect the political opinions of London, especially in the occa-

Drinking mug or 'canette'. Metropolitan slipware with design trailed in white on red body. Clear glaze. About 1650. Height 8 inches. (Museum of London)

centres used similar slip techniques. There were various other methods of decoration. White clay was often applied in relief and slips were occasionally coloured dark brown or black. The use of green slip or glaze was not widespread until the late eighteenth and nineteenth centuries.

Potteries at Barnstaple, Bideford and Fremington in Devon used the highly plastic local

sional use of pious inscriptions such as 'Be not hy minded but fear God 1638'.

White tin-glazed earthenware

The sixteenth-century increase in European trade saw the importation into England of two major types of continental ware and the subsequent use of similar manufacturing techniques in England: one was saltglazed stoneware from Germany which is dealt with later, and the other was European tin-glazed earthenware, known as 'maiolica'. White tin-glazed earthenware was imported via the Low Countries where it was made by Flemish potters. The industry was later centred in Holland at Delft and the white tin-glazed pottery was often known in England as delftware. In France, tin-glazed ware was known as faience, after the Italian city of Faenza which was one of the principal centres of manufacture in Italy.

Early tin-glazed earthenware

White tin-glazed earthenware was first recorded as having been made in London in around 1570, by Jacob Janson, a potter from Antwerp who arrived in Norwich about 1567 and founded the Aldgate pottery three years later; it is not known whether or not Janson was the first tin-glaze potter in England. Dishes, drug jars, vases and jugs were made continuously from 1575 at Aldgate and Southwark and later at Lambeth. The wares were decorated with stylized floral and bird designs very similar to contemporary continental designs.

Production did not begin in earnest until the early seventeenth century when potteries were established in London as well as Liverpool and Bristol. It is significant that all these locations were ports and so particularly subject to foreign influence. Clay, from Norfolk and Suffolk, was excellent for the production

Blue dash charger painted in blue, yellow, brown and purple, showing William III and the cypher 'W. R.' Lambeth. Diameter $15\frac{1}{4}$ inches. (British Museum)

of this ware and, as well as supplying the English centres, it was exported to Holland during the seventeenth century for the use of the Delft potters. Cornish tin-mines were the source of tin for both England and Holland.

The greatest attraction of tin-glazed earthenware was its white surface, which was relatively easy to obtain, smooth and pleasant to handle and provided an excellent surface for painted decoration. It also resembled Chinese porcelain, which was beginning to reach England in considerable quantities and was greatly admired.

Unfortunately, tin-glazed ware chipped easily, revealing the red porous body; only a limited number of forms were made, such as tankards, pill and ointment pots and wig-stands. The flat dishes or chargers were most noteworthy because they presented a suitable surface for painted decoration. Many of the dishes were decorated with blue strokes round the rim and were known as blue-dash-chargers. Blue, green, yellow and brown were the chief colours used in the decoration. Early designs copied those of Renaissance Italy, but slowly an English style developed, characterized by bold, freely drawn designs often possessing a naïve simplicity. Informal portraits of kings and queens and other personalities, which were almost caricatures, decorated the dishes; other subjects were biblical, especially Adam and Eve, and formal floral designs of tulips and carnations.

New drinking habits arose during Commonwealth times in the mid-seventeenth century, and tea, coffee and chocolate were often preferred to alcoholic drinks. Cups or mugs were made to hold the non-alcoholic drinks and the production of the full, round-bodied wine bottles with narrow necks, imitating the form of contemporary German stoneware bottles, which had hitherto been very popular, ceased.

Continuing the oriental tradition, a wide range of vessels for the use of apothecaries was made which included spouted pots for syrups and oils, globular drug jars, cylindrical and squat jars for powders, pills, ointments and confections, and pill slabs. Decoration often included the name of the contents as well as floral designs. Barbers' bowls were another popular form; they were often de-

Small bottle for holding decanted wine, in the shape of contemporary imported German saltglaze pots. The device, painted in blue, carries the initials and date 'E. C. 1640'. Height about 8 inches. (British Museum)

Below left: Barber's bowl, shaped to fit the neck, with designs painted in blue, showing the barber's tools. Lambeth. (Museum of London)

Earthenware flower vase. Tin-glazed with painted decoration. Bristol. c 1760. (Victoria & Albert Museum, London)

Above Lidded boxes, extruded and assembled, stoneware with painted and resist decoration. David Frith, *c.* 1982.

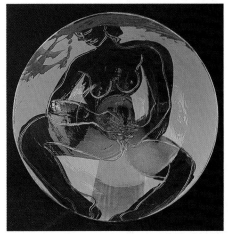

Right Bowl with painted and incised decoration, earthenware, 15 inches across. Bruce McLean, 1986.

Below Bowl, handbuilt with coloured clay inlays, stoneware, about 7 inches across. Ruth Duckworth.

Above Container form, thrown, with matt surface decoration, stoneware, about 10 inches tall. Hans Coper.

Above right Limb form with painted and modelled decoration, about 24 inches long. Jill Crowley, 1987.

Centre
Jug forms, thrown, with trailed glaze decoration, tallest about 15 inches. Janice Tchalenko, 1987.

Below right Form, handbuilt, stoneware, about 11 inches tall. Sarah Radstone, 1986.

Plate, stoneware, with trailed and poured decoration, about 14 inches across. John Glick.

Blue and white jug, 12 inches tall, earthenware. Alison Britton, 1987.

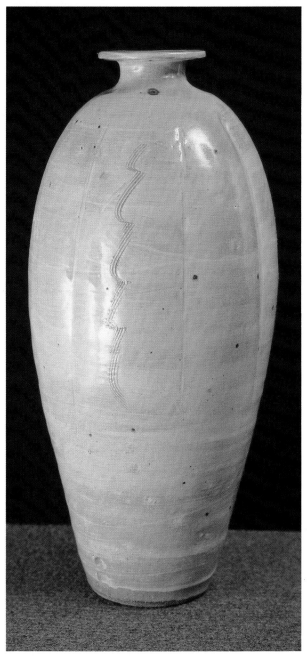

Bottle form, thrown and pressed, with white slip and glaze, stoneware, about 10 inches tall. Bernard Leach, *c.* 1965.
(Cleveland Craft Collection)

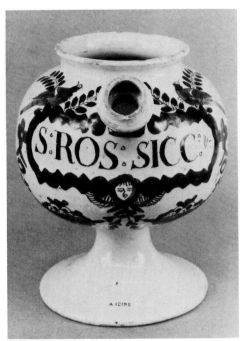

Maiolica drug jar for holding liquid medicine and carrying its Latin name. Containers for use by the apothecaries were made by the maiolica potters and so continued the tradition started in the Middle East by the Islamic potters. Mid-seventeenth century. Height about 8 inches. (Museum of London)

corated with scissors, combs and other tools of their trade, painted in blue on the white glaze.

Towards the end of the seventeenth century, the palette used by the tin-glaze decorator was becoming brighter and had been extended to include red; shapes became more diverse, some being modelled and moulded after the work of the French potter Bernard Palissy (c 1510–90), who supplied rustic pottery to the King and Queen Mother of France. His work included pots and dishes modelled with snakes, fish, shells, coloured with lifelike colours. Constant contact between Dutch and English potters brought other foreign influences into Britain, though the English potters never attained the sophistication of the Dutch work which, in some cases, managed to imitate Chinese porcelain almost exactly. The naïve combination in England of Chinese and English design motifs has a unique charm. One design, for example, had English soldiers set in an English landscape with a band of Chinese mythological heads as a border.

Towards the end of the eighteenth century the colours developed a softer look and took on a pleasant watercolour quality. Forms had been extended to include rectangular flower-

Above right: Earthenware candlestick made in the form of a cat. Press moulded, tin-glazed and dabbed with underglaze colour. Dated 1674. (British Museum)

Liverpool maiolica tea-caddy, octagonal shape, painted in greyish blue. The increasing popularity of tea during the seventeenth century stimulated the production of many beautiful and precious tea utensils. Height $4\frac{1}{4}$ inches. (British Museum)

Earthenware, tin-glazed flower holder in form of a book. Made at Lambeth or Southwark, dated 1658. Height 4¼ inches. (British Museum)

Saltglaze mug with moulded relief decoration with hare hunting scene and inscription:
On Banstead downs
A hare wee found
Which lead us all
A smoaking round
Top half has iron pigment. Fulham, dated 1721. Height 4 inches. (Hastings Museum)

holders, pen-and-ink stands, puzzle jugs and the full tea-drinking equipment of cups and saucers, sugar bowls, milk jugs, teapots and tea caddies. The introduction and success of industrially made cream-coloured ware in 1765 by Josiah Wedgwood brought about the decline of tin-glazed ware until its production virtually ceased around 1800.

Stoneware and saltglaze ware

German stonewares and saltglaze had been imported into England since at least the end of the fifteenth century, and many attempts were made to produce it. Early production is slightly confused as potters often made both sorts of ware. Stoneware is made by firing pottery to a temperature above 1200°C (2191°F) when the clay vitrifies and becomes non-porous. Saltglaze stoneware (usually known as saltglaze ware) is fired to a similar temperature but is glazed by introducing common salt into the kiln at maximum temperature. The technique of firing pottery to a high temperature was introduced into England from the Continent, and two types of ware were made. One type, based on pots which came originally from China and known as dry red stoneware, was not glazed but was made from carefully prepared red-firing clay. The other was saltglaze ware from Germany. While giving the pottery a glassy surface, saltglaze also limited the colours to cream and brown as no colouring oxides were then used.

By the sixteenth century many saltglaze pieces were being manufactured in Germany specially for the English market, some having English coats-of-arms and the like as relief decoration. The finest of these pots were highly prized and often beautifully mounted with silver. The large quantities of Rhenish imported salt-glazed bottles and drinking mugs were curtailed in 1671 when war broke out between England and Holland. This encouraged the efforts of potters in England to make saltglaze ware for themselves.

The second major stoneware influence came from China. The activities of the Dutch East India Company in that country had resulted in large quantities of Yi-hsing ware being imported into Europe during the seventeenth century. Yi-hsing ware, sometimes known as red-ware, was hard, unglazed red stoneware made mainly in the form of teapots and in England and on the Continent it encouraged the popularity of tea. Many experiments were carried out both in Holland and in Germany to discover how the ware was made, and the successful results were brought to England.

John Dwight

A patent is recorded in England as early as 1636 for the manufacture of stoneware, though it is not known for certain whether or not any pots were made. John Dwight (1637–1703), a university graduate and man of letters, took out a patent in 1671 for the manufacture of stoneware in London, though his real interest lay in the search for the secret of porcelain manufacture. Dwight worked at a pottery at Fulham, London, where he employed immigrant potters from the Continent to make saltglaze mugs and bottles following the German style. Unlike the softer tin-glazed ware, stoneware could be made thinly without loss of strength, though the high temperature required in its manufacture precluded the use of lead glaze and colours painted in the tin-glazed earthenware style. Following the German example, Dwight decorated the pots with relief decoration known as sprigs made in metal moulds. The fine detailed modelling on the sprigs of such things as busts, animals and foliage was picked out and heightened by the saltglaze. Dwight continued his search for the production of white porcelain and, attempting to produce a white body, he mixed calcined flint with his clay which enabled him to produce a hard white stoneware. Unfortunately, his ignorance of china stone, an essential ingredient of porcelain, prevented the discovery of true porcelain.

Elers brothers

Despite his patent Dwight was not alone in manufacturing stoneware in England. John, Philip and David Elers, Morley of Nottingham and others set about making it. The Elers brothers of high Saxon-Dutch descent, and originally silversmiths, were the most inventive. It is thought they studied the art of saltglazing at Cologne and, following the crowning of William of Orange, came to England and worked in Dwight's pottery in Fulham, London. In the 1690s they moved to a remote part of England, Bradwell Wood near Newcastle-under-Lyme in Staffordshire, and produced, by methods they tried to keep secret, unglazed red stoneware in the Chinese style. Their processes of careful clay preparation and the use of relief decoration made in sprig moulds were soon discovered by the local potters, who used the technique themselves. Elers ware is characterized by fairly simple clean forms, based on the Chinese Yi-hsing wares. Small teapots, coffee pots, tea canisters, teacups and jugs made from finely prepared red clay were first thrown on the wheel and were then turned on the wheel or lathe while leather-hard to give them a smooth, sharp contour. Some were left plain and on others sprigs of relief decoration, often with Chinese motifs, were subsequently added. Plum blossom in the Chinese style, and birds and figures, also appear.

Staffordshire saltglaze wares

Most Staffordshire clays will not withstand the higher temperatures required for stoneware without warping and distorting. It was only with the discovery that calcined flint, when added to a clay body, could enable it to

Saltglazed jug with applied relief decoration and incised scrolls picked out in cobalt blue. Staffordshire, c 1770. (Victoria & Albert Museum, London)

withstand still higher temperatures, as well as whiten the body, that stoneware could be produced. This discovery has been attributed to various potters, and it is possible that it may have been made by more than one.

With the introduction into Staffordshire of moulds around 1740–50 it was possible to make thin-walled pots in asymetrical and angular shapes. Many had ornate carved designs which included humorous and fantasy figures; teapots were made in the shape of kneeling camels or houses, some with 'Chinese' designs.

The imported Chinese fine white porcelain continued to challenge the pottery industry and the high temperature white-clay body was widely adapted by the potters as an alternative to porcelain. Following the success of the Elers brothers at achieving high temperatures and their possible introduction into Staffordshire of the saltglazing technique, a good white domestic saltglaze ware was being widely produced in Staffordshire by about 1720. It is said that when salt was

Saltglaze agate
candlestick in the shape
of a cat. (British
Museum)

being thrown in the kilns the whole area was covered in a thick grey fog, indicating the prevalence of the technique. At its best, Staffordshire white saltglazed stoneware rivalled porcelain in its thinness, delicacy and refinement of decoration but not in the richness and depth of the glaze.

Around 1720 scratched blue saltglaze ware was developed. Designs were incised into the surface of the white clay before it dried and the scratches filled with cobalt-blue stain. The limited blue and white palette and the unsophisticated designs prevented the fairly crude decorative technique from looking harsh or gaudy and the finely thrown and turned pots were, in many cases, further enhanced.

Other centres making saltglaze wares

From the end of the seventeenth century, brown saltglaze ware was manufactured in the Midlands at three main centres: Nottingham, Chesterfield and Derby. Nottingham had been a major production centre of earthenware since medieval times and in 1693 James Morley started up the production of

brown saltglaze. Loving cups, mugs, puzzle jugs and jugs in the form of bears with removable heads, which were used as cups, were made. The suitable Midland clays and the mastering of the technique gave the saltglaze wares produced here a rich, smooth, brown, lustrous quality, produced by using an iron slip under the glaze. Delicately potted, thin-walled and lightly made, these pots were very popular. Decoration, instead of being in relief, consisted of bold, freely drawn scrolls, foliage and flowers scratched into the soft clay, as well as incised lines.

Unfortunately, the hard, slightly rough surface of saltglaze abraded silver cutlery and production of most saltglaze wares stopped towards the end of the eighteenth century in the face of the growing popularity of cream-coloured ware made by the larger pottery industries which developed in Staffordshire. The production of the more decorative saltglaze ware continued throughout the nineteenth century and culminated in the saltglaze vases made by Doulton's factory and in the studio pottery made by the Martin brothers from 1877 to 1914.

Saltglaze tankard made by the Morley Family and carrying the owner's name 'John Bond'. Nottingham, c 1720. Height 4 inches. (Hastings Museum)

7 GREAT BRITAIN (1700-1850)

Earthenware teapot. Whieldon ware. Transparent brown glaze with green and bluish colouring oxides applied in spots. Sometimes known as tortoise-shell ware. *c* 1760. Height 7 inches. (City Museums, Stoke-on-Trent)

The Industrial Revolution brought many changes in social and economic conditions. The population was expanding and industrial changes introduced new technology and different patterns of work. Pots which had been made in small potteries for local needs were not suited to mass-production methods and the mood was towards greater refinement and low prices. Tin-glazed wares, though bright and cheerful, chipped easily, while saltglaze ware wore away silver cutlery; country earthenwares were not accepted by the well-to-do, who preferred the imported Chinese porcelains.

Cream-coloured ware and the industrialization of pottery in Staffordshire

As explained in the last chapter, many small potteries were firmly established by AD 1700 in north Staffordshire and during the following 20 years a whole series of technical improvements were made. The subsequent development here of the industrializing of the pottery industry is marked in the eighteenth century by three stages. The first was brought about by the Elers brothers who made fine red stoneware from carefully levigated clay; the pots were then turned on the lathe to precise

shapes. Secondly there was the addition of calcined flint to the body enabling the production of a near-white saltglaze. Stage three was the production of cream-coloured earthenware body used for making thrown and turned shapes finished with a nearly colourless lead glaze. This was manufactured on an industrial scale by Josiah Wedgwood in 1765. Cream wares, as they are often known, eventually replaced tin-glazed earthenware throughout Europe and caused the production of country earthenware to be greatly reduced.

Until the second half of the eighteenth century the Staffordshire potters tended to work in small family units employing about eight people. Overcrowding and soot and smoke pollution resulted in the working conditions in the area becoming worse as the industry grew bigger. Clay was dug as near the pottery as possible and clay pits often grew to a dangerous size. Usually the home and workshop were one and the same building. Roads were little more than tracks and during wet weather degenerated into quagmires. It was not until serious attempts were

A Staffordshire 'hovel' kiln, showing the firebox below, the glaze compartment in the centre, and the biscuit compartment above.

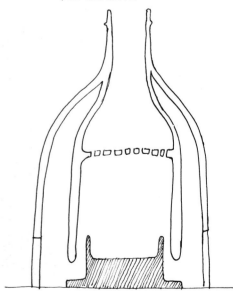

126

Above left: Teapots, made in a press mould, based on vegetable and fruit shapes. Wedgwood, c 1760. (Victoria & Albert Museum, London)

Milk jug made in agate ware; form based on contemporary silver vessels. Lead-glazed. Staffordshire, c 1750. (Victoria & Albert Museum, London)

Fine red ware teapot, engine-turned, with applied decoration. Elers factory, c 1690. Height $4\frac{1}{2}$ inches. (Victoria & Albert Museum, London)

established his own pottery. Much of Astbury's work resembles that made by the Elers brothers in thinness and in the use of applied and stamped relief decoration. However, Astbury also made earthenware; the reliefs are commonly made out of white pipe-clay with the vessels finished in a lead glaze with a yellowish tone. He used clay which varied in colour from red to buff and appeared much darker under the transparent glaze. The stamped reliefs, often crudely done, had motifs of harps, stags, birds, lions and shields.

In 1725 Astbury, with his son Thomas, established a pottery at Shelton where they are credited with having used white Devonshire clay to make lighter-coloured bodies. They are also said to have introduced the use of calcined and ground flint as an ingredient of the body, which gave an even lighter-coloured body. Early pieces made from this body could be the earliest cream ware made, though the glaze was still tinged brown or yellow.

Ralph Daniel

One of a large family of Cobridge potters, Ralph Daniel is said to have brought the method of making plaster of Paris moulds, for casting pottery forms, to Staffordshire around 1740. Some hollow wares were made by pouring liquid clay slip into plaster of Paris moulds previously made from a 'block' or model. Most moulds, however, were filled by pressing thin slabs of clay into them with enormous skill and precision. Aaron Wood (1715–72), who was the most famous 'block' cutter, worked for several potters, and was responsible for many contemporary designs.

Thomas Whieldon (1719–95)

One of the foremost potters of his day, Thomas Whieldon started his pottery at Fenton Low in 1740. He incorporated the technical developments made, primarily by Astbury, into his work and extended them. He is known chiefly for the production of 'agate' and 'tortoise-shell' wares. Agate ware was made by combining clay of different colours with the result that the finished pot had a marbled look which resembled agate stone. Tortoise-shell ware was made by dusting colouring oxides on to the glaze. At first only manganese, which gave brown, was used, but the method was soon extended to the use of other colouring oxides, which were absorbed more or less irregularly into the thick soft glaze. Green, yellow, dark brown, purple and grey were employed in this way.

Saltglaze wares were another of Whieldon's products, including the so-called 'scratched-blue' ware.

Top: Double tea-caddy, cream-coloured earthenware. Staffordshire. c 1750. Height 5¼ inches. (Victoria & Albert Museum, London)

Centre: Butter-dish with cover and stand, cream-coloured earthenware, Leeds, c 1790. Height 13½ inches. (Victoria & Albert Museum, London)

made in the eighteenth century by the industry to form itself into larger units that conditions in the area began to be organized and improved. Most of the ideas for these changes came from Josiah Wedgwood.

Many of the technical developments which were introduced in the eighteenth century have become identified with individual potters, mainly through the writings of Simeon Shaw in the early nineteenth century. Though it is convenient to use much of his information, developments cannot all be so easily classified.

John Astbury

In 1710 the Elers brothers left Staffordshire and John Astbury (1686–1743), who is said to have worked for the Elers brothers and learned many of their manufacturing secrets,

Further technical improvements and refinements were made during 1754–59 when Josiah Wedgwood was Whieldon's partner. A green glaze was perfected and used over teapots and other vessels in such natural forms as pineapples and melons which reflected the interest in newly imported exotic fruit. More homespun vegetables, like cauliflowers, were also made. Fine workmanship and richness of colour prevented these wares from appearing crude; they possessed a freer, less restrained quality which is absent from much of Wedgwood's later work.

Enoch Booth

A potter in Tunstall, Enoch Booth, is credited with having introduced into Staffordshire, around 1750, the practice of biscuit-firing earthenware. This made the ware easier to handle as it was stronger, and gave it a suitable surface to absorb the glaze of lead, flint and clay which was now mixed in liquid form. The practice of biscuit-firing had been used long before by the potters who made tin-glazed maiolica wares.

Transfer-printing

In 1753 the Battersea enamel factory started using transfer-printing, which is thought to have been invented by John Brooks (c 1720–60). These transfers enabled detailed designs to be mass-produced for the first time. Colour was applied to a glued paper and transferred to the raw glaze. Messrs Sadler and Green further developed the process in Liverpool where many pots were taken from Staffordshire to be decorated.

Josiah Wedgwood (1730–95)

It was mainly due to the endeavour and skill of Josiah Wedgwood that the universal acceptance of the English cream-coloured earthen-

Jasperware copy of the famous Portland Vase. Wedgwood, c 1786. (Victoria & Albert Museum, London)

wares came about. Wedgwood had an extra-ordinary gift for organization and this, combined with a high standard of technical excellence, resulted in the industrialization of the pottery industry – the first major step of the industrial revolution.

The thirteenth child of the potter Thomas Wedgwood, Josiah became an apprentice potter at the age of fourteen to his brother Thomas. In 1754 Wedgwood joined Thomas Whieldon of Fenton and in 1759 opened his own factory at Burslem, making pottery of all the contemporary Staffordshire types. Wedgwood not only incorporated all the eighteenth-century technical improvements in his work but continued to develop these in the successful production of creamwares. In 1764 he secured the patronage of Queen Charlotte and renamed his ware Queen's ware. In 1769 he opened a brand new 'ideal' factory at Etruria where he further developed his creamwares by adding china stone and china clay to the body he was using to give a whitish-blue, more resonant body which could be made even more thinly without loss of strength. This pearl ware, as it was called, rivalled porcelain in its delicacy and colour.

Strong simple shapes formed the basis of Wedgwood's creamware and, though the work of the silversmith was often emulated in the decoration, the clay was used in a straightforward and successful way. Decoration was limited to simple feather-edged

Above left: Pot and cover in cream-coloured earthenware with brown painted decoration. Wedgwood, c 1780. (Victoria & Albert Museum, London)

Left: Cream ware, Staffordshire Teapot and stand with pierced decoration. At their best, cream-coloured wares were refined and elegant. Late eighteenth century. (Victoria & Albert Museum)

Below: Saltglaze teapot decorated with a portrait of Frederick the Great of Prussia in enamels. The shape of the spout and handle imitates wood and was popular with many potters. 1757. Height 5 inches. (Hastings Museum)

mouldings and beading and some pierced designs, but little or no painting. Only later did Wedgwood apply transfer and enamelled designs to his wares.

Contemporary excavations at this time at Pompeii and Herculaneum held the public interest and encouraged Wedgwood to develop his neo-classical taste. He made dry, unglazed pots which in surface quality and colour imitated stones such as jasper, basalt and onyx; these were decorated with fine translucent applied reliefs with classical motifs such as draped figures and garlands of flowers.

Leeds and other cream ware centres

Leeds was the main centre for the production of cream ware outside Staffordshire. Some of the ware had heart- and diamond-shaped pierced decoration and small moulded flowers often decorated the junction of handle and pot. Handles were often made of woven strands of clay. The clear glaze used by the Leeds potters tended to run pale green in the angles and crevices. Much of the work is, however, very similar to that of Staffordshire. Liverpool and, later, Bristol were also sites where cream ware was made at this time.

The result of all this activity and the developments in the production of cream-ware was that during the eighteenth century the pottery industry changed from a pattern of small, locally based potteries, often producing rich folk art, to a major industry mass-producing large quantities of pots for home and export markets. In north Staffordshire the potteries had spread from the original five towns of Burslem, Stoke, Hanley, Tunstall and Longton to include Longport, Fenton, Cobridge, Shelton, Lane Delph and Lane End. In 1774 the completion of the Grand Union Canal ensured easy access for the transport of raw materials and products and encouraged the growth of the industry. The success of the industry was such that in many parts of the world imported Queen's ware was cheaper than home-produced pots.

Porcelain

The discovery of the manufacture of true porcelain, that is, porcelain fired to a high temperature in the manner of the Chinese, and sometimes known as hard paste, was made in Europe for the first time at the beginning of the eighteenth century. In due course the discovery had a profound effect on the design and production of contemporary earthenware. Johann Friedrich Bottger, a German chemist, worked out the secret of how to make porcelain, while working for the Elector of Saxony, in 1709. On the basis of this

Top right: Teapot, cream-coloured ware, with double reeded handle, moulded flowers and floral knob on lid. Enamel floral design. Leeds, c 1775. Height 5 inches. (Hastings Museum)

Cream-coloured earthenware teapot decorated with enamel colours. Leeds, late eighteenth century. (Victoria & Albert Museum, London)

discovery the Meissen factory was established in 1710, under his direction, to produce pots and ornaments for the use of the Royal family. Pots were put on the market in 1713. Later, factories were set up in other countries by renegade Meissen workmen.

The so-called 'soft-paste' porcelain, made by adding a glassy frit to the clay, was invented by factories who wanted to produce porcelain wares. The technique led to production difficulties because the ware has to be fired to a precise temperature; if it is slightly exceeded, the ware distorts and loses its shape in the firing. However, the advantage was that a thin, translucent body resembling

true porcelain was obtained at earthenware temperatures. The first soft-paste porcelain factory using a frit of this kind in England was founded at Chelsea in 1745 by Nicholas Sprimont. The three English factories which did succeed in making hard-paste porcelain were Plymouth, Bristol and New Hall, Staffordshire, though none produced porcelain of great technical sophistication or design. William Cookworthy learnt the secret from the American potter Andrew Duché, and helped to introduce the process in different factories.

The invention of bone china, a form of porcelain, was peculiar to England and is attributed to the first Josiah Spode around 1800. This discovery overcame many of the earlier difficulties of loss of shape, since bone ash is not in itself a glass but reacts with the other ingredients of clay, flint and feldspar to produce a translucent body.

A porcelain factory was founded at Worcester in 1751 and established an impressive tradition of finely made and decorated wares, many fired to high temperatures. It exists to this day. At Sèvres, in France, soon after 1800, Alexandre Brongniart devised an exceptionally hard and refractory body which remained in use for most of the century. Production of fine wares at Sèvres still continues.

Mocha, lustre wares and other novelty earthenwares

Cottage earthenware, cheaply produced in small pottery factories, reflected the popular taste of the time. The enlarged populations of the towns particularly during the nineteenth century encouraged a taste for novelty, and mocha and lustre wares were made as a result of this interest. Wedgwood had first tried lustre on a large scale around 1780, though its use only became widespread during the first part of the nineteenth century. When applied thickly, the lustre took on the appearance of metal and was used on forms copied exactly from silver, though this technique lost favour when electroplating was discovered. When used thinly, lustre took on an iridescent quality with bluish, reddish, purple or mother-of-pearl reflections. Its use was often combined with other techniques, notably those of transfer-printing and 'resist' which left parts of the pot without lustre. Verses and quotations were common forms of decoration and were usually applied to jugs and plates. Swansea, Leeds, Newcastle and Sunderland were principal centres of manufacture. The printed designs, apart from their decorative quality, also have a documentary interest, reflecting contemporary events, celebrities, pious expressions and licentious verses.

Mocha ware was so called because of the dendritic patterns resembling an ornamental quartz called mocha stone. By careful preparation of the slips, patterns of trees, feathers and moss which seemed to have a natural quality could be obtained. Backgrounds of brown, cream, orange and green were usually decorated with brown or black designs. Ale mugs, chamber pots, jugs, pitchers and shrimp and nut measures were the forms most usually decorated.

Another novelty ware was the ornately moulded jugs usually made of an unglazed white-clay body, though occasionally terracotta was used. The tradition was started by Josiah Wedgwood towards the end of the eighteenth century but emulated by many other firms. An advertisement of 1855 shows a wide variety of these jugs with titles such as Stag, Apostles, Oak, Grape Gatherer and Babes in the Wood; each jug was modelled in the appropriate Gothic, rococo or Renaissance style and the jug and modelling were cast as one.

Transfer-printing, especially of the very English blue and white willow pattern, was also a novelty feature. Transfers were mainly of pictorial subjects and pots were made especially to show this decoration to its best advantage. Local or exotic scenes with Chinese details, a rural cottage with crows and rustic figures, intricate baroque borders, and Gothic designs were all used at different times.

Parian porcelain, made by mixing feldspar and china clay, was first used for figures and later for hollow wares, notably at the Belleek factory in Ireland where it was covered with a

Fruit basket in cream-coloured earthenware. Newcastle-upon-Tyne, c 1830. (Victoria & Albert Museum, London)

Below left: Jug with moulded design of vine leaves, masks and scrolls. Impressed W. Ridgway. Hanley. Height 6 inches. (Hastings Museum)

Below right: Jug with copper lustre and transfer-printed scenes of Mariners' Arms and Sailor's Farewell. Such decoration was common and popular on Sunderland pottery. c 1870. Height 7 inches. (Hastings Museum)

white iridescent glaze. It was a low-temperature type of porcelain and the various pots were made extremely thin in quite complex shapes. W. H. Goss, in Stoke-on-Trent, using a similar body, made what was known as Heraldic China chiefly, it seems, for seaside souvenirs. The demand for these no doubt came about through the increasing popularity of holidays and day trips to the seaside advertised by the railways.

'Maiolica', the term which had been used to describe the technique of painting coloured oxides on a white opaque tin-glaze, was now corrupted to 'majolica' and used to describe pots decorated with coloured glazes painted on to moulded forms with raised decoration. Minton's factory introduced the new technique around 1850 using designs based on

vegetable and floral forms. Green-glazed plates with moulded leaf designs are another example of this so-called majolica.

In the Great Exhibition of 1851 much of the work on show was typical of contemporary design, especially with regard to pottery. While the objects displayed at the Exhibition served to show new and magnificent technical developments in the production of pottery, the standard of design generally could not have been lower. French Sèvres porcelain was imitated slavishly by the large English factories; the work seemed to have lost any sense of the capabilities and limitations of clay, whilst the reproduction, though technically excellent, seemed mechanical and lifeless. Vessels, badly designed, were overloaded with decoration. In 1857 the South Kensington Museum was established with the aims of showing the 'application of fine art to objects of utility' and 'the improvement of public taste in design'. As a result the Museum tended to display forms which were fashionable rather than those which were well designed.

Ironstone china plate, M. Mason. Blue transfer decoration in the 'willow pattern' style. c 1825. Diameter 9 inches. (Victoria & Alber Museum, London)

Flagon, red clay with impressed and inlaid design, commemorating a wedding. Sussex pottery, 1819. Height 12 inches. (Hastings Museum)

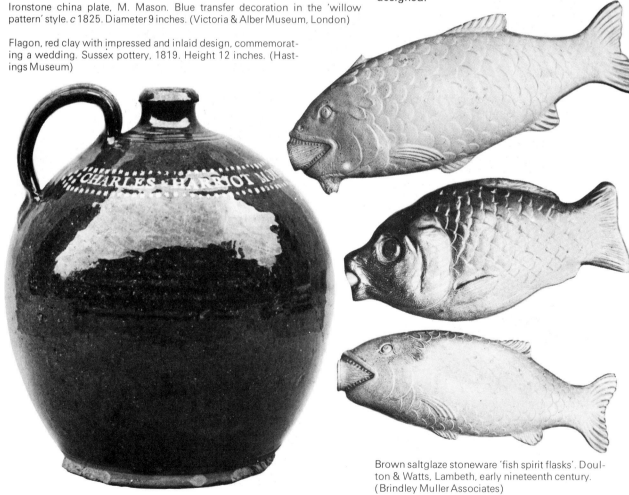

Brown saltglaze stoneware 'fish spirit flasks'. Doulton & Watts, Lambeth, early nineteenth century. (Brindley Muller Associates)

Country earthenwares

Regional country potteries, many set up during the eighteenth century, continued throughout much of the nineteenth century. They made a wide range of thrown pots, usually from red earthenware clay and finished with a clear lead glaze for local markets. Llewellyn Jewitt's *Ceramic Art of Great Britain* of 1877 lists numerous small potteries, many of which lasted for only a short time. Main products seem to have been pitchers, mugs, bottles, bowls, vinegar kegs and settling pans with simple but strong forms, well suited to their use. Candlesticks and tans or

carpet bowls were also in common production. Local styles of decoration which had developed during the eighteenth century were often maintained during the nineteenth century. For example, many potteries in Kent, some using the dark-red-firing wealden clays, continued the slipware tradition started in the seventeenth century. In Sussex, Burgess Hill was noted for its agate ware which included goblets, posset pots and basins. At Rye and Brede, large full-bodied jars and pipkins were decorated with impressed patterns, sprigs of leaves and printer's type. Fuddling cups with intertwined handles, and basins and salt pots

Stoneware teapot. This 'caneware', by Turner, was in the form of bamboo. Late eighteenth century. Height 4¾ inches. (Victoria & Albert Museum, London)

Below right: Jug, fine red stoneware. This type of ware was discovered by the German chemist Bottger who was attempting to discover how to make true porcelain. *c* 1708. Height 5 inches. (Hastings Museum)

Spirit flask with inlaid pattern made from printer's type – a feature of some Sussex pottery. Dated January 17th 1797. Diameter 8 inches. (Hastings Museum)

Mug, saltglaze stoneware, with iron dip on top half. Staffordshire, *c* 1720. Height 2½ inches. (Victoria & Albert Museum, London)

Left: Mug, saltglaze stoneware with extruded handle. English, dated 1747. (Victoria & Albert Museum, London)

Right: Mug, saltglaze stoneware with applied decoration in the form of scenes after Hogarth's 'Midnight Conversation'. Iron dip on top half. Fulham, c 1740. It has strong similarities with the Hastings Museum mug on p. 122. (Victoria & Albert Museum, London)

with incised decoration, were made near Ilminster in Somerset. From Devon came pilchard pots, harvest jugs, ovens and lamb feeders, while spice chests, money boxes, puzzle jugs and cradles were made in Yorkshire.

Saltglaze wares continued to be produced by many small potteries in the London area, notably at Mortlake, Lambeth and Vauxhall. Outside London, production centred on Nottingham, Bristol, Waverley Pottery, Portobello, Glasgow, and at Crich, Chesterfield and Denby in Derbyshire.

8 ANCIENT AMERICA (UNTIL AD 1500)

Southwest area of NORTH AMERICA c.1000 AD.
showing main tribal areas

NEVADA

UTAH

COLORADO

Colorado

Hopi

Navajo

N. Rio Grande

CALIFORNIA

Little Colorado

Zuni
○Acoma

ARIZONA

NEW MEXICO

Colorado

Gila   *Salt*

Hohokam

Gila

Mimbres

Rio Grande

TEXAS

Eastern Woodlands (Tennessee)

Pacific Ocean

MEXICO

Pottery in both North and South America developed quite different styles from pots made in other parts of the world. Potters in America were protected from invasion, and therefore influence, until explorers and settlers arrived in the sixteenth century. The earliest pots have two major characteristics. Firstly, they are all hand-built either by the use of coils or rings of clay; or hand-built with moulds. No potter's wheel was used. Secondly, they are all decorated with coloured clay slip or pigment. Glaze was not known. Settlers from Europe brought very different methods and techniques.

Geographically, the areas in which the majority of pottery has been made in America

are diverse and include hot, swampy lowlands, deserts, highlands and cultivated valleys. Early nomads, probably of Mongol descent, coming from the north of America, settled in the warmer areas of Central America, and it is here that most pottery was made. Early American pottery is unique in several ways. Separation from the remainder of the world for some thousands of years allowed a Neolithic-type society to develop without help or hindrance until visited and, in due course conquered, by invaders' from Europe. The invaders found a fantastic and totally alien society, with artistic standards quite different from their own.

Metalworking was not developed in

Water bottle, orange ware with painted spiral design in dark pigment which was typical of the eastern woodlands area of the U.S.A. as a whole. Perry County, Tennessee. 10 inches high. (Museum of the American Indian, Heye Foundation)

enabling the black colouring associated with reduced firing to be obtained. The pottery shapes themselves tended to be squat. Seed and maize, the basic food, had to be stored and many pots were made for this purpose. Cooking pots, which constitute the largest group of wares, show the characteristics of pots used by a primitive society living at ground level; for example, rounded bottoms, to sit in the fire or rest on soft surfaces, are common, as are bowls with tripod legs to stand on uneven floors. Faces modelled on pots point upwards so they can be clearly seen when the pots are sitting on the ground.

Basket-making undoubtedly played a large part in influencing pottery form. Three methods of building pottery – coiling, moulding and modelling, used separately or in combination – allowed almost any shape to be made. This is in strong contrast to the use of the wheel which imposes a limit on the shape of the pot.

Decoration was rarely naturalistic, in that it did not attempt to reproduce natural forms such as animals or flowers as they exist in nature. Such motifs were interpreted stylistically and adapted to the medium of clay. In Mimbres ware, for example, insects were simplified and shown as patterns and designs. Scenes on Mayan pots were highly stylized while depicting the events accurately. Geometric designs were the most common motifs and occurred throughout most of the region. In some areas the patterns were clearly influenced by contemporary textile design, while in others they seem fairly basic geometric shapes used in satisfying divisions of space.

The custom of burying pots with the dead, practised by many tribes, has preserved much pottery, often in good condition. Most other evidence of the long-departed groups of people has been destroyed either by the sixteenth-century conquistadors or by the very nature of the material; for example, adobe, a mixture of mud and straw used for building houses, has not the permanence of stone.

The form and design of the pots made by individual groups of people closely reflect the contemporary way of life. In some groups, notably in the Mochica culture of Peru, the pots were painted with, or had modelled on to them, many aspects of contemporary life, from eating and hunting scenes to ones of love-making and punishment. The pottery of early America not only serves as a social record uniquely preserving in detail events otherwise unrecorded, but it is also an art form in its own right, reflecting the thoughtful and aesthetic success of communities following a unique stream of development. Three natural

America until the ninth or tenth century AD; the wheel was either unknown or not developed, and mules and sleds were used for transport generally, while litters carried the rich or important. Basket-making developed very early, preceding pottery in many areas, and a similar technique to the coiling method of building baskets was used for making pots. Glaze was unknown except in rare cases and then it was used for decorative rather than functional purposes as, for example, on pottery made in the south-west of North America.

From out of this rather primitive background a distinctive pottery style, using only hand-building methods, emerged. The pots were decorated in a wide variety of ways using either incised or relief decoration or coloured slips. Kilns were primitive, but in some areas they were sufficiently developed to allow the atmosphere to be controlled,

Bowl with design of insects painted in black pigment in white slip. A beautiful example of Mimbres ware, New Mexico, U.S.A. Diameter 9 inches. (Peabody Museum, Harvard University)

geographical divisions provide three convenient groups of American pottery.

South-western North America
Pueblo Indians

The south-west area of North America roughly covers the modern states of Arizona and New Mexico. Here Indians settled in villages or pueblos and were given the general name Pueblo Indians. Maize was the staple diet and pottery was one of the main art forms. Early pottery was coil-built and the outlines of the coils were often left on the outside, showing quite clearly the method of construction. Made from grey clay, the pots formed the basic cooking vessels and are known as corrugated wares. Later, coloured slips, mainly black and white, were used for simple geometric designs of rectangles, triangles, zig-zags, frets, spirals and chequers either hatched or painted.

Thin-walled bowls, cylindrical jars, ollas (jars with rounded sides and necks), handled pitchers, ladles and mugs were all made out of carefully prepared pink or red clay. Although the local pottery techniques have undergone some changes, much of the traditional pottery made today employs methods similar to those used hundreds of years ago. Decoration has probably changed slightly and shapes have developed, but basically they are much the same. Each tribe had a distinctive style of decoration. Zuni pottery, for example, made in the upper Little Colorado, comes from an area occupied continuously by Indians. Zuni pottery had characteristic painted decoration which often covered the whole of the pot. Black and dark red paints were used on a pale grey background. Designs often showed deer enclosed in a structure which could be a house, near to a sunflower which is thought to be its food. On the deer, the internal organs

Bowl with coloured slip-painted decoration of two parrots and a scroll. Arizona, fourteenth century.

Three bowls. Pueblo Indian Zuni. Designs painted in black and dark red on a grey white background. 10 inches high. (British Museum)

of the throat, mouth and thorax were indicated. The base of the Zuni pots tended to be rounded, unlike the more pointed bases on the pots from Acoma, nearby.

Acoma pottery was decorated with a band of pattern covering the upper two-thirds of the pots. The design, often floral, was painted in black and yellowish-red. At Santo Domingo a white slip background was decorated with pure geometric and more openly spaced black designs. Hopi pottery, made in northeast Arizona, was decorated with black designs on a yellow slip.

Hohokam Indians

The Hohokam tribe who lived in the Gila and Salt valleys in Arizona developed the use of the paddle-and-anvil method of pot building. A sharp shoulder on the pot, formed by the junction of the rounded base with the straight walls, which probably developed out of the building method, is characteristic. Mimbres ware, made in the Mimbres Valley in the south-west of New Mexico, combined technical and cultural influences to produce one of the most beautiful and distinctive wares of America. Bowls are the chief form which have survived, probably because they were buried with the dead. Often they had a small hole knocked in the base, no doubt to render them useless to robbers, though there is a theory that certain tribes, believing that the inanimate as well as the animate possessed souls, deliberately broke burial objects in order to release their souls. The bowls, fairly simple in form, are notable for their painted decoration. Some had complex and beautifully executed geometric designs in black and white slip in which solid black and hatch-work designs were combined and covered much of the

Oval bowl with a painted design of two jack rabbits in a lively juxtaposition. Mimbres ware, 900–1050 AD Diameter $11\frac{1}{4}$ inches. (William Rockhill Nelson gallery of Art, Atking Museum of Fine Art, Kansas City)

Two jugs from the Upper Gila area and Salt River Valley, Arizona, U.S.A. The sharp shoulder is often found in this ware. Height of tallest jug 5 inches. (British Museum)

Left: Oval bowl with black painted design, c 1000–1130 AD Diameter 7 inches, height $2\frac{1}{2}$ inches. (Peabody Museum, Harvard University)

surface. Other bowls had realistic though slightly stylized animal designs which are, perhaps, the most characteristic. These designs are not only beautifully drawn but spaced in such a way as to imply tension and a concern for the finer aspects of art. Frequently shown in opposite pairs, creatures such as insects were painted in black on a white background. The black was quite often replaced by dark brown. Production of the ware ceased around the fourteenth century.

Central America
Mexico

The development of the area which chiefly comprises modern Mexico can be broken down into three phases after the archaic period. The period from 1500 BC to AD 300 is known as the 'formative', AD 300–900 as the 'classic', and AD 900–1520 as the 'post-classic'. Geographically, the area is large, with many local tribes and customs and it is only

Polychrome incense pot used for burning balls of copal gum and rubber on ceremonial occasions. Length 23 inches. Mixteca Pueblo Culture. (British Museum)

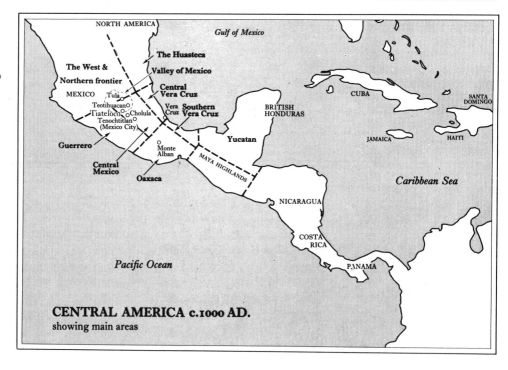

CENTRAL AMERICA c.1000 AD.
showing main areas

possible to mention the main centres. Though each group developed an individual style of decoration and customs, they all had a common background; this included hieroglyphic writing, bark-paper or deerskin books, maps and calendars, astronomy and a curious ball game, tlachtli, played with a rubber ball in a carefully prepared court.

During the classic period each city state existed peacefully. Independent cities were controlled by the priesthood and all the advantages of peace were enjoyed: trade flourished and pottery was widely sold. The end of the classic period is marked by the fall of Teotihuacan, the fantastic city in the Mexican highlands, and heralded a period of violence and aggression in which wars were waged to secure sacrificial victims and large-scale human sacrifice took place. Eventually the Aztecs gained a dominance they retained until overthrown by Cortez (AD 1519–21).

Mexican formative period
(*c* 1500 BC–AD 300)
During the formative period, most basic pottery shapes were common throughout the area. Bowls, neckless jars, long-necked bottles, spouted trays, bowls and jars with three

Above: Three-legged bowl with slip-painted design. Clay rattles were left inside each leg. Puerto Rica. Similar pots were common throughout much of Central America. Diameter about 5 inches. (British Museum)

Pot with pouring spout, painted in black and modelled in the form of an animal. This type is often known as a chocolate-pot. Huastaca, Gulf Coast of Mexico. Height 8 inches. (British Museum)

tall feet and jars with stirrup spouts were all made. Hollow 'mammiform' legs, in the shape of breasts, were often used on flat dishes.

Decorative techniques involved covering the pot in a fine slip of black, brown, red or white. This was often burnished by rubbing with a smooth pebble to produce a shine (sometimes called polishing). Some pots were left plain while others had simple geometric patterning. Incised designs were carried out, sometimes before the pot was fired, sometimes after: the latter gave a finer, drier line. 'Negative' painting was a method of decoration in which the design was painted on to a pot with hot wax or another similar resist substance; the pot, subsequently dipped in a different coloured pigment, was left with the design in the colour of the body showing through. The wax burnt away in the firing.

Mexican classic period (AD 300–900)

The classic period is marked by the growth of independent cities in which much time was spent in the study of astronomy and the service of numerous deities. Large temples and pyramids were built, and sculpture, pottery and painting were used for ritual purposes.

Teotihuacan, in the Mexican highlands, is a typical example of one of the cities. Here the pottery was technically accomplished if, in its early stages, dull and uninspired. Later, a polychrome style of decoration developed in which the 'champlevé' technique was used in which the pots were covered in a dark brown or black slip which was scraped away to show the dark body which was sometimes painted in with cinnabar. A stucco technique was also used in which the surface of the pot, usually a cylinder with three feet, was covered with plaster; this was carved and the design filled with coloured clays. The result, fragile and impractical, seems to have been highly regarded, more for its technical virtuosity than for its artistic importance.

The Maya

The Maya tribe, geographically situated in the Yucatan Peninsula, Guatemala and British

Cylindrical tripod vase with hieroglyphic design incised through layer of dark slip. The technique is similar to that of 'fresco' decoration in which coloured slips were inlaid in the walls. Teotihuacan, Mexican highlands, classic period. Height about 6 inches. (British Museum)

Honduras, developed fairly independently in an area relatively secure from invasion. They showed little interest in military expansion until the post-classic period. Early work shows strong influence from Teotihuacan, but after about AD 600 a decorative effect, involving the use of coloured pigments of great brilliance, was developed by firing the pots to a lower temperature. Durability was sacrificed for aesthetic beauty. Hieroglyphics and animals were used as decoration, but the most beautiful designs are the scenes of Mayan ceremonial life. Sacrificial cups in the shape of animals were also made.

Mayan post-classic period
(c AD 950–1325)

The Mayan post-classic period is reckoned from about AD 950. War was generally glorified during this time and an air of militarism prevailed which resulted in an expansion of the Mayan tribe. Tough, professional warriors, taking their names from such animals as the coyote, jaguar and eagle, led the tribe into Mexico. The main group, called Toltecs, meaning the artificers, established their capital, Tula, near Teotihuacan in Mexico and were led by King Topiltzin who claimed the title Quetzalcoatl, or Feathered Serpent, the hero of Mexican mythology.

The style of the decoration on their pots generally became more severe and abstract. While many local pottery styles continued, two styles predominated. The first, known as the Mazapan style, is characterized by a decoration of painted parallel wavy lines in red or white slip. Plates, jars, cylindrical vases, bowls and bi-conical cups were made in fine orange ware and had a hard, lustrous surface. The second main group, known as plumbate ware, so called because its black lustrous appearance was originally thought to come from lead, was in fact the result of careful kiln control. Forms were varied but all were black, hard and shiny.

Aztecs (AD 1325–1420)

In 1325 the Aztecs founded Tenochtitlan (Mexico City) and became the dominant ruling tribe. They founded a society based primarily on ecclesiastical rather that secular power, involving horrible rituals in which priests carried out mass human sacrifices; children, for example, were sacrificed to bring rain and the more they cried the more effective they were thought to be.

Pottery consisted of thinly made, well-fired, orange-coloured ware. Bi-conical and chalice-shaped cups were made for the old

Twelve small pots joined in a circle with modelling of gods or animals. Oaxaca, Monte Alban, Zapotec culture. Probably made during the classic period of the Mayas. (British Museum)

Jug with slip decoration in the form of a butterfly pattern. Mexico, Aztec period. (British Museum)

Right and below right: Two stirrup-handled pots. (a) Jar with painted scene of formalized warrior. Mochica, classic period. Height about 10 inches. (b) Guord-shaped pot with geometrical design in red slip. Mochica, formative period. Height about $6\frac{3}{4}$ inches. (British Museum)

is possible to separate the north and south of the region on stylistic grounds.

Chavin or Cuprisnique culture
(*c* 1200 BC–AD 1)

In the north, the early or formative period from 1200 BC to about the birth of Christ saw the

men to drink pulque, a potent alcoholic drink made from the fermented juice of maguey. Decoration, painted in black lines, was often geometric, though later it included birds, animals and floral patterns.

Mixteca polychrome pottery was one of the finest and most esteemed of the Aztec wares. It was made at Cholula and was decorated with several coloured slips. It is said that this was the only pottery King Montezuma would use. It was primarily a luxury ware using cream, yellow, red ochre, burnt sienna, grey and black colours. Human figures, religious and secular symbols, feathers and scrolls were some of the decorative devices and the designs had a full, busy quality. Much pottery was traded and the Spanish soldier, Bernard Diaz, reported seeing 'every sort of pottery, made in a thousand forms from great water jars to little jugs' at the great market at Tiateloco, near Tenochtitlan.

South America

The west coast and western mountains of South America, embracing Peru and Bolivia, known as the Andes, produced pottery which, though still made without the use of the wheel and lacking glaze, has a style different from that made in Central America. Little trading of goods seems to have occurred between the people of Central and South America, though raw materials were certainly exchanged. Because the land of the Andes is long north to south and narrow east to west it

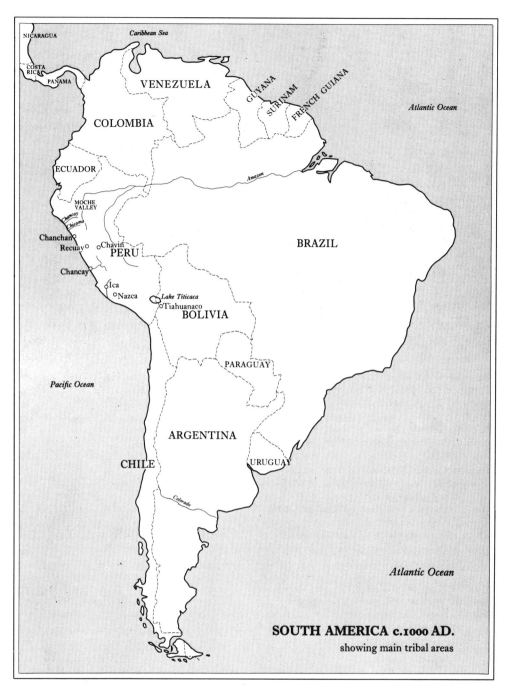

SOUTH AMERICA c.1000 AD.
showing main tribal areas

early beginnings of the Mochica culture centred in the north coastal valleys on the Chicama River. Chavin or Cuprisnique pottery, made around 800 BC, was characterized by gourd-shaped pots in white or buff body sometimes decorated with a red inlay, topped by a stirrup handle. Resinous paint was often applied to the pottery to make it waterproof. 'Negative' painting as well as incised decoration was used. The stirrup handle became a significant feature of later Mochica work

made in this area and was so called because of its resemblance to a saddle stirrup, and provided both a comfortable carrying handle and an efficient drinking or pouring spout, as well as protecting the contents from dust and contamination.

Mochica culture (*c* AD 1–1200)

The Mochica culture emerged around AD 1 and lasted until about AD 1200. The Mochica were brilliant engineers and built complicated

147

Three portrait heads.
Mochica, classic
period, Peru. Height
about 8 inches. (British
Museum)

irrigation systems involving aqueducts. Adobe brick, rather than stone, was the chief building material and so no large masonry structures were built. Mochica pottery is well known through its careful preservation in tombs and has been closely studied for the light it sheds on contemporary life. Maize, potatoes, beans, peanuts, gourds, cotton, cocoa and fruit were the main agricultural crops and pots were often made in the shape of fruit of, for example, pineapple or squash. The pottery was distinctive and was made by different methods from those used in North or Central America. Moulds made out of fired clay were the chief method of production, though the pots often had additional modelling. Though technically excellent, the pots have a characteristic mechanical quality because of this. Designs, often taking on the appearance of human or animal figures, were carefully executed and well considered.

Mochica art had a strong stylistic tradition similar in many ways to that of the Egyptians. The human figure was conventionalized into three sections, each showing its broadest aspect. Legs were shown from the side, usually in a striding position suggesting movement. Bodies were shown frontally with shoulders square, while heads were depicted in profile, though the eye remained in full front view. Royal figures were sometimes exceptions to these rules, and this also applied to relief figures on pottery. Decorations on pots, as opposed to other forms of art, seems to have been allowed slightly more freedom of

expression. Art, concerned with religious symbolism and secular ceremonial scenes of pageantry and warfare, contrasts strongly with animals and birds modelled on pots with refreshing directness which could only have come from close observation. No attempt was made to suggest perspective or volume in pottery decoration.

Modelled and painted scenes from daily life on the pottery provide superb documentary evidence of the contemporary life of this period. In warfare it seems the Mochica were vigorous and successful, using axes, clubs, spears, shields, helmets and drums. Architecture included religious and military structures, as well as simple thatched houses. Numerous gods are reresented, indicating a polytheistic religion. The gods of maize and other agricultural products are shown and a feline deity is very much in evidence. Wind and percussion musical instruments made from clay, for religious and secular occasions, included the flute, trumpet, bugle and rattle. Though the roads were good, no wheeled vehicles seem to have been used. Instead, long trains of llamas were used, and the coastal islands had boats and rafts. Fish, a valuable source of food, were caught by a variety of methods – harpoons, hooks and nets supported by gourd floats. Dress, more elaborate and ornate for the men, especially the complex head-dresses, is shown in detail.

Portrait jars, enabling individuals to be recognized, had faces looking upward; while originally mould-made, the pots were embel-

Chimu, as the people are known, were successors to the Mochica; they used moulds to produce forms similar to those made by the Mochica, but their pottery lacked the high quality of the Mochica work. The pots were mainly monochrome in grey, black or red, and many were burnished and reduction fired. The Mochica modelling tradition, reintroduced on Chimu pottery, perhaps by small independent tribes, lacked the spirit of the early work. Stirrup spouts and double whistling vases continued to be made.

Southern area Nazca culture

In the south, the Nazca culture flourished at a time similar to that of the Mochica. Again, a lot is learnt about contemporary life from the pots, many of which have survived. Unlike the Mochica work, the Nazca pots rely for effect on their decoration and the forms of the pots tend to be less interesting, having smooth contours which lack the strength of the Mochica forms.

The pottery may be described as colourful, as the slips were brightly coloured and wide ranging. Eight colours – black, red, white, yellow, green, brown, violet and cream – are known, though it was usual to use only five on any one pot. Designs were often outlined

Stirrup vase. Black reduced ware. Peru, Inca period. Height 7 inches. (Anthropological Museum. University of Aberdeen)

Two vases from Peru, Chimu culture. (a) Vase with flaring spout, moulded in form of bi-valve shell. Black reduction-fired ware. Height 6½ inches. (b) Four small pots, stirrup handle with model of animal at base. Burnished and reduction-fired ware. Height 7 inches. (British Museum)

lished to show individual characteristics such as scars.

Whistling jars, in the form of birds, were common and were so built that when water poured from the spout it caused air to be sucked in through a whistle.

Chimu people (c AD 1200–1450)

Following the gradual collapse of the Mochica culture after AD 1000 and the spread of influences from the south, a new state emerged around AD 1200 in the north with its capital at Chanchan. In many ways the

Bowl with concave sides, hard, burnished orange or dull red with a pattern derived from woven textiles. Painted in black, white and red. This is characteristic pottery of the southern area of Peru. Inca period. Height 8 inches. (British Museum)

Below: Double spouted globular jar with polychrome painted design of heads. Nazca culture, southern Peru. Height 11 inches. (British Museum)

in black. Early designs were based on animals and fruit set on a plain red background. Gradually the themes were broadened to include religious and mythological subjects.

Other southern cultures

The Tiahuanaco culture, centred on or near lake Titicaca in Bolivia, was politically highly organized; evidence of huge gateways and walled cities has survived. The pottery is severe and lacks the warmth of other cultures. Tall, concave cylinders are typical pots of the city-building stage of this culture's development (AD 1000–1200).

Vase with modelled features of corpulent man holding a cup. Red body, white slip, details painted in brown. Chancay, Peru. Height 14 inches. (Anthropological Museum, University of Aberdeen)

In the Chancay Valley a distinctive if un-ambitious pottery style developed. Thin and porous jars were made in egg shapes with the bottom more rounded than the top. Humanoid features, often diminutive, were applied in relief and were often combined with black and white painted decoration.

The Incas (*c* AD 1450–1550)

The Imperialist period (AD 1450–1550) saw the rise to power of the Incas, who took and maintained control over the whole inhabited Andes region in South America. By means of a network of roads, conquered peoples were controlled, though they were not allowed to travel on them. Rigid bureaucratic control was exercised by the Incas, who seem to have had a genius for administration.

Two bowls with rounded bottoms and straight sides. Geometrical patterns painted in slip. Diaguite, northern Chile. Height 3 inches. (British Museum)

Pots with painted
decoration. Ucayali
river, Upper Amazon,
Peru. (British Museum)

Pottery seated figure,
Tumaco. Height 15½
inches. (Museo Del
Banco Popular,
Bogota, Colombia)

forms and designs were carefully worked out
and controlled. Shapes showed little change
over a period of time and fall into three types:
the aryballus or narrow-necked water jar,
made in many sizes, the largest of which were
carried on the back with a rope; plates with
small, bird-head handles; jars and flat-based
bowls, many for cooking purposes, with
broad strap handles. Decoration, which was
usually restricted to small areas, consisted of
geometric shapes, carefully painted, and included bands, hatched diamonds, triangles,
stylized plants and, rather incongruously, butterflies and bees.

The European conquest of America destroyed or dispersed many of the ancient
tribes and their cultures. Knowledge of these
ancient societies has, in most cases, been the
result of excavations and further work will no
doubt increase this knowledge.

Technically, the Inca pottery was excellent.
But though it was fine-walled, well made and
strong looking, the forms and designs lacked
the free and inventive qualities associated
with the best pottery of South America. Nothing, it seemed, was left to chance; both

9 MODERN TRIBAL AND PRIMITIVE SOCIETIES

In certain parts of the world, groups of people have survived independently of other and more advanced civilizations. In many cases the cultures that exist are only slight developments of Neolithic models but other societies have developed complex social and economic structures often using basic technological skills. I have put them here under the general heading of 'tribal'. Africa, Oceania, Melanesia and Indonesia as well as parts of the Middle and Near East are areas where such societies have continued. Many tribes have survived in areas heavily protected by natural barriers such as forests, mountains, deserts or seas which have allowed cultures to develop slowly and without hindrance. Their pottery, for the most part, reflects a social need which is either religious or functional; it is rarely

made for its own sake. Most pots, even the most basic, usually incorporate some form of decoration which serves no practical purpose, but is thought to enliven and enhance the form. In many countries the hot climate and scarce water supplies have resulted in an abundance and variety of vessels for water storage which take a wide variety of forms. In Nigeria, for example, pitchers, bowls, ewers, small flagons and large urns are all made. Generally these pots have rounded bases for resting on sandy floors or sitting in the embers of a fire and strong rims for ladling and pouring the liquid.

Technically, the pottery is simply but skilfully hand-built by men and women who tend to specialize as pot-makers. Others may concentrate on the firing. Local clay which, by

A pottery seller in a village of the Punjab, Pakistan. (Pakistan High Commission)

153

Left: (a) Jug, rounded bottom, impressed textured surface, contrasting well with plain burnished neck. Nigeria. Height 9 inches. (British Museum) (b) Round-bottom cooking pot. An almost ideal shape for cooking. Nigeria. Height 4 inches. (British Museum)

Top right: Water pot in the form of a woman. Brazilian Indian. (British Museum)

Earthenware pot, Nigeria.

Earthenware handbuilt pot with vegetable varnish on the underside. Height 8½ inches. Melanesia. (Anthropological Museum, University of Aberdeen)

experience, has proved suitable is carefully prepared; stones are removed and in some cases the clay may be first dried and then ground before being mixed with sand, shell or grit to improve its working quality. Pots may be made by any one of a variety of hand-building methods, each method brought to near perfection. The Eile tribe of East Africa, who were at one period slaves to the Arabs, learnt and retained from their former masters the use of a simple pivot-wheel turned by hand, but this is a rare exception to the rule.

Most tribes have either no knowledge of, or have not adapted, the wheel for the use of the potter.

In Nigeria, firings are usually one of three types: open bonfire, in which any number from one to a thousand pots can be fired; grate firing, in which a circular enclosure, eight feet in diameter with a wall four foot high and nine inches thick, is packed with pots and kindling wood and covered with dry grass; clamp method, which consists of a permanent structure of sun-baked mud built in the form of an elongated oven. In this last method pots and kindling wood are packed inside the oven and the heat is fairly evenly distributed throughout the kiln. None of these firing methods allows a glaze of any sort to be used and, in fact, the development or use of glaze is not associated with primitive societies. To give the pots a shine, vegetable resins prepared from such

Pedestal bowl, decorated with yellow, red and black geometrical designs, side handle, red clay. A typical and beautiful example of the pottery of the great Berber tribes known as the Kobyles, who live in Algeria. They have an ancient tradition of making and decorating pottery. Nineteenth century. Height 8 inches. (Anthropological Museum, University of Aberdeen)

Below: Earthenware pot in the form of a bird. Basuto. (British Museum)

things as locust beans or tree bark are painted on to the pots, often while they are still hot from the firing. While the resins lack the permanence of true glaze and will not stand up to cooking use, they do add to the decorative qualities of the pots as well as making them more waterproof.

The style of most tribal pottery is based on shapes and forms which have evolved slowly. Over the years the pots that have proved to be most useful continue to be made and shapes continue to be refined. Most shapes are either copied from, or developments of, naturally occurring forms, such as gourds, though many societies will rapidly adapt new forms or different styles of decoration for their purposes. The tribes of northern Nigeria, for example, have incorporated into their pots the narrow necks from the pottery of the Islamic invaders from the north. Other Nigerian tribes have incorporated western objects such as aeroplanes into the traditional incised decoration. Shapes tend, on the whole, to be rounded, full and even.

It is in the decoration that local and even individual styles of pottery can be more clearly recognized. In West Africa each of some eighty tribes has its own style. Decoration is often limited to patterns that can be made in the clay, through incising, or applied clay patterns. Inlay work, made by filling incised patterns with clay of a contrasting colour, is made in, among other places, Ceylon.

A pottery water-cooler from Hunkuyi village, Hausa. Africa. (Commonwealth Institute, London)

The designs can have either religious, secular or abstract themes. Fingernails, corncobs, twisted vines, roulettes, shell fragments and hollow flower stems have been used to decorate pots by pressing them into the clay to give it a pattern. In the Sepik River area of north-west New Guinea, although there are many local styles, the predominant motif is a highly stylized representation of the human face, carried out in a variety of ways. Decorated 'appliqué' strips of clay are applied to the coarse red-brown pots in the New Hebrides in the form of geometric patterns.

Burnishing the clay by rubbing it before it is fired with a stone or small pebble smooths and polishes the surface and gives it a dull shine and strengthens the pot. It also helps to make the pots waterproof. The Hausa in Nigeria decorate many of their pots by this method.

10 MODERN AMERICA (1500-1800)

The arrival of Christopher Columbus in America in 1492 and the subsequent conquest by Spanish settlers brought an end to most of the early American pottery, except in remote, protected areas. The Pueblo Indians in the distant areas of Southern North America continued to make their traditional shapes and designs until the late nineteenth century, but they were only in comparatively small numbers. During the sixteenth and seventeenth centuries European settlers arrived in large numbers on the east coast of North America.

American folk pottery

The traditions of American folk pottery derived from designs, styles and techniques introduced from England and Europe. As the demands of the community, the changed way of living, the availability of raw materials and skilled labour encouraged inventiveness and gradually distinctive shapes and styles began to emerge. Two distinct types of ware can be recognized: earthenware produced from about 1640 until 1785, chiefly made in the New England colonies, particularly in Massachusetts and Connecticut, and also in East Pennsylvania; and stoneware, production of which started around 1700 and lasted until about 1900.

Red wares

Imported pots for the use of the new communities were expensive and by the early part of the seventeenth century potters had started to make their own wares. Philip Drinker, who arrived at Charlestown, Massachusetts in 1635 is one of the first potters whose work is recorded. Pots, made at Jamestown, Virginia between 1625 and 1650 included storage jars, jugs, pitchers, bowls, cups, mugs, porringers and milk pans, made on the wheel from red earthenware clay. Decoration was simple often made directly in the surface of the pots. Straight or wavy lines were incised with pointed sticks to heighten the strong shapes.

Two sorts of potter's wheels came into use: the English 'kick' or treadle wheel, which was revolved by pushing a treadle connected by an arm to the flywheel, and the Continental

Below left: Salt-glazed stoneware jar with painted cobalt decoration. Attributed to the Cheesequake, New Jersey, pottery of Captain James Morgan which operated during the last quarter of the eighteenth century. (John Paul Remensnyder Collection, Smithsonian Institution)

Saltglazed stoneware cakepot ornamented with bands of coggled decoration and stamped with the marks of potters Thomas Warne and Joshua Letts who were in partnership in South Amboy, New Jersey, 1805–13. (John Paul Remensynder Collection, Smithsonian Institution)

wheel. This was much simpler and was operated by the potter pushing the large flywheel round with the foot. For this reason it was sometimes known as a 'paw' wheel. Lead powder usually imported from England was dusted on the surface of the pots, and provided a thin, but serviceable coating of glaze. Later, with the introduction of biscuit firing the pots were finished in a more substantial coat of liquid glaze. Occasionally lead could be oxidized from the linings of tea chests but the more expensive imported lead was preferred. Other raw materials such as iron oxide could be gleaned from the blacksmith's anvil, while yellow ochre and umber were dug from local deposits. Manganese oxide was readily available and produced shades of brown in the glaze. Copper oxide which coloured the glaze green was expensive though an adequate substitute could be obtained from burning old copper utensils in the kiln.

Pots were fired in wood-burning brick kilns, built with an arched roof, some 10–12 feet long with a packing door at one end and a chimney at the other. Temperature was judged by the colour inside the kiln and the length of the escaping flames. More sophisticated methods used glazed 'draw trials' which were hooked out of the kiln and examined to check the melted glaze.

Records exist of the conditions under which potters took on apprentices to train and teach. The growing communities continually called for more and more pots so being a potter offered a reasonable livelihood. Apprentices were indentured from about the age of 14 for seven years; the potter supplied them with clothing and lodging, and taught them to read and write. In return they had to work long hours and learn all the pottery processes.

By the mid 1700s the pottery industry was well established. Most pots were glazed inside and out and some wares were decorated with colouring oxides or slips poured down the pots – a method popular in Connecticut. German potters who settled in Pennsylvania after 1730 introduced their own styles which were gradually adapted to the new society in which they lived. For example, pie dishes and bean pots were new forms they soon learnt to make. Red earthenware clay, white clay for decoration and lead for the glaze were abundant and were used in the production of the wares. The white slip, which contrasted well with the red body, was trailed on to the surface in lively semi-abstract patterns or provided a bright clean-looking lining inside dishes and plates onto which designs could be painted or scratched. 'Tulip' motifs were commonly used in decoration of Pennsylvania Dutchwares.

Improvements in making methods and more sophisticated firing and decorating techniques were introduced by itinerant potters who travelled from one pottery to another working to supply local needs before moving on.

By the time of the Revolution in 1776 earthenware had lost much of its popularity to the much tougher stonewares which were then being made. The public too was becoming increasingly aware of the defects of earthenware, in particular the health hazard posed by the lead glazes. An article in the *Pennsylvania Mercury* in 1785 suggested that the use of lead glazes should be banned as 'unwholesome', observing that not only did it tend to scale off the pot but is 'imperceptibly eaten away by every acid matter; and mixing with the drinks and meats of the people becomes a slow but sure poison'. Production was greatly reduced and by 1800 very few potteries continued to make earthenware pots in any quantity.

Stoneware and saltglaze

Production of stoneware in America started around 1720, introduced by potters from Europe: Anthony Duché, a French Huguenot immigrant, and his elder sons, made stoneware in Philadelphia in the 1720s. Twenty years later James, one of his sons, went to New England to help Isaac Parker start up stoneware production, but the venture was not a success.

While most deposits of local clays can be used for the production of earthenware, stoneware can only be made from beds of high-firing clays, which are much less common. Suitable beds of clay exist in and around New York City and this became one of the earliest centres of production. William Crolius, a German potter from Coblenz, set up a pottery around 1730 which remained in production until 1887. Another German immigrant potter, John Remmey from Neuweid, married a relative of Crolius and set up a pottery nearby which continued production until 1820.

Potteries were set up in Massachusetts (using clay shipped from New Jersey) and Connecticut, and their wares soon offered

Saltglazed stoneware water cooler, inscribed 'Mr Oliver Gridley/Newburgh July 1 1825'. Mr Gridley is thought to have been ironmaster of Queensborough furnace below Newburgh, New York. Made in New York, 1825. (John Paul Remensnyder Collection, Smithsonian Institution)

Vase in albarello shape. Tin-glazed earthenware with painted decoration. Influence from immigrant potters from Europe was often evident in the pots made. Mexico, 1800. Height $8\frac{3}{8}$ inches. (National Collection of Fine Arts, Washington)

strong competition to the earthenwares. Some potters, learning the new processes, made both sorts of ware at the same time, as did, for example, some German Pennsylvania workshops. Most stoneware was fired and glazed by introducing salt into the kiln, a technique brought over from Germany.

Like New York, Philadelphia was a pioneer centre in the production of stoneware. Excellent deposits of suitable clay, an expanding thriving population and excellent seaports encouraged increased production of wares,

Red earthenware dish
with slip-trailed
decoration bearing the
word 'Concord', and
lead glaze. A typical
pie-dish made in large
quantities. (American
Museum in Britain,
Bath)

much of which were made to very high
standards. Pots of high quality were also
made at Yorktown in Virginia. Most of these
stonewares were once-fired and saltglazed,
giving subdued mottled brown and grey surface colours. Other glazes were developed for
use at high temperatures most notably by the
use of dark iron-bearing clay slips which fired
a shiny black and brown. Decoration, often
scratched onto the surface of the pots, was
simple and direct. Incised straight and wavy
lines as well as stylized floral patterns were
used to great effect by potters in New York.
Some designs were coloured in with cobalt
blue, an oxide which withstands high-
temperature firing. Potters working in the
Shenandoah Valley favoured a lively wood-
pecker design, well placed and swiftly drawn
on the side of the pot. A variety of fish, birds
and flowers were also used, some scratched,
some painted, but invariably crisp and im-
pressionist in feeling. Many of these designs
have a primitive, untrained freshness which
totally enhances the form. Jugs, pitchers and
other containers were often stamped with the
name of the factory and a number, pre-
sumably referring to the capacity of the pot.

By 1790 the skills of the potters were well
advanced; they had to have knowledge of

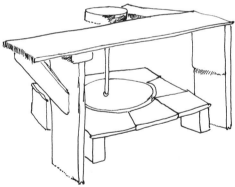

American potter's wheel, c 1775.

clay preparation, throwing, glazing and decorating, and also kiln design, stacking and
firing. The flourishing economy of the newly
established country attracted many more skilled European craftworkers who liked the
idealism, democracy and high wages. Wares
were thinly thrown and had crisp simple
shapes.

Like the earthenware, the stonewares were
practical and highly functional and, after the
establishment of the Federal Government in
1789, a tariff was imposed with duty on all
imported goods. Ordinary stoneware vessels

American earthenware dish with the slip motto 'Money Wanted', probably made for display in a shop window at a time when barter was quite common. Length 14 inches. (Shelburne Museum, Vermont)

American oval-shaped dish with slip-trailed decoration. Such dishes were made in large quantities for use in the home. Diameter 19 inches. (Shelburne Museum, Vermont)

were too expensive to ship from England and the demand for home-produced pots increased.

Flowerpots, vases, pie plates, baking dishes and porringers were made in stoneware though as earthenware had a greater resistance to heat shock many baking dishes continued to be made in earthenware. Some wares, like milk pans, churns, crocks and lard pots, with variations of local styles, continued to be made for more than 200 years with little change in either shape or function. It is these pots which are some of the best American folk pottery. In time potteries were set up at all western frontier settlements.

Industrial production

By 1800 a wide range of pottery was being produced in the United States of America, though the rich continued to favour imported wares from England and Holland. During the nineteenth century industrial wares continued to develop in scope and quality. All manner of pots were produced from red and black glazed teapots and coffee pots to lustre pitchers. Early attempts to produce the finer white wares in competition with the imported European pots were not always successful. The discovery of fine white clay near Philadelphia prompted several attempts but none were successful. Andrew Duché, another son of the German stoneware potter Anthony

American earthenware basin, coated with slip and decorated with coloured and clear glazes. Diameter 15 inches. (Shelburne Museum, Vermont)

American earthenware slip-decorated dish, probably made in Pennsylvania, 1796. Diameter 13¼ inches. A formal but fresh design based on traditional German motifs. (Shelburne Museum, Vermont)

Duché, claimed to have successfully produced true porcelain in Savannah, Georgia in 1758 by using china clay from the Cherokee Indian territory and went to England to sell or exploit his discovery. Back in America he was not able to repeat his success. However, American china clay was imported into England at the request of Josiah Wedgwood during the eighteenth century until the large deposits in Cornwall, England, were discovered. By far the most important attempt was the shortlived Bonnin and Morris factory at Southwark, Philadelphia, which from 1770 to 1772 produced fine white American china on a commercial scale. Clay from the banks of the Delaware was mixed with calcined bones to make a low-temperature porcelain body for pots based on contemporary styles of English wares. Bowls, jugs, fruit baskets, and plates with cut decoration were produced, some with painted decoration, others transfer-printed in underglaze blue.

Other potteries were less ambitious and more successful, and did not make true porcelain. William Ellis introduced both Queen's ware and stoneware at the well-established Moravian pottery at Salem, North Carolina. A wide variety of red earthenware pots were made here during the eighteenth century, often with slip-trailed decoration of simple lines and formalized flowers. Ellis introduced the method of making pots from press-moulds, and a wide variety of animal forms were produced as well as the more refined pots based on European creamwares.

Pottery factories in the European style, however, were not set up until the 1830s, when they developed very rapidly. Mass-production techniques, based on the use of patterns and moulds, were quickly taken up and important potteries developed near deposits of suitable clay, most notably around Bennington, Vermont; later factories were established at East Liverpool, Ohio and Trenton, New Jersey.

At Bennington, Captain John Norton, a

veteran of the Revolutionary war, first made earthenware in 1793 and twenty years later was producing stoneware. The 'American Josiah Wedgwood', Christopher Webber Fenton, joined the Norton pottery in 1837 and production expanded to include Rockingham ware, characterized by a mottled brown glaze. Later this ware was improved by sprinkling different coloured oxides on the pots to give a blue, yellow, orange and green glaze mottled effect. A huge range of well designed products was offered which included every sort of domestic pot as well as a wide variety of decorative and ornamental wares.

From 1853, Fenton named his enterprise the 'United States Pottery Company' and was producing a wide range of well made wares which included plain white earthenware, yellow earthenware, Parian porcelain and semi-porcelain, as well as various other speciality ranges like 'lava' or 'scoddled' ware. The variety of objects included almost every-thing that could be made in clay from water and coffee urns to footbaths and spitoons, as well as the more ordinary domestic table-wares. Perhaps the factory was too ambitious, for it collapsed in 1858.

By the time of the civil war in 1860 distribution was well established and many small potteries existed producing industrial wares. Some earthenwares continued to be produced particularly during and after the war when communications broke down, and stoneware potteries were being reduced in number. Advances in technology and the emergence of an industrial society eventually brought the production of 'folk' pots to an end. By 1880 most small potteries in the northern and middle eastern states closed down, leaving flourishing potteries in the southern highlands. As a network of roads and railways transported cheap and efficient mass-produced pots to remote areas so even these workshops were finally forced to close.

11 THE ARTS AND CRAFTS MOVEMENT (1850-1910)

General view of the International Exhibition, London, 1862, showing one of the stands displaying pottery and porcelain. (Victoria & Albert Museum, London)

Throughout the nineteenth century massive social and economic changes continued to take place which affected the production and design of pottery; mass-production techniques were perfected and methods of decoration were brought to a high degree of refinement. Traditional country wares which relied on the potter's skill on the wheel began to suffer from declining markets and a preference for the industrially made alternatives. Tin and metalwares as well as glass containers were equally cheap and often more practical choices. The middle classes had no taste for the crude 'peasant' wares.

Britain

In Britain the expansion of towns, the increase in population and availability of huge overseas markets encouraged the growth of a pottery industry which was to lead the world both in the quality and quantity of its products. One technical improvement quickly followed another. There was little the pottery industry could not do and all too often ingenuity seems to have been used to produce odd and complex forms rather than those which were clear and simple. Sumptuous, ornate and spectacular porcelain objects made by such firms as Minton and Worcester were shown with great pride at the 1851 Great Exhibition, but did little to boost the confidence of British designers who began to feel that there was something wrong with British design. In many ways the Great Exhibition can be seen as the starting point for modern applied art in Europe, for it helped bring about the realization that before the Industrial Revolution, industry and art were not separate; craftworkers were also designers and artists. The Industrial Revolution separated designer and producer; manufacturers and art drifted apart and processes which had been a part of each other had to be forced back together. The ornate, skilled, but aesthetically disastrous artifacts shown in the Great Exhibition encouraged the setting up of art schools and the eventual application of 'art' to industry, hence schools of 'applied art'. Museums were set up in many towns and cities and for the first time artists could admire pots and objects from many distant countries. Particularly popular were the ethnographical objects from Central and South America, Africa and the Far East. The more exotic and brightly coloured decorated wares from Persia and Turkey were equally inspiring.

The growth of the large well-to-do middle classes who wanted reasonably priced art objects encouraged the production of handmade work which eventually resulted in the Arts and Crafts movement. For the first time the work of the craftworker was recognized as 'art' and devotees sought to elevate their status to that of the 'fine artist'.

Equally important were the ideas of the aesthetic movement who wanted 'art for art's sake' and did not want to justify in any sense the production of any object, however useless, in terms other than its beauty. They

Tea cup and saucer, white earthenware. Designed by Felix Summerley (Henry Cole) and made by Mintons, *c* 1846. (Victoria & Albert Museum, London)

Decorated earthenware tiles produced by Morris & Co. (Fine Arts Society, London)

wanted to extend 'art' to include ordinary everyday objects such as flower vases and tableware made in the factory; factories set up art pottery departments and encouraged designers to produce fashionable and topical designs, many of which were based on the vogue for debased Chinese and Japanese styles.

Different countries in Europe, and the United States of America, reacted in different ways, yet there was an underlying common philosophy, particularly in the Arts and Crafts movement, which included a more honest approach to function and materials, and a belief in the enjoyment of the making processes. Central to these developments are the ideas of William Morris.

William Morris

William Morris (1834–96), friend and colleague of Burne-Jones and D. G. Rossetti, and follower of John Ruskin, was one of the first advocates of the Pre-Raphaelite school of painting in the 1850s. He lectured and

wrote extensively about his ideas on art and craft which, as far as he was concerned, were inseparable. The effects of his teaching were far-reaching and no doubt were instrumental in encouraging many of the experiments made by individuals such as his friend William de Morgan or by pottery producers such as Doulton's or the Martin Brothers.

Morris voiced ideas which reflected the growing concern about the separation of the maker from the user. As a socialist many of Morris's ideas on reforms were inspired by the dislike of ugliness and the soul-destroying effects of industrialization. He was also concerned about the need he saw for a change in society which would do away with poverty, corruption and exploitation so that a free fair and egalitarian community could be built. Art and craft, he argued, had a major role to play, both in helping to bring this change about and in the new society which would develop. Ideally, he said, art should be made by the people, for the people, for the enjoyment of both the maker and the user. Practically he encouraged craftworkers and, with a group of artists, helped to set up the Morris, Marshall and Faulkner Company in 1861. He commissioned designs from artists for furniture, stained glass, metalwork and fabrics, all of which had to be beautiful to look at and practical to use. Their products proved so popular that a factory with larger premises

Earthenware dish painted in underglaze and rich red lustre with design of deer and tree. William de Morgan. (Victoria & Albert Museum, London)

was opened at Merton Abbey, Surrey, in 1881.

Morris's ideas were central to the efforts of the Arts and Crafts movement which attracted craft workers from many different crafts to work out their ideas and philosophies. They organized exhibitions and societies to share common interests.

William de Morgan

The potter most closely associated with the ideas of the arts and crafts, and particularly with the work of William Morris was William de Morgan (1839–1917). He was a follower of the Pre-Raphaelite school and a friend of Burne-Jones and Rossetti and established his own pottery studio in 1872. His main interest was in decoration rather than form and in particular in the lustre colours on the Hispano-Moresque pots and the bright Persian underglaze colours. He decorated many tiles with complex designs of animals, strange beasts and ornate swirling foliage. Flat dishes also appealed to him for the opportunity they offered for decorative treatment.

His so-called 'Persian' colours had a vivid yet harmonious quality, especially the blues, greens and turquoises which were painted on to a white slip under a clear glaze. Pots of oriental form were decorated with ships, foliage, animals and other motifs. De Morgan organized his workshop carefully, employing skilled craftsmen to carry out his instructions and to paint his ornate designs. His importance in the world of pottery lies in his studies of the use of lustre colours and underglaze colours and their use on decorative tiles and vases.

Industry made various attempts to respond to the Arts and Crafts movement; some set up special 'art' departments, others employed designers, but the factory to embrace the ideals most firmly was that of Doulton's in London.

Doulton of Lambeth

John Doulton had gone into partnership in a pottery in 1818 at Lambeth, producing brown saltglaze ware. During the 1820s and 1830s the factory produced a wide range of pots and utensils for use in industry and the home. Among their products were spirit flasks with ornate decoration, but the rough finish of much of the work eventually caused them to lose favour. The factory, however, continued to produce utilitarian wares such as oven pots, water filters, ginger-beer bottles and most importantly drain pipes which were laid throughout London, providing the much-needed sewage system. Under the management of Doulton's son, Henry Doulton, the factory was brought into close contact with

Left and centre: Biscuit barrel and lidded pot with incised decoration by Hannah Barlow, 1895. Right: Saltglaze Doulton stoneware vase decorated with birds, by Florence E. Barlow, 1883. (Doulton Museum, London)

the Lambeth School of Art. The then head-master and Henry Doulton worked out a scheme whereby students from the school could use the facilities of the factory to decorate pots made in the workshop – in fact, to apply 'art' to industry. The results of the liaison were displayed in 1871 and 1872 in exhibitions in South Kensington. The pots were greatly admired even by Queen Victoria and Professor Archer of Edinburgh, writing about the exhibition in the *Art Journal*, a contemporary magazine which reviewed the arts, said that no tricks were played with the clay by trying to make it do more than it was capable of doing well.

Following the success of these exhibitions the Lambeth factory employed decorators to work on shapes which were specially de-signed and then made in the factory. The pots were fired in large saltglaze kilns sitting among the sewage pipes. Hannah B. Barlow is especially noted for her incised sensitive animal designs; her brother Arthur and sister Florence also worked in the factory as decor-ators. Later, experiments in the factory were extended to include the making of faience, using it as a term to describe any earthenware with relief modelling decorated with coloured glazes. Towards the end of the century over 300 employees worked in the 'art' studio.

Division of labour, however, continued to be practised in all aspects of the production of art pottery and the makers were quite separate from the decorators. No workshop had yet been set up in which one person carried out all the processes from start to finish or one in which form and decoration were related in any meaningful way.

Art studios

Other firms attempted to put the ideas of the movement into practice in other ways. In 1872–3 the large pottery firm of Minton es-tablished their Art Pottery Studio in Kensing-ton Gore with a curious kiln designed, so it was claimed, to consume its own smoke. Pots made in Staffordshire were brought to London to be decorated by artists who could make full use, it was announced, of both the local horticultural gardens and the South Kensington Museum. This was one of several experiments which tried to relate the indus-trial production of pottery with the work of the artist.

Other large factories, such as Wedgwood and Royal Worcester Porcelain set up small 'art' departments where 'art pots' could be designed which would be produced in the factory. Such wares were aimed at the fol-lowers of the aesthetic movement. One family of potters did however work in a very different way and make very different sorts of pots.

Martin brothers

The Martin brothers were the first group of potters who worked most like the studio potters of today. Hitherto, all potteries had either made traditional country pots or indus-trial wares; the Martin pottery, however, con-stituted the first break with this system in

167

Photograph of three of the Martin brothers working in their studio at Southall. A wide variety of their work can be seen, including the 'owl pots' and 'face pots'. Late nineteenth century. (Victoria & Albert Museum)

Right: Saltglaze stoneware vase with carved decoration in organic form. Martin Brothers, 1903. (Victoria & Albert Museum, London)

England, although each of the four brothers tended to specialize in a particular aspect of production rather than carrying out all the processes involved in the making of a pot. Robert Wallace Martin (1843–1923) was the eldest of the brothers, and organized the studio. After training first as a sculptor, he later worked as a modeller at Doulton's factory in Lambeth. In 1864 he attended the Royal Academy Schools, and the terracotta sculpture he made was subsequently fired at Doulton's saltglaze factory. He gained production experience from a pottery in Devon and for a brief period, around 1871, in Staffordshire. Later, he decorated pots which were fired at Dwight's old Fulham pottery. In 1873 with his brothers he set up a decorating studio in Fulham; on the strength of its success they opened a fully equipped studio at Southall, Middlesex, in 1877.

The pots were saltglazed in subdued colours, with painted oxides used to give dark blue, purplish-brown and dark brown. Decorative vases and jugs were made with relief, incised or painted decoration, as well as fireplaces and fountains, chess sets and some tableware.

Production continued at the pottery at Southall for some forty years though the pots met with little popular success. The products can be roughly divided into three chronological periods. Angular shapes, with decoration carved in deep relief together with incised patterns, marked the first period which lasted until the early eighties. In the middle period the pots were more carefully thought out and the beginning of a more individual style can be recognized even though the colours and decoration were very subdued. Cobalt-blue colour painted on a grey stoneware body as well as a rich, deep brown glaze were popular. Shapes became simpler and more rounded. Incised patterns were used sparingly and Renaissance designs of formally arranged foliage also appeared. In the last period, from around 1895 until 1914, attempts were made to integrate form and decoration and some very pleasing pieces were produced. A wider range of colours and textured surfaces derived from plant forms and fish, were used with considerable success.

Face jugs and pots in animal form made throughout the forty years are a particular feature of the Martin products. The grotesque, fantastic, almost medievally styled animals seem to conjure up the ideas of a mysterious underworld. The heads of these owl-like creatures were removable from their bodies. Face jugs, in much the same spirit, had the modelled features leering out of the side of the jugs. Of the four brothers, Charles died in 1910, Walter in 1912 and Edwin, the youngest, in 1914, after whose death Robert closed down the workshop.

Other art wares

As the Arts and Crafts movement gathered momentum in the later part of the Victorian period many art potteries were started throughout Britain. The pottery established in 1879 at Linthorpe near Middlesbrough by Henry Tooth is typical. Many of the designs were prepared by Christopher Dresser (1834–1904) whose influential book on Japanese art and industry was based on his visit to the country in 1877. Dresser designed pots for Minton, as well as for the Linthorpe and Ault potteries. One of his ranges, the so-called 'Peruvian pottery', were based on pots made in ancient Peru; Dresser's pots were highly glazed and characterized by speckled, richly flowing colours. In 1889 he moved and established the Bretby Art Pottery at Woodville in Derbyshire, where umbrella stands, 'jardinières', vases and hanging pots were made. Earthenware, made to resemble hammered copper, bronze and steel, as well as carved bamboo was produced by the pottery.

Vase inspired by pre-Columbian pots, modelled and impressed with a human mask in flowing white and green glaze over brown ground, c 1879–82. Designed by Christopher Dresser, made at Linthorpe Pottery. Height 6½ inches. (Fine Arts Society, London)

Earthenware pottery vases with thickly applied metallic crackle glaze in gold and platinum. Elton Pottery, c 1900. (Royal Academy of Arts, London)

The London store, Liberty's, in 1879 sold and popularized various 'art' pots as well as commissioning special designs. One range they included were the Barum wares of Devon in which thrown shapes were decorated with sgraffito or painted slips. Aller Vale wares, made at Newton Abbot from 1881, were heavily decorated on fashionable shapes. Students from the local art school carried out the decoration. In Somerset the Elton wares, dating from around 1882, followed many ideas of the Pre-Raphaelites. Asymmetrical relief patterns of flowers and foliage built up of coloured slips with sgraffito outline stood on a background of mottled shades of blue and green. From 1894 to 1906 the Della Robbia pottery at Liverpool produced white opaque glazed ware decorated with painted underglaze decoration. Much of it was in the form of tiles for architectural use, though hollow wares with vivid green glazes on modelled shapes were also made.

Art nouveau

The art nouveau style first made its appearance around 1883 and was taken up by potters and designers. The ideas of William Morris and of the other Pre-Raphaelites encouraged artists, especially in France, to look at natural plant forms which developed into an extravagant art style employing trailing and climbing plants in an exotic linear manner. New ideas associated with, and developing out of, the renewed contact with Japanese art encouraged the new style. Japanese stonewares were, perhaps, the major single influence on the pots made in the last 25 years of the century. Trade had been re-established with Japan in 1859 and large quantities of Japanese artifacts were brought to Europe. In pottery, as in other fields, art nouveau was evidenced by a break away from imitation of the past. Shapes from nature were adapted into stylized decorative patterns and a new feeling for colour was developed which continued to influence designs in the manufacture of pottery in the twentieth century. Particularly important are the later pots made by the Martin Brothers and the decorative wares produced in the art departments of the large factories, all of which reflected art nouveau style.

United States of America

Art potters in the United States of America were part of a general artistic movement which developed in the country after it settled down following the Civil War, and was part of the genuine development of an indigenous American style in all the arts. As with art pottery made in other countries, production followed two major paths: there were a few individual artist potters working either by themselves or in small workshops, and there were the factory-produced art pots, designed specifically for particular markets, which involved potters and decorators working on shapes made in the factory.

Cincinnati was the birthplace of American art pottery. In 1871 the ceramic chemist Karl Langenbeck started experimenting with a set of china-painting colours he had been sent from Germany. In this he was helped by Maria Longworth Nichols. The following year the local art school started a china painting class primarily for socially prominent women, one of whom was Mary Louise McLaughlin, who pronounced that 'tidings of the veritable renaissance in England under the leadership of William Morris and his associates had reached this country'.

Their work, shown in the Centennial Exhibition at Philadelphia was well received. Also on show in the exhibition were oriental wares and French slip- and underglaze-decorated ware made by Ernest Chaplet. Inspired by these pots, Miss McLaughlin set about decorating her work in a similar way, showing the results in New York in 1878 and at the World's Fair in Paris. Known as 'Cincinnati Limoges', the pots were much admired and the following year the Woman's Pottery Club was started by Miss McLaughlin so that women could learn the skills. Confusion and disagreements with Miss Nichols resulted in her setting up a rival establishment in 1880 in an abandoned schoolhouse: she named her pottery 'Rookwood' and set about putting it on a sound economic basis.

The Rookwood pottery

During the 1880s Rookwood's style gradually emerged; the forms became simpler and were decorated with naturalistically rendered plants and animals; colours became more refined and in 1883 the use of finely sprayed colours was introduced which eventually resulted in 'Rockwood Standard' ware. Subtle changes of colour from dark brown to orange to yellow and green prompted the description 'Rembrandtesque tones'.

Rival potteries set up in Cincinnati were short-lived, but in other cities, most notably in Zanesville, Ohio, sometimes known as 'Clay City', S. W. Weller successfully produced a ware based on Rookwood. In 1896 J. B. Owen's factory made similar wares and four years later the Roseville Pottery followed suit.

The Robertson family

Almost as important as the Rookwood pottery was the work of the Robertson family. They made ordinary brown wares in Chelsea, outside Boston, in 1866 and later in an enlarged workshop known as 'Chelsea Keramic Art Works' they produced pots in a chaste Greek style. After seeing the French and Oriental pots in the 1876 Philadelphia Exhibition they developed a range of slip-decorated wares and experimented to make rich red glazes. After many failures and near bankruptcy a new company, the Chelsea Pottery, was formed under Hugh Robertson. An attractive crackle glaze became the main product, used on decorative and functional wares. In 1896 the pottery moved to Dedham, where production continued much as before. The workshops finally closed in 1943. Closely associated with Robertsons was the work of John Low and the J. & J. G. Low Art Tile Works. Father and son had worked at the Chelsea Keramic Art Works before setting up their own tile business in 1878.

European influences

The influence of art nouveau around the turn of the century extended to most wares. Pots by the French potters Delaherche and Chaplet shown at the Chicago World's Fair in 1893 combined form and decoration and were finished with mat glazes. Inspired by these wares William H. Grueby experimented to find similar glaze. His firm, the Grueby Faience

Company produced ornamental vases, often decorated with vegetal forms in low relief, as well as architectural tiles. The vases were thrown by hand and were decorated by women following designers' patterns. His business was conceived as a 'happy merger of mercantile principles and the high ideals of art' and was in many ways a pure realization of the Arts and Crafts movement.

The idea that women could be trained in a craft which would enable them to make an honourable living was seen as one of the main tenets of the Arts and Crafts movement, and one which formed the basis of the Newcomb Pottery of New Orleans. Men made the pots,

Earthenware vase with smooth matt green glaze over carved decoration. Grueby Pottery, Boston. c 1900.

women learned to decorate them, mostly with naturalistic designs based on local plants and vegetation. The pottery was started in 1895 at Newcomb College, the women's division of Tulane, by William Woodward and employed Mary G. Sheerer, a skilled china-painter as design-teacher.

Influences such as art nouveau were also important in the work of potters. Artus Van Briggle (1869–1904) who first trained as a painter before learning to be a potter at Rookwood, based his work on the flowing style of Art Nouveau. Two years study in Paris introduced him, not only to contemporary decorative styles but to the oriental wares on show in the museums. Back in America he started to develop 'matt' Chinese glazes and to model pots in which design and decoration merged. In 1899, suffering from tuberculosis, he left Rookwood to move south and set up his own workshop helped by his wife. His pots made to a high standard were highly acclaimed and production still continues.

Other individual potters worked on a smaller scale and were influenced by other ideas and styles. Louise McLaughlin experimented to discover how to make true porcelain which she eventually used for pots, on which she did highly skilled decoration very much in the art nouveau style. They were successfully exhibited in America and Italy.

Adelaide Alsop Robineau

Adelaide Alsop Robineau was a major figure in the ceramic movement; she was not only a great potter but also interested in making ideas and techniques widely known. In 1899 she started puplication, and became editor of *Keramic Studio* a magazine aimed principally at the amateur potter and china painter. Articles by the French potter Taxile Doat on making porcelain stimulated her to try her hand and she began classes with Charles Binns, one of the leading teachers of the time, at Alfred University, where classes had been held since 1901. Pots were mostly decorated with incised and carved decoration enhanced by the jewel-like quality of the matt and crystalline glazes. Her greatest success was the award of the Grand Prize for fifty-five pieces shown at the International Exposition of Decorative Art in Turin in 1911.

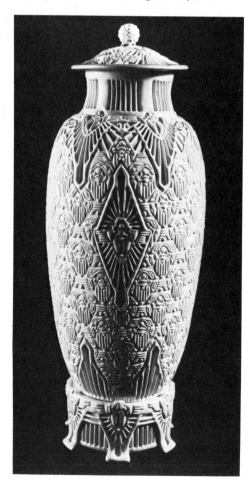

Adelaide Alsop Robineau 'Scarab Vase', porcelain with incised and carved decoration, 1910. Height 16½ inches. (Everson Museum of Art)

Porcelain 'Gourd' vase with matt glaze by Taxile Doat, University City Pottery, Missouri, 1912. Height 9 inches.

Louis Tiffany

Also important was Louis C. Tiffany, who acknowledged William Morris as the leader of the Arts and Crafts movement and based his work on the ideals of the movement. The first Tiffany pottery was shown in 1904 under the trade name 'Favrile'. Most was made on the wheel and decorated with plants and animals. Glazes were rich and ornate, such as splodged green resembling moss, and another ranged from light yellow to black suggesting old ivory.

Other influences

Influences on potters came not only from foreign wares, but from articles in *Keramic Studio* and from potters who came to work in America from overseas. Frederick Hurten Rhead from England brought a sense of modern design which inspired designers in several factories. He wrote articles for *Keramic Studio* and in 1902 went to work for Samuel Weller. In 1904 he was made art director of the Roseville Pottery. Much of his work incorporated conventionalized modelled or applied decoration.

Art nouveau designs continued to influence many potters, though there were attempts by some potteries like the Clifton Art Pottery at Newark, New Jersey to look at traditional American Indian pots and try and evolve a style based on them. Others like the Fulper Pottery at Flemington, New Jersey or the Pewabic Pottery looked to the Chinese pots.

France

The first artist potters emerged in France as early as the sixteenth century when Bernard Palissy (c 1510–90) was making highly individual tin-glazed pots modelled with realistic animals and plants. Charles Avisseau (1796–1861) of Tours emulated his work. It is, however, Theodore Deck (1823–91) who can be identified as the first artist potter in the modern sense. Eventually he became art director at Sèvres but before then he had opened his own workshop in Paris in 1856 to make decorative earthenware. Like de Morgan in Britain Deck was inspired by the Isnik and Persian pots and lustrewares on which he based much of his work. Technically his work was excellent and inventive; the colours were smooth and rich though the shapes were less interesting. Only later was Deck's work influenced by the imported Japanese stonewares which were seen at the Paris Exhibition in 1878 and which inspired him to make red-glazed pots fired in the reduction kiln.

Other potters felt much freer to experiment and improvise and interpret the oriental influences in their own way. Ernest Chaplet (1835–1909) produced rich deep glazes and was a major influence on succeeding potters. He also worked on slip-decorated wares at the Laurin and later Haviland factories before setting up his own workshop at Choisy-le-Roi. Auguste Delaherche, Albert Dammouse and Adrien Dalpayat were all influenced by his work and all contributed to the remarkable blossoming of studio ceramics. Artist potters

Earthenware plate richly painted in brown, blue, green and turquoise, in a design based on Turkish Isnik pots. Theodore Deck, France. Like William de Morgan, Deck studied Isnik and Persian wares and attempted to reproduce the brilliance of their designs. 1860/1870.

Left: Tankard, modelled by Gauguin and glazed and fired by Ernest Chaplet. (Museum of Decorative Art, Paris)

173

laherche as well as the sculptor Jean Carries, Georges Hoentschel and Emile Decoeur. In southern France the Clément Massier pottery at Golfe-Juan produced richly iridescent, nacreous glazes, and shapes which reflected the influence of art nouveau. French artist potters, unlike their contemporaries in England, had an attitude towards studio pottery which related it very clearly to that of fine art; collaboration between potters, painters and sculptors was not unusual, as for example Gauguin and Carries and Chaplet who produced new and exciting work. These experiments preceded the ceramics of Picasso at Vallauris which borrowed from the traditional brightly coloured tin-glazed earthenware made in Spain and southern France.

Other European countries

Artist potters in other Continental countries were slower to respond to the new ideas. It was not until the last ten years of the century that the ideas of the arts and crafts movement began to affect the work of artist potters. Max Läuger was an important teacher who helped spread ideas; his own work was experimental and reflected the shapes and decoration of art nouveau. Hermann Mutz of Altona and his son Richard studied Japanese pottery and created rich glazes. Julius Scharvogel set up a workshop in Munich where he made stoneware, after working first with the large firm of

such as Taxile Doat collaborated happily with factory production. Jean-Charles Cazin (1841–1901) also worked with stoneware in a Japanese style but his work in France was brought to an end when he had to flee from the troubles of 1871 to London. As a teacher at Lambeth School of Decorative Art he brought new ideas in stylistic influences. He taught Robert Martin as well as making his own pots.

The influence of art nouveau was absorbed happily and fruitfully by artists such as De-

Red earthenware with white inlaid decoration, designed by Van der Hoef, Holland. (Gemeentemusea, Amsterdam)

heart in them, and be a joy to hold, they must be human, vital and warm' wrote a Danish potter, and is a belief at the heart of Scandinavian design as much as that of Britain and was evident in much of the work produced. In Denmark the first studio pots were made by Thorvold Bundesboll in the 1880s. Here, as in France, earthenware was very much the chosen material. Herman A. Kahler took over his father's pottery at Naestved in 1872 and is notable for his lustre-decorated earthenware.

In Finland the Central School of Arts and Crafts was founded in Helsinki in 1871, and marks the start of the arts and crafts movement in that country. The work of A. W. Finch and the 'Iris' workshop was significant. Finch,

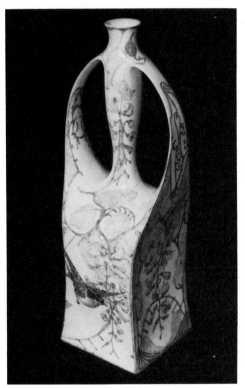

Paper-thin porcelain vase designed by Theodorus Colenbrander and made at the Rozenberg factory. (Gemeentemusea, Amsterdam)

Ludwid Tschiesche, stoneware vase with dappled blue and green glaze, showing the influence of 'art nouveau'. Bohemian, c 1900. (Victoria & Albert Museum, London)

Vase with inlaid and painted decoration. Designed by T. Nieuwenhuis, made by the de Distel workshops. (Gemeentemusea, Amsterdam)

Villeroy and Boch in Mettlach. Later Scharvogel was appointed director of the Grand Ducal Ceramic Factory in Darmstadt and concentrated his efforts in producing stoneware with rich glaze effects.

Later, other German potters were influenced by this work and today much German studio pottery is enhanced by rich lustrous Japanese glazes, or the more spectacular crystalline glazes which have become their hallmark.

'The things we make should have life and

Herman A. Kahler, pot with white tin glaze and splashed and lustred colours. Made at Noestrad, Denmark. 1894. (Victoria & Albert Museum, London)

Below: Red earthenware mug and dish with incised decoration through a coloured slip. Made by A. W. Finch at the Iris Workshop, Porvoo, *c* 1900. Finch's work was surprisingly modern and forward-looking and is clearly related in feeling to studio pottery. (Victoria & Albert Museum, London)

born of British parents, trained in Belgium where he learnt to make earthenware pottery. In the late 1890s he went to Finland and helped to set up the 'Iris' workshop in Porvoo (Borga). Domestic pottery with practical shapes with linear decoration cut through the slip were made. Later Finch taught at the Central School in Helsinki until the 1920s and helped spread ideas and methods which were reflected in the work of later potters.

Generally the techniques of higher-temperature firing were introduced and used by the factories who often set up smaller design studios where artist potters could work. Notable are Villeroy and Boch in Mettlach, Germany, the Gustavsberg factory in Sweden, the Porsgrund porcelain factory, Norway, Arabia, Helsinki, and the Royal Porcelain factory and Bing and Grondahl, Copenhagen.

A particularly rich flowering of the ceramic art took place in Holland. At the Hague in 1884 the German ceramist W. Von Gudenberg and Theodorus Colenbrander began making highly sensitive work at the Rozenberg factory. Influences came from imported Japanese wares, from traditional Japanese batiks and from the emerging ideas of art nouveau; the paper-thin wares, decorated with colourful stylized flowers and insects were made with great success and factories imitated the work. At the Delft factory of De Porceleyne Fles a range of dark brown earthenware with running glazes and incised ornament were made.

The ideas of the English arts and crafts movement were more influential in the small workshops at Amstelhoek and later at Distel, set up to make domestic earthenware. The individual potter W. C. Brouver worked at Gouda and then at Leiderdorp producing chunky vases from coarse clay glazed green or yellow. Some were decorated with designs cut in relief and coloured a darker tone. Mendes da Costa's work is also significant. His stoneware figures and pots, often saltglazed, have vigour and strength despite the sombre greys and browns of the glaze.

12 THE TWENTIETH CENTURY

Traditional country potteries struggled on during the first years of the century, but the First World War finally brought most of them to an end. In an attempt to extend the appeal of their wares many workshops had turned away from traditional functional pieces to more 'art' pots, but mostly without success. By 1920 the air of change was in the air and artists, designers and craftworkers set about discovering new ways of working; in Germany the Bauhaus was established which affected the ideas of potters in Germany and later in other European countries and in America. In 1920 Bernard Leach returned from Japan to set up the St Ives pottery, where, with the help of a small team, he made domestic pottery based on traditional English earthenwares, and also experimented with high-firing stoneware techniques learnt in the East. In time the model he created influenced studio potters in many countries throughout the world.

Britain
Early potters

The Martin Brothers' Southall pottery, described in the last chapter, had had little effect in stimulating other potters to follow suit, or indeed, on the work of studio potters in the twentieth century, and when it finally closed in 1914 it disappeared with little notice. The potter nearest to their ideas and methods, though it was unlikely that she knew their work, was the Australian Denise Wren (1891–1979). In England she studied design at Kingston upon Thames School of Art and went on, with her husband Henry D. Wren to set up the Oxshott pottery in Surrey. Together they built a number of small high-temperature coke-firing kilns and made reduced stonewares and saltglazed wares. They were later assisted by their daughter Rosemary D. Wren who eventually took over the pottery.

Some art schools had started small pottery departments, often employing throwers from the industry in Stoke-on-Trent to teach basic skills. Richard Lunn, an instructor in pottery at the Royal College of Art, London wrote what must be the first how-to-do-it book for potters, *Pottery*, in 1903. Among his students

was Dora Billington who went on to teach and inspire many students at the Central School of Arts and Crafts in London and its Principal W. B. Dalton became passionately interested in the subject and experimented with stoneware made in the Chinese tradition.

Reginald Wells (1877–1951) a sculptor who became a potter, also attended Camberwell School of Art. He later set up his pottery in Wrotham, Kent where he made red earthenwares decorated with white slip very much in the manner of traditional wares of the area. Later experiments with high-fired wares resulted in pleasant matt glazes in blue and grey-white.

Another Camberwell student was Charles Vyse (1882–1971), also a sculptor who turned to pottery. With his wife Nell, an able chemist, he made a range of fine stonewares strongly influenced by classical Chinese wares. Technically competent and visually very attractive, the pieces were quiet explorations of the strong shapes and decoration of the Chinese wares rather than being particularly inventive. They also made a series of lively colourful earthenware figures, many based on traditional English characters, which are as much admired as a social record as for their skill in modelling.

The Omega workshop

It was to Camberwell that Roger Fry (1866–1934) went to study pottery, after having had lessons from a traditional flower-pot maker in Mitcham. Fry's shapes, however, were futuristic and 'modern' and in the end too challenging for contemporary taste, but the experimental 'Omega Workshop', which tried to link the arts and crafts by inviting and commissioning designs from artists, is historically important. Contacts between Leach and Fry, though established, do not seem to have been fruitful.

The Omega Workshop in Bloomsbury, London, started by Fry in 1913 in association with Duncan Grant, Vanessa Bell and Wyndham Lewis, sold, made and commissioned many sorts of artefacts for the 'modern' home. This included pottery which, seen today, seems to lack technical skill and craftsmanship but which is, from a design point of view,

Earthenware teapot and cup and saucer. Roger Fry, Omega Workshops, London. Though lacking in technical skill, the far-sighted originality of the design can still be admired. *c* 1912. (Victoria & Albert Museum, London)

Vase and cover by Katharine Pleydell-Bouverie, Wiltshire, 1929–30. The sides have been carved and the ash glaze combines well with the simple but strong form.

Stoneware lidded box with white crackle glaze, Charlotte Epton, *c* 1930. (Victoria & Albert Museum, London)

potters in many countries is Bernard Leach. In many ways he can be considered to be the first studio potter, both because of the working methods he introduced, which were strongly influenced by the ideas of William Morris and the arts and crafts movement, and by his philosophical approach which involved every aspect of life.

Bernard Leach (1887–1979) was born in Hong Kong but came to England at an early age to go to school. In 1909 he travelled to Japan where he was so inspired by the raku process of making pots he decided to learn to be a potter. He returned to Britain in 1920 with the Japanese potter, and his fellow student, Shoji Hamada (1892–1978) and started a studio pottery in St Ives in Cornwall. In Japan Leach had studied pottery under the sixth Kenzan after a period of training as an artist at the Slade School of Art in London. As well as learning the raku processes which was closely associated with the tea ceremony, Leach also learnt the techniques of high-temperature stoneware firing. Despite early difficulties production was started; slip-decorated earthenware was made, as well as the high temperature stonewares. Public response was limited and only gradually were outlets established.

Leach's style was also slow to develop but at their best his pots combined a great feeling and sympathy for the East and the best qualities of traditional English slipware. Form, rather than decoration, became his principal concern and the pots he made were conceived from an aesthetic as well as a func-

Stoneware vases with incised decoration and runny ash glaze. Bernard Leach, Leach Pottery; St Ives.

original and forward-looking. Clean white or rich blue glazes over simple shapes foretold the future of pottery design in an extraordinary way. But England was not yet ready for that revolution and the work failed to attract much serious attention. The Workshop was finally brought to an end by the conditions of the First World War, though as individuals the artists such as Duncan Grant and Phyllis Keyes continued to make and decorate pots, vases and plates.

Bernard Leach

Undoubtedly the major figure who looms over studio pottery in Britain and influenced

tional point of view. Together with the other workers in the pottery, he was involved in all the making, decorating and firing processes, successfully combining the traditional work of the potter with that of an artist. Much of his work shows a strong eastern influence, but he attempted to express this through understanding rather than emulation. At the St Ives pottery Leach organized the production of a well-designed and aesthetically pleasing, low-priced range of domestic stoneware made by a small team of potters of whom he was one. He also made individual pots with subtly incised, carved or slip decoration. His skill as an artist was especially evident in his control and use of brushwork.

Regular visits to Japan and, in the thirties to China, sustained his interest in, and development of, oriental shapes and ideas. In the fifties visits were made to America and it was there that he met his third wife, the potter Janet Leach, whose own understanding of Japanese pottery, particularly that made by the Bizen potters, influenced his ideas. Pots made since the fifties had a freer, more assured strength.

Not only did Bernard Leach establish the first studio pottery in England but he took pupils who developed his ideas. Notable among these early pupils were Michael Cardew (1901–1983), Katharine Pleydell-Bouverie (1895–1985) and Norah Braden (born 1901). Since 1945 many foreign students have spread Leach's ideas internationally, most notably the American Warren Mac-Kenzie who lives in Minnesota, the Canadian John Reeve, the Belgian potter Pierre Culot and the Australian potter Gwyn Hanssen.

Leach also wrote *A Potter's Book*, first published in 1940, which has now gone into many editions and has been translated into many languages. In it he outlined his philosophy as well as describing the methods he used: for many artists it was their first introduction to pottery and is regarded by many potters as a sort of bible. It, perhaps more than any other single factor, has influenced studio potters throughout the world.

Michael Cardew (1901–1983)

By far Leach's most important pupil was Michael Cardew who, though he now makes high fired stoneware in a style very much his own, started by making slipware. After working in the Leach pottery, Michael Cardew took over the old traditional country pottery at Winchcombe in Gloucestershire in 1926. He sought out a retired traditional potter and revived the production of slipware. In 1939 he left the pottery in the hands of Raymond Finch, who had been one of his students and was then a partner, and established the Wen-

ford Bridge Pottery in Cornwall. In 1942 he accepted the post of ceramist at the West African Institute of Arts, Industries and Social Sciences, Achimota in the then Gold Coast, where later he founded the Volta Pottery at Vume. Much of the experience gained in this period formed the basis of his book *Pioneer Pottery* published in 1969, which covers in detail native Nigerian pottery and includes technical notes which are an invaluable guide for the studio potter. The book also deals with Cardew's philosophical attitude and the nature and role of the studio potter in modern society. Many of Cardew's pots are derived from traditional African shapes. He favours dark-coloured bodies and dense opaque glazes, many derived from naturally occurring materials. Brushwork decoration too reflects African influences with simple divisions of the surface enlivened with animal motifs.

Harry Davis (1910–1986)

Harry Davis, with his wife May, both students at the Leach pottery in the thirties, were

Earthenware cider jar with incised decoration, made at Winchcombe Pottery by Michael Cardew, 1936.

important in developing Leach's ideas. They continued the tradition of making well-designed, functional ware very much influenced by Bernard Leach. They started the Crowan Pottery in Cornwall in 1948 where they combined enormous technical understanding with a sensitive feeling for form and produced a range of consistently well-designed and hard-wearing stoneware and porcelain. They left England in 1962 to start a pottery in New Zealand, where they established a workshop using indigenous raw materials. Both Harry and May have spent time in Peru working with the Peruvians trying to introduce new potting techniques and processes which would help to form the basis of new small industries.

William Staite Murray (1881–1962)

In contrast to Bernard Leach, William Staite Murray worked in a very different way and put forward radical ideas which challenged many contemporary attitudes to the making and selling of craftwork. William Staite Murray was an early champion of studio pottery who worked to raise its status and promote the pots as art rather than as craft. His ideas about studio pottery were based on ideas current in France and were very different from those advocated by Leach. Originally trained as a painter he became interested in high-fired stonewares. He was particularly impressed by Hamada's pots made in Britain in the early twenties, and from then on concentrated on making individual pieces. His idea was that pots were works of art which should be able to stand by the work of the fine artist. To this end he successfully exhibited his own pots along with paintings by such artists as Ben Nicholson and Christopher Wood in galleries which usually showed only paintings. His large, almost monumental high-shouldered

Thrown stoneware pot with iron brush decoration by William Staite Murray. (Victoria & Albert Museum, London)

vases with their swirling brushwork have strength of form but somehow fail to impress in the way Leach's work does. Murray's greatest influence was as a professor of ceramics at the Royal College of Art where his ideas often made a lasting impression on many of his students. Most notable of these were Thomas Samuel Haile (1909–48) whose lively slip-decorated jugs and plates reflected the freedom and spontaneity of much of Picasso's work. Henry Hammond, another student, went on to become head of ceramics at Farnham School of Art, and to make pots in the oriental style with strong and vigorous brush decoration.

The end of the Second World War in 1945 introduced, for the studio potter, a time of recognition and expansion. The work of Bernard Leach, the growth of his followers and his generosity in publishing *A Potter's Book* in 1940 making his working methods and ideas generally available, and the work of William Staite Murray in promoting the value of studio pottery encouraged individual potters to establish small studios, and art schools to start courses in studio pottery. Leach's ideas based on eastern philosophy continued to dominate much of the pottery design, but they were becoming less strong under such influences as Lucie Rie (born 1902), Scandinavian design, and the experimental use of clay as 'a means of artistic expression' by potters in the United States.

Lucie Rie

Lucie Rie originally studied pottery at Vienna under Michael Powolny, and had been influenced indirectly by the ideas of the Bauhaus. She came to England in 1939 having already established a reputation as a potter, and set up her studio in Paddington, London. At first she made earthenware but meetings with W. B. Honey, head of the Ceramics Department of the Victoria and Albert Museum, and Bernard Leach who impressed her with his concern for 'completeness' in a pot, eventually led her to make oxidized stoneware and porcelain in her electric kiln, producing a range of simply designed pots and bowls. Typically, her work is finely thrown and delicately balanced. Dry, gritty, textured surfaces are combined with yellow or white glazes and decoration scratched on to a matt dark-brown pigment. Shape always seems to predominate and decoration, whether in the form of simple lines or bubbling textures, is always subservient to it. Today Lucie Rie's work is exhibited round the world and she is considered one of the world's leading potters.

As a teacher at Camberwell School of Art, Lucie Rie influenced many students and her

Thrown stoneware bowl with incised line decoration through black lustrous matt glaze. Lucie Rie, London, c 1971.

Thrown and assembled pot in the form of a pilgrim bottle. Hans Coper, London, 1956. (Victoria & Albert Museum, London).

Thrown stoneware pot with painted decoration. David Leach, Lowerdown Pottery, England, 1978.

Thrown pot with ash markings. Leach Pottery, St Ives, Janet Leach, c 1972.

work inspires many potters today. By far the most important potter whose work is often linked with that of Lucie Rie is Hans Coper (1920–1981). Coper went to work for Lucie Rie in her workshop in 1947 and stayed, sharing her workshop until 1958. Coper's work, often based on ancient Egyptian or Mediterranean pots or metal forms, is matt glazed and richly textured and explores a limited number of shapes, each one building upon and illuminating that which has gone before. His work manages to combine the best traditions of the craft with a rare degree of individual expression. For some years he taught at the Royal College of Art in London and helped revive interest in hand-built forms.

The Leach tradition

The end of the fifties and the beginning of the sixties saw the development of studio pottery along two lines, on one hand there was the production of well-designed useful pottery and individual pieces very much in the Leach tradition of high-fired stonewares, and on the other were the experimentors and hand-builders trying to break away from clay as a potter's material and find out what else it can do.

Within the Leach tradition many potters established workshops producing well-designed, hand-made domestic pottery at reasonable prices which does not merely celebrate 'hand-madeness'. Raymond Finch, at Winchcome Pottery, Gloucestershire, and David Leach, eldest son of Bernard, at Lower-down Pottery, Devon, are two potters in this tradition. David Leach, very much in the style of his father, made and still makes sensitive interpretations of oriental forms as well as a range of domestic pots.

Developments in the Fifties

The opening of the Crafts Centre of Great Britain in 1948 and the Craftsmen Potters Association ten years later did much to promote and foster the work of the growing band of studio potters. New small craft shops and galleries also sold pottery. Many art schools also promoted this tradition. Most had at least one lecturer who had a direct or indirect association with the Leach tradition.

A wider interest in pottery, following the work of T. S. Haile, was reflected in the work of William Newland, Margaret Hine and Nicholas Vergette (labelled by Leach as the three 'Picassettes'), who used traditional pottery materials to produce decorative objects such as bulls, birds and goats and pots which had a sculptural quality. While some of their work appears to have a whimsical and amusing quality, unlike the contemporary work made by Lucie Rie or Bernard Leach and does not have the classical quality of oriental pottery, it was a liberalizing influence on studio pottery in England. James Tower made pots based on

fish shapes with strong black and white decorations. Such ideas were keenly taken up by a few students in art schools though were not developed until the sixties which was very much a time of expansion and experiment.

Some potters, notably Alan Caiger-Smith at the Aldermaston Pottery and the Briglin Pottery, set up in London in 1948, made earthenware with white tin-glaze decorated with colourful underglaze designs usually brushed on. Alan Caiger-Smith's experiments in the

Earthenware bowl with sgraffito decoration through white glaze. Nicholas Vergette, 1954. (Victoria & Albert Museum, London)

Thrown lidded jar with green ash glaze. Richard Batterham, England.

Stoneware jugs thrown in two parts, with iron painted decoration over rich brown glaze. Michael Casson, 1978.

Object, stoneware with dry matt glaze. Gillian Lowndes, 1978. Height 4 inches.

last fifteen years with traditional reduction-fired lustres have resulted in beautiful colours and textures.

The majority of studio potters continued to make high-fired stonewares; notable among them are Robin Welch, Richard Batterham, the Australian potter Gwyn Hanssen, Colin Pearson, Michael Casson and Geoffrey Whiting.

The Sixties

The sixties also saw the development of potters who were more interested in the ceramic form than the ceramic function. Some, like Tony Hepburn were inspired by the work of American potters and made slipcast forms of everyday objects such as telephones, milk bottles, as well as lustre-decorated non-functional cups and saucers. Other potters, such as Ian Auld, Gillian Lowndes and Dan Arbeid were more interested in hand building methods and the pot as a sculptural form. Some reacted against the Leach tradition and deliberately avoided brown glazes and reduction effects.

Recent developments

The seventies saw an even greater widening of the spectrum of ceramic activity. Domestic potters continued to flourish and produced the majority of studio pots that were made. The establishment of the Studio Pottery course at Harrow School of Art indirectly promoted Leach-influenced wares fired to high temperature in a reduction kiln. Many other art schools set up similar courses, geared to a vocational training in workshop pottery techniques. Recently the opening of the Dartington Training Workshop, which is a pottery which also trains apprentices, is a recognition of the need for this sort of pottery teaching.

Techniques too have broadened. There has

been a revival of interest in wood-burning kilns, partly as a result of increased oil prices and partly because of the rich effects of the flame and wood ash on the wares. Likewise, saltglaze has found new favour, because of its direct and attractive effect on the clay body. Difficulties with pollution which results from saltglazing restrict its use, but experiments with alternatives to salt are yielding reasonable results.

Potters like Jane Hamlyn, Walter Keeler and Sarah Walton run small workshops making domestic tableware fired in a saltglaze kiln: the pots are lively and inventive often with simple clay decoration. The muted saltglaze brown, oranges and yellows are often heightened by dashes of colour from such oxides as iron to give a dark brown and cobalt to give blue. Many potters have been attracted to the purity of the traditional English slipwares, particularly the slip-trailed wares made in Staffordshire, but few have been able to develop the unsophisticated qualities of these pots in any meanful way. Peter Dick's work based on these wares is a creative development. He makes slip-decorated and trailed domestic pots with a lead glaze, fired to a higher temperature in a reduction atmosphere, which transmutes the colours and gives the wares a deep, rich quality of their own.

A growing number of artist-potters use clay for its own qualities and look to the traditions of the hand builder rather than the thrower. Mary Rogers, who trained as a graphic designer before taking up pottery, makes small

Porcelain vase thrown and modelled, with matt white glaze. Oxidized. Eileen Lewenstein, 1979. Height 10 inches.

Handbuilt optical bottle decorated with painted slip pattern. Elizabeth Fritsch, 1975. Height 10 inches. (Crafts Council)

Porcelain objects, thrown with added modelled decoration and rich crackle glazes. Colin Pearson, 1979. Tallest pot 12 inches high.

Bone china bowl with modelled chicken decoration. Jacqueline Poncelet, London.

'Eight Double Squares', stoneware, by Graham Burr. London, 1978.

fine bowls by pinching and squeezing stoneware and porcelain clay. Her shapes are based on natural flower or organic forms and the decoration often derived from such patterns as the dappling on an animals's back or the strata of rocks. Delicate and sensitive, her pots are poised and precise with an almost intellectual authority.

Elizabeth Fritsch is another hand-worker; she has been influenced by Peruvian and African shapes. As a student at the Royal College of Art she learnt much from Hans Coper. She builds her pots with coils of clay, slowly smoothing and scraping down the walls to make them flat and even. Some shapes are symmetrical and rounded, while others take on a more organic feel: in some pieces a flattened side is added to act as a strong contrast. All the pots are decorated with coloured slips painted onto the surface. Some have geometrical rythmic patterns, others are designed to give a more optical effect. Elizabeth Fritsch's work is still solely aligned to the traditional pottery vessel but in forms and decoration relates closely to contemporary ideas in the visual arts.

Ceramic sculptures too retain their strong allegiance to the tradition of clay and the firing processes. Gordon Baldwin, Graham Burr, Colin Pearson and Eileen Nesbit use throwing or hand building techniques usually in combination to make objects which use the qualities of the material. For instance all four potters fire to stoneware temperature and use either stoneware or porcelain. Some young potters have been inspired by the hyper-realistic ceramics of the West Coast of America, such as Sarah Kaye or Simone Lyon, but so far such work has been made only rarely. While potters have not been particularly attracted to low-temperature firings and bright colours, there has been a renewed interest in the materials and techniques of industrial ceramics, particularly by students at the Royal College of Art. Jacqueline Poncelet's experiments with bone china, which she used to cast up bowls and dishes which were then decorated with delicate carved patterns and designs, were particularly successful. The same materials also enabled Glenys Barton to obtain precise and clean effects on sculptural pieces. Some earlier geometrical forms were often decorated with transfer-printed patterns. Other forms were based on the concept of man as an object in the world. Recent interest in the more ethnic forms and processes, in particular sawdust firing and polishing, again relates back to the use of clay as a material which can be moulded and formed by the hand.

Decorators such as Jane Osborn-Smith have worked with industrial bodies like parian paste to produce small precious finely moulded pieces which are then decorated with painted scenes and narrative stories with on-

'Conveyer', press-moulded and assembled objects. Paul Astbury, 1978.

Below: Porcelain pot with variegated lustre decoration. Geoffrey Swindell, 1979. Height 3 inches.

'Time at Yagul' by Glenys Barton. The base is cast-pressed in bone china. The figure and upright slabs are cast in bone china, unglazed and hand pressed. A photolithographic transfer of clouds has been applied. Made at Wedgwood, limited edition of four, 1978.

Handbuilt jug with incised and coloured decoration, Alison Britton, London, 1978.

Top: Pinched porcelain pots with dappled decoration. Mary Rogers, England, 1979.

Porcelain bowl with green speckled glaze. Emmanuel Cooper, London, 1976.

work to a wider audience, the Crafts Council has helped bring a new awareness of the skills of the craftworker. It has also encouraged work of high technical standard and helped to foster the 'new wave' of artist potters.

United States of America

Studio pottery in America slowly evolved from the art pottery workshops, from the ceramic departments of art schools and from the inspiration and ideas of potters who arrived in the country from Europe between the wars.

Early studio potters

One of the first potters to tackle the training of studio potters was Charles Fergus Binns (1857–1934) who is often known as the 'father of American studio pottery'. Binns, served a traditional apprenticeship at the Royal Worcester Porcelain works in England before he eventually moved to the U.S.A.; he was made head of the new ceramics school at Alfred University and set about designing a thorough and practical course. In his teaching he firmly embraced the ideas of the arts and crafts movement but extended the course to include all stages of pottery making. He continued to inspire and influence the ideas and work of many students for many years as well as establishing Alfred University as a highly regarded and serious course for students.

Binns published papers on various technical aspects of the craft, wrote three books; *The Potter's Craft*, *The Story of the Potter* and *Ceramic Technology*, and contributed to various technical and educational magazines as well as making his own fine pots. Some of the students Binns taught also continued to pot during the twenties and thirties; among them were Myrtle French, Arthur E. Baggs and William G. Whitford.

Different ideas were current on the West Coast where Glen Lukens was one of the early leaders. Inspired by Egyptian faience, he used the alkaline deposits of the arid Death Valley Desert to produce bright glazes such as 'Mesa Blue' and 'Death Valley Yellow' which were trailed and dribbled onto his pots. For many years he taught at the University of Southern California.

European influences

During the period 1920–45 immigrant potters arrived in America from Europe bringing new and different ideas. Trained in Finland, Maija Grotell brought refreshing liveliness to her pots, many of which were thrown freely on the wheel and decorated with 'modern', semi-abstract designs. Equally important were the

glaze enamels. The forms, such as scent bottles or lidded boxes, are often small and are perfectly in tune with the delicate decoration.

The publication of *Ceramic Review* since 1970 has also contributed to the spread of ideas and information and has encouraged a broad approach to the craft which is not only based on the ideas of Leach and his followers. The magazine has helped to bring about an understanding of pottery as a creative medium in its own right. Equally important has been the setting up of the Crafts Council by the British government to promote the work of the artist craftworker. Through a system of direct grants to craftworkers and loans as well as various educational and advisory schemes aimed at promoting craft-

Above: Bowl, earthenware with brown and turquoise matt glaze. Height 8¾ inches. Maijá Grotell, 1956. (Syracuse University Art Collections)

Stoneware vase with incised decoration of boys with a kite. By Marguerite Wildenhain.

potters Frans and Marguerite Wildenhain. Both studied at the Weimer Bauhaus and fled from Europe in 1939, Frans to stay in New York, Marguerite to set up her own workshop at Pond Farm, California. With a direct, unstudied approach, Marguerite Wildenhain's work contrasts strongly with the academic precision of Charles Binns. Full, flowing, 'organic' forms, with wood-ash glazes or coloured slips highlighted the clay quality of the work. As well as the more decorative pieces, functional pots such as teapots, covered jars, planters, bowls, cups and candlesticks were made which related much more to European studio pottery than to pots made in America at that time. The workshop was, and still is, open to students, and Marguerite Wildenhain continues to be an important influence in studio ceramics.

The two potters Gertrude and Otto Natzler arrived from Vienna in 1938 and concentrated on working out highly attractive glazes. Gertrude made the forms such as bottles and bowls, while Otto perfected the glazes, which range from crater-like surfaces to crystalline and lustre finishes.

Post-war ceramics

Ceramists working in the States started to develop a style and approach very different from their peers in Europe, particularly in the early fifties. Along with artists working in the fine arts, they responded to ideas which reflected the post-atomic age. Potters were influenced by two major philosophies – that of Zen Buddhism and the ideas of the abstract expressionist artists. The philosophy of Zen Buddhism, which came from Japan, had an effect not only on the pots that were made, but stimulated attempts to link the act of

making and firing pots with the Zen concepts of beauty which are applied to lifestyle as well as to art.

Bernard Leach visited the States in 1950 to talk to students and potters and three years later returned for a further widely acclaimed tour with the potter Shoji Hamada, and the director of the National Folk Museum of Japan Soetsu Yanagi. Other visitors brought first-hand knowledge of oriental aesthetics to large and appreciative audiences.

Potters also drew on the work of the visual artists. In Europe, Picasso and Leger, Miro and Chagall had worked or were working freely with clay, while the ideas and energies of the abstract expressionist painters, such as Mark Tobey who had earlier worked with Leach at Dartington in Britain, and Jackson Pollack, had their effect. Later the work of pop artists seemed equally relevant and applicable to ceramics.

Potters on the West Coast were first to respond to these new energies, and to develop these ideas. Leading potters were Rudy Autio, who developed anthropomorphic forms, and Peter Voulkos. Voulkos, after producing functional wares, was inspired by the ceramic work of European painters and started to produce non-functional sculptural forms which challenged the craft-oriented traditions of pottery. Students flocked to his classes at the Otis Art Institute, Los Angeles, and among them were Paul Soldner, Kenneth Price, John Mason, Billy Al Bengston, Henry Takemoto and Jerry Rothman, all of whom took up and developed Voulkos' ideas and produced their own styles: Takemoto as a lively decorator, Price as colourist dealing with precise form and mass, while Mason, very much influenced by abstract expressionism, made huge wall pieces. Later, his large pieces became minimalist and monumental. Paul Soldner concentrated on making large-scale raku pieces decorated with figures derived from magazines and newspapers. In 1958 Voulkos moved to Berkeley and the University of California where he continued his work. Notable students included Ron Nagle, Jim Melcher and Stephen De Staebler.

On the East Coast a quieter revolution took place, with Alfred University and its more academic tradition acting very much as a stabilizing force. Robert Turner, Karen Karnes, Val Cushing and Ken Ferguson made functional wares, experimenting with high-fired stoneware and saltglaze. Other artists, such as David Weinrib, who worked at Black Mountain College, built structured slab pots; Daniel Rhodes, who became head of ceramics at Alfred University explored sculptural forms. It was Rhodes' best-selling book *Clays and*

Wheel thrown vase, unglazed, with iron, copper and rutile stains stencilled over the figure. Smoked after firing. Height 16 inches. Paul Soldner, 1971. (Ceramic Review)

Thrown and slab built pot, stoneware. By Daniel Rhodes. (Victoria & Albert Museum)

Left: Porcelain cup with photo transfers and lustre decoration. By Erik Gronborg.

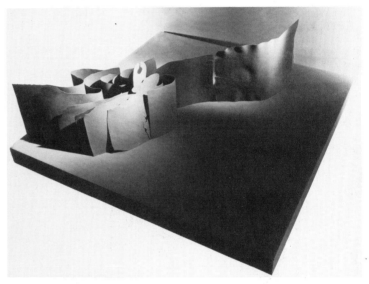

'Lithos Sculpture', ceramic monoliths on sand. Height 4 inches, width 4 inches. Le Roy Saucier, 1978.

Glazes for the Potter which, along with *A Potter's Book* by Bernard Leach, became the standard reference book for potters and students alike both in the United States of America and in Britain. Warren Mackenzie and his wife Alix returned from their time as apprentices at the Leach Pottery and set up a workshop in Stillwater, Minnesota: their work, mostly functional, reflected strong oriental influences. As Professor of Art at the University of Minnesota, Warren Mackenzie has inspired many students.

Expressionist ceramics

If the fifties were restless, the sixties were frenetic. Ceramics as a medium of expression seemed as legitimate as painting and sculpture and, following renewed interest in the ideas of Dada and Surrealism, 'funk art' was born. Improbable, impossible, outrageous, even disgusting, it embraced a wide range of objects, often deliberately badly made, which challenged concepts of 'correct' or 'incorrect' and what was a 'legitimate' use for clay. The work of David Gilhooly and Robert Arneson is particularly significant. Typical mid-sixties sculptural objects by Arneson includes 'Toasties' in which fingers stick out of an electric toaster, 'Typewriter' with red lacquered finger nails replacing keys, and 'Call Girl' – a tele-phone with breast. Realism and the use of everyday items – tinned foods, sexual imagery, make-up and the more socially unacceptable display of sexual genitalia made the work humorous, intellectual or outrageous, but reflected the political and social unrest of the time.

Gilhooly invented a mythical frog world in which he could legitimately satirize society and particularly its art. 'Bad taste' or even 'gross taste' was the aim of Clayton Bailey; many of his carefully made pieces, often with lurid and realistically modelled sexual organs caused faces to redden and critics to deplore them as 'tasteless and obscene'.

Other funk artists did not seek such crudely made or sensational effects but wanted to create precise, technically accomplished objects which conveyed visual and intellectual comment, whether serious or humorous. The techniques of the ceramic industry, such as plaster moulds, white clays, smooth industrial glazes and screen-printed transfers as well as

Hand built porcelain forms. Ruth Duckworth. 1973.

David Middlebrook, 'Hot Quake', ceramic with low temperature; an example of super-realism. Height 4 inches. 1979.

enamel colours were used. The work of pop artist Roy Lichtenstein also used these techniques to explore themes of 'reality' and 'illusion'. In one piece he assembled a pile of commercially produced cups and saucers decorated with screen-printed dots; the cups and saucers were real, but unusable, while the dots appeared to cast contradictory shadows. Richard Shaw became very much associated with this movement: his 'Ocean Liner Sinking into Sofa' made in 1966 was one of his first 'super-realist' objects and a worthy forerunner of his recent 'super-realistic' pieces.

Contextual art statements using collage, assemblage, *trompe l'oeil* and realist representation developed in Seattle with important contributions coming from Howard Kottler, Fred Bauer and Patti Warashina.

Realism continues to be a major aspect of American sculptural ceramics. It ranges from the hyper-realist objects of artists such as Richard Shaw, David Middlebrook and Kenneth Price to the 'sharp-focus realism' of Marilyn Levine whose leather objects and clothes look totally convincing. Only through touch can the 'unreal' nature of the objects become apparent and convey the idea that things may not be what they seem. Other ceramists deliberately seek out sculptural qualities in their work and notable here is the work of Mary Frank and Ruth Duckworth.

Ceramists, like all artists continue to be influenced by current social and economic conditions. The excesses and extravagances of the sixties were replaced by the more sombre seventies and as economic restraint affects university places and commercial success, there are signs of a move away from

Right: 'Woman', by Mary Frank, unglazed ceramic. A strong and powerful sculptural piece. Length 98 inches. 1975. (Collection of Mr and Mrs Al A. Lippe)

Below: Part of a dinner set, with painted decoration by Dora De Larios. 1977.

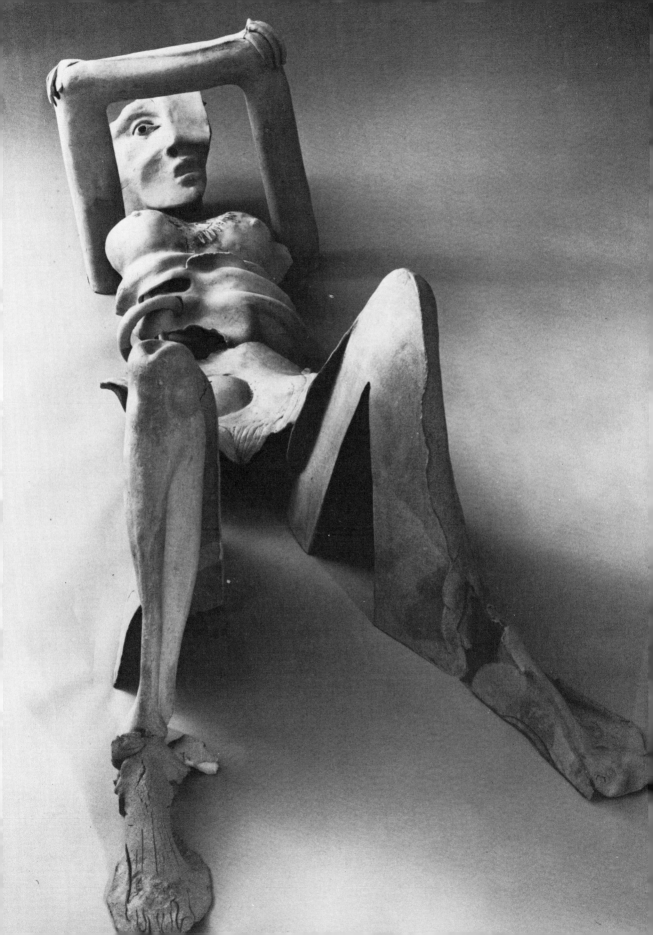

Thrown stoneware jug by Karen Karnes. (Photograph: Eileen Lewenstein)

decorative arts to more vocational and practical courses. The backbone of American ceramics remains the production of domestic pottery for use in and around the home. Less sensational than 'art' 'funk' or 'punk' objects, they reflect the high level of skill required, but are of far less 'news' or exhibition interest. Pots by artists such as Karen Karnes and Robert Turner hover on the boundary between function and object. They draw the best from tradition and relate their work and ideas to the present day. Potters such as John Glick and Stephen Jepson, using oriental techniques of highfired reduced stoneware, produce attractive tableware.

Canada

Unlike the United States, potters in Canada have been slower to develop their own styles, and influences have been absorbed from the States as well as from immigrant British and foreign potters. Until the late sixties the majority of Canadian studio potters produced

domestic tablewares influenced by the Leach-made stonewares. The opening of excellent ceramic departments in art schools, notably at Halifax under the direction of Homer Lord and Walter Osborn has brought a deeper understanding of the craft. Osborn's strong, rounded, saltglazed forms, such as lidded jars, are particularly successful. John Reeve returned to Vancouver after his apprenticeship at the Leach Pottery and helped explain the ideas of Zen Buddhism, and its philosophical application to the making of practical pottery. John Chalke, an English

Butter dish, thrown and saltglazed. Bill Rowland, Canada.

Black porcelain (basalt) bottles, thrown, with mocha diffusions in manganese with orange and white slips. Height 12 inches. Robin Hopper, Canada.

Raku bowls. Cheryl Russell, Canada.

potter who trained in Britain in the sixties, emmigrated to Canada and in his work, some of which is thrown, some hand-built, he continues to explore the ideas of Zen Buddhism extended to include non-functional wares.

Other potters, reflecting the influence of West Coast American ceramics, have been making ceramic objects, many with 'funk' elements. David Gilhooly spent time in Canada and inspired others to explore the fantasy world he described. Harlan House has made sports cars and highways decorated with low temperature enamels and bright colours, very much in the 'funk' vogue. Realism, introduced by the work of Marilyn Levine, inspired Stanley Tanira to explore this quality in his models of iron stoves.

Europe
The pottery industry

Studio potters on the continent have been inspired by three major influences: oriental stonewares and porcelain, the design ideas of the Bauhaus, which were closely associated with the arts and crafts movement, and the large porcelain factories, many of which were established in the eighteenth and nineteenth century often under royal patronage. Porcelain was highly valued and its manufacture was considered to be a mark of great prestige. In Germany the first porcelain factory at Meissen was established in 1709. The Rosenthal factory, founded in Bavaria in 1879, encouraged the consideration of the form of the pots rather than their decoration, though it was primarily a machine-made rather than a hand-made form. During the 1920s the functional ideas of design developed by the Bauhaus were applied to work made here.

Many students trained in the Rosenthal factories moved to other countries where they continued to work in similar ways. Since 1950 Rosenthal has produced a particularly adventurous range of ceramics, commissioning designs from artists such as R. Loewy and W. Wagenfield. 'Studio-Houses' were opened in several European cities to market its own wares, as well as those of other factories and studio potters.

In Finland the Arabia factory, one of the largest in Europe, was established in Helsinki in 1874. In the early part of this century pots in the art nouveau style were produced, notably by Thure Oberg. Modernization during the thirties led to the production of clean, modern designs. Since the last war, the factory has maintained a high standard of well designed pots based on plain, almost austere forms. The domestic range of pots has managed to combine the warmth of hand-made ware with the

Left: Zoltan Popovits, ceramic objects. Height 12 inches. Zoltan Popovits, Finland, 1979.

Right: Handbuilt pots, stoneware with oxide colouring in impressed decoration. Height 6 inches. Else Kamp Jensen, Denmark, 1979.

Below left: 'La Verità', terracotta. Anita Milbreta, USSR, 1978.

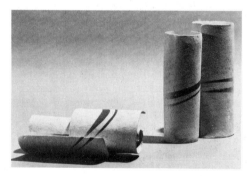

best qualities of machine production. Recently potters such as Toini Muona and Kyllikki Salmenhaara have been encouraged to develop their own ideas independently while working in the Arabia factory with full technical resources at their disposal. The work of the individual potters seems to be primarily concerned with decoration as a means of breaking away from the eveness of machine production and this is the best quality of the work.

The Rorstrand pottery and porcelain factory (originally founded near Stockholm in Sweden in 1725), the Royal Copenhagen factory (1775) of Denmark, and the Norwegian Porsgrunde factory have all played a major role in their own countries. Each has recently been concerned with encouraging

Bowl, stoneware by
Alev Siesbye, 1979.
Alev Siesbye has
worked in Denmark
since 1963 at the Royal
Danish Porcelain
Factory and in her own
workshop.

the work of individual potters within their
factories. This has encouraged the development of pots often characterized by simple
forms and rich decoration. Bright, rich glazes
such as red and blue are often used on small
areas set against dark textured unglazed surfaces on simple, often straight-sided forms.
Designs, often of geometric shapes as well as
stylized animals, are richly worked in relief
decoration.

Germany

Between the two World Wars the influence of
the Bauhaus was felt in most countries and
influenced potters working in factories and as
individual potters. In 1919 Walter Gropius
(1883–1969) succeeded Henry Van de Velde
as head of the School of Arts and crafts in
Weiner and the Bauhaus was born. It was
primarily a school of architecture and included within this all objects and fittings
which went in the building such as furniture,
as well as all kinds of domestic utensils.
Gropius followed the ideas of William Morris
and the arts and crafts movement and developed the notion that machines should not

emulate the work of human hands, and set
about finding out what machines could do
well. The result, sometimes called 'functiona-
lism', swept away the old ideas of fussy
ornament, and the designs, in comparison
with what had gone before, look clean, naked
and austere. So successful was the Bauhaus
that today much design is based on the
principles which the school established.

The ideas of the Bauhaus, as far as ceramics
was concerned, were expounded by several
artists, notably Gerhard Mareks, Otto Lindig,
Theodor Bogler and Marguerite Wildenhain.
The attempt to link art and industry covered
furniture and design generally. Many students
throughout Europe came under the Bauhaus
influence and potters were no exception. In
Vienna, the teaching of Otto Wagner, that an
object which from a practical point of view
was unsatisfactory could not be beautiful,
encouraged the search for good as well as
beautiful design. Michael Powolny (1871–
1944) as a potter and teacher at the Kunst-
gewerbeschule was another major influence.

In 1933 the Nazis closed the Bauhaus and
the staff dispersed, carrying with them its
ideas; many went to America.

194

Porcelain with incised decoration. Karl Scheid, West Germany, 1972.

'Provisional', stoneware. Height 14 inches. Pierre Baey, France, 1978.

Slipcast and assembled porcelain forms. Kurt and Gerda Spurrey, Austria, 1971.

Bottle and jug, stoneware, wood-fired kiln. Yves and Monique Mohy, France, 1971.

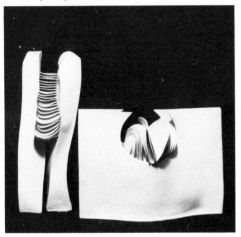

Not all potters were so concerned with making functional objects but pursued more artistic aims. Hubert Griemert, who worked in the twenties and thirties, developed rich glaze surfaces on strong basic forms. Glaze effects, some spectacular, some subdued, have become the hallmark of much German ceramics. Since the war two principal aspects of ceramic work can be identified: sculptural and decorative work and functional tableware influenced by the ideas of Bernard Leach.

German potters have maintained their reputation for decorative glazes with crystalline effects as well as traditional Chinese glazes, often used on sculptural or bottle forms. Notable are the artists Ursula and Karl Scheid, Lotte Reimers and Margarette Schott.

Recently more decorative work, sometimes sculpture, sometimes as humorous pieces, has produced interesting work from artists such as Robert Sturm, Antje Briggemann and

Tom Heinrich. All the work is made to a high technical level both in the form and the glazing.

France

The aims and ideals of the artist-potters working in France continued into the twenties and thirties, but with greater emphasis on decoration and colour, rather than form. Figure modelling too became popular. Since the war the work of Pablo Picasso at the Madoura pottery at Valluris has prompted other painters and potters to experiment with decorated ceramic forms. As well as decorating shapes made specially for him, Picasso also built up sculptural forms by joining different pieces together. Always made in earthenware and often with bright, colourful decoration Picasso's ceramics stimulated the formation of a whole colony of potters around Vallauris. The painter Joan Miro also worked successfully with the Spanish potter Artigas to produce decorative ornamental pieces.

Other potters looked in different directions, some to oriental stoneware forms, others to the traditional saltglazed pots made in Central France in the district around La Borne. La Borne has a long history of pot-making which some authorities claim goes back to the thirteenth century. A flourishing industry has been there producing wood-fired stonewares for over four hundred years. Until some twelve years ago there were still some half-dozen potters working with the huge kilns producing pots in much the same way, but these potters have now all but disappeared. The huge walnut-oil bottles, wine bottles and salting vats, as well as the objects for everyday farm and kitchen use, have ceased to be made. Now potters are attracted to the area because of the richness of the clays and the varieties of effects that can be achieved, and by the traditional methods of firing using wood from the nearby forests. Some potters make rustic tablewares, but many have turned to more decorative and sculptural forms. The work of Janet Steadman, Ives Mohy and Elizabeth Joulia are particularly notable.

Holland and Belgium

Other European countries have undergone similar sorts of development. Between the wars in Holland 'De Porceleyne Fles' encouraged the making of architectural pieces. Since the war, exhibitions of ceramics have been held and an enlightened and liberal attitude from the museums of decorative art has done much to promote the work of the potter. In Holland some potters have looked to traditional techniques and make domestic tablewares, while others such as Johnny Rolf and Jan de Rooden make sculptural forms with a strong awareness of the material they use. Some potters, for example Adriana Baarspul, produce domestic pottery, but their main interest lies in sculptural forms. Jan Van der Vaart makes hard-edged 'pipe' forms, while the artist Jan Van Leeuden's 'hyper-realist' cast male torsos, without arms or legs, draw on contemporary ideas in art and link them with the classical tradition in a particularly inventive way.

Similar attitudes exist in Belgium where the work of Pierre Culot, who trained as a potter at the St Ives pottery, now makes large and strongly conceived sculptural pots, often with ash glazes. Carmen Dionyse and Oliver Leloup make more figurative pieces, but all have a strong 'clay' feel about them.

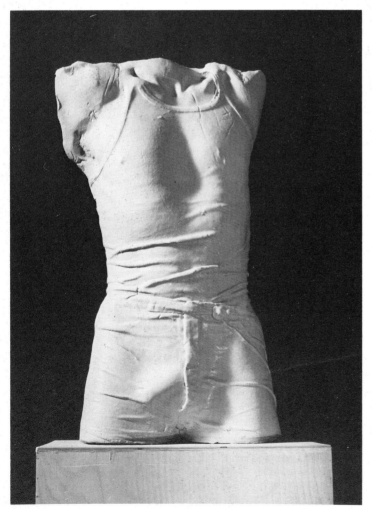

Ceramic figure. Jan van de Leeuden, Holland, 1978.

Jan de Rooden 'Pressure', stoneware, handbuilt. Height 20 inches. Jan de Rooden, Holland, 1970.

Scandinavia

In the last ten years many individual potters have broken away from the strong tradition of hand-thrown pots made in association with industry, and have turned to the more sculptural objects. Much of this work is influenced by and comments on contemporary social and political conditions.

Influences from surrealism and pop-art, as well as more traditional sources like the Far East, have given rise to ceramic sculptors, most notably in Sweden. Britt-Ingrid Persson uses her ceramic sculptures to comment and often attack consumerism and many aspects of contemporary society. Hertha Hillfon and Marit Lindberg-Freund work on a smaller scale and comment on more human sensitivities.

In Denmark the work of potter/designer Finn Lynggaard is notable, as are the earthy rounded pots of Alev Siesbye. Anna-Maria Osipow in Finland and Marjatta Lahtela both explore the surrealistic qualities of the forms they make, using naturalistic modelling contrasted with unlikely shapes and forms. In Norway Erik Ploen makes attractive

Objects, stoneware, made and designed by Raija Tuumi at the Arabia factory, Finland.

reduction-fired domestic stoneware, while Finn Hald and Dagny Hald make modelled forms, often incorporating the figure in various sorts of relationship.

Australia

One of the first recorded accounts of pottery-making in Australia appeared in the *Sydney Gazette and New South Wales Advertiser* in September 1803, which advertised for earthenware. In 1830 James King set up a workshop making water jars, cups and jugs at Irrawang, NSW and in 1857 George Guthrie was producing bottles, jugs and jars at Bendigo, Victoria. Gradually, potteries making wares for local needs were opened mostly using clays from the area. Flowerpots, jars, teapots, filter bottles and inkpots were being made semi-industrially to supply the needs of the newly settling country. James Silcock opened his pottery in Lithgow Valley in 1879 which continued production until 1973.

One of the first artist-potters was Merric Boyd, who set up his workshop at Murrumbeena, Victoria in 1911. His work, directly inspired by natural forms, had jugs with 'tree-trunk' handles, and large pots decorated with animal and human figures.

Other early potters include H. R. Hughan (born 1893) who learned his craft from Leach's *A Potter's Book* and by studying Chinese ceramics displayed in the National Gallery of Victoria. Hughan learned hand-building methods with F. E. Cox, a potter in Melbourne, and became the first artist-potter in Australia to specialize in stoneware: he continues to make reduced-fired high-temperature wares. A major influence has been Ivan McMeekin who, after training with Michael Cardew and running the Wenford Bridge pottery, moved to Australia in the early fifties and set up the Sturt Pottery at Mittagong. He researched local materials and produced fine stoneware and porcelain, strongly influenced by the Leach tradition and the great Sung pots of China. His students included Gwyn Hanssen and Les Blakeborough. McMeekin's book *Notes for Potters in Australia*, published in 1967, has been influential in helping to encourage potters to use Australian materials and indirectly to develop their own styles. As a teacher at the University of New South Wales, McMeekin helped inspire young potters. The establishment of art schools with pottery courses, the immigration of potters trained in Europe and the increase in the number of studio potters led, in 1956, to the formation of the Potters' Society of Australia. Peter Rushforth, Ivan McMeekin, Mollie Douglas and Ivan England, all of whom produce distinctive

wares, were involved in the setting up of the Society.

Potters absorbed influences from oriental high-fired wares with many potters spending study periods in Japan. Much influence also comes from the strong colours of the landscape, the starkness of desert areas and the shapes and forms of plant and animal life unique to Australia. Particularly successful is the work of Peter Rushworth who as head of ceramics at the National Art School in Sydney, has had a great influence on young potters. His work combines influences from medieval English wares, as well as from oriental pots. His strong, simple ash glazed forms have great strength and beauty.

Recently Gwyn Hanssen, whose training included working at St Ives pottery and for Michael Cardew is, with her husband John Piggot, setting up a pottery in Tasmania producing finely made tablewares fired to high temperature. Other potters have experimented with ceramic form, notable of whom is Shunichi Inone and Maria Gazzard. Decorative ware by Peter Travis and Stephen Skillitzi often reflects influences from the Australian countryside. Vic Greenaway is another young potter whose work combines a strong feeling for form with the 'natural' glaze

Opposite: Head, built out of thin slabs of clay; unglazed dark stoneware body with free silica to produce cracks. Gerald Makin, Tasmania.

Peter Rushforth 'Blossom Jar', stoneware with salt and ash glaze. Height 12 inches. Peter Rushforth, Australia, 1978.

Left: Ceramic forms, handbuilt and coloured with slips. Fired in gas kiln to about 1160°C (2120°F). Peter Travis, Australia.

Below left: Four cup teapot, jug and sugar bowl. Tomato over oatmeal glaze, wax resist pattern. Janet Kovesi, Australia.

Below: Saltglazed thrown jar. Height 18 inches. Janet Mansfield, Australia.

Above left: Thrown
stoneware lidded jars
with Shino glaze and
resist decoration. Janet
De Boos, Australia.

Above right: Landscape
jar. Post-reduced
earthenware, clear
glaze over white slip,
clay appliqué and
sgraffito, cupric oxide
wash. Height 12 inches.
Jeff Mincham,
Australia.

Porcelain forms with
lustres and on-glaze
enamels over a satin-
matt white dolomite
glaze. Height 24 inches.
Vincent McGrath,
Australia.

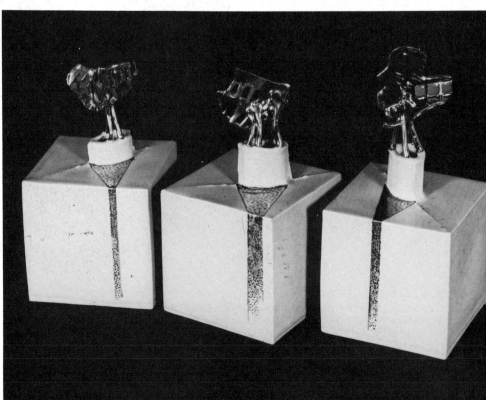

qualities associated with ash and ground igneous rocks.

Organizations such as the Potters' Society of Australia which organizes exhibitions of work and the Society's magazine 'Pottery in Australia' do much to encourage new ideas and spread information. Recently the series of international exhibitions at Bendigo have stimulated much interest.

New Zealand

Production of pottery in New Zealand started first with the manufacture of bricks, pipes and tiles; towards the end of the nineteenth century local potteries made saltglazed crocks, bottles and jars for industrial and domestic use. Luke Adams in Christchurch expanded production to include cast and moulded domestic ware while the Temuka Pottery in South Canterbury was equally successful.

Early studio potters drew support and encouragement from the ceramics industry, whom they persuaded to fire their pots. During the 1920s to 1940s, Brian Gardiner, Olive Jones, Elizabeth Lissaman and Elizabeth Matheson began to make pots. Robert Field built a wood and coke kiln in 1935 and ten years later started a series of pottery classes. During the fifties there was a great surge of interest in the craft as contacts were made with the work and ideas of Bernard Leach. Grants to potters such as Len Castle and Peter Stitchbury to travel abroad and for some to work with Bernard Leach and Michael Cardew brought a wider view to the craft as well as increased experience and technical knowledge. In 1962 Harry and May Davis set up the Crewenna pottery at Nelson, producing high-fired stoneware very much in the Leach style, made from native materials. Domestic pottery is still produced in substantial quantities by such potters as Peter Stichbury and Mirek Smisek, and many others. Other influences from organic forms such as gourds and shells have inspired some strong shapes from Ned Grant and Len Castle. A focus for activity was the establishment of the New Zealand Potters Society in the late fifties and the annual exhibition it promotes. It also publishes the magazine *The New Zealand Potter* which keeps members informed of events and records and reports on contemporary work.

Israel

Potters in Israel drew on traditional ideas and shapes for much of the domestic ware; particularly of interest are the smooth earthenware forms of Hanna Charag-Zuntz. Many ceramists in Israel are more concerned with

Thrown plate, stoneware with wax resist decoration, 1970, by Harry and May Davis, New Zealand.

Bottle with impressed decoration. Len Castle, New Zealand, 1970. Len Castle specializes in handbuilt forms often based on natural shapes such as shells.

decorative and sculptural themes. New buildings are often decorated with architectural ceramic panels, both on the inside and on the exterior. A good example is the mural by

203

Three objects, with glaze and oxide decoration. Edith Ady, Israel.

Gedula Ogen on the Ceramic Museum, Tel Aviv. Gedula Ogen also makes decorated work much of which relates to native plant forms.

Lydia Zavadsky has carried out some relief panels with sensitive designs. Potters such as Edith Ady and Agi Yoeli have made anthropomorphic sculptural objects with a sure awareness both of the form and the qualities of the clay. The official recognition of the work of studio potters came in 1968 with the setting up of the 'Ceramic Arts Association of Israel' with the support of the Ministry of Education and Culture.

Africa

In Africa the two major influences on studio potters have been the traditional African pots and the introduction of Western making and firing techniques. Traditional African pots are usually hand-built from local red coloured clays, fired either in simple kilns or in open bonfires. Strong direct shapes, many relating to natural forms such as gourds, have inspired contemporary potters such as Isaac Olusegun Aina in Nigeria. Other potters have combined traditional influences with oriental high-firing techniques. Esias Bosch in South Africa started making earthenware decorated with Bushman motifs but later changed to reduction fired domestic stoneware decorated with powerful iron brushwork. Sculptural work by Barbara Greig touches upon more social concerns and recently potters are finding an appreciative audience for decorative work.

Stoneware jar with ash glaze. Height 9 inches. Esias Bosch, 1972. Esias Bosch worked in England with Ray Finch and Michael Cardew before setting up his workshop in the Republic of South Africa.

13 NEW DIRECTIONS

One of the major concerns of potters throughout the 1980s has been the search for new forms which reflect changing economic and social attitudes, as well as major technological developments. Broadly, there has been a move away from the traditional work of the studio potter, whose output of hand thrown pots on the wheel intended for use in the home continues the work of the country potter, towards more special, usually hand-built, pieces often fired in an electric kiln or in low temperature raku or sawdust firings. Integral to these changes is the question of whether potters, in the broadest sense, are artists or craftspeople, with the corresponding differing status of their work in terms of price and whether their objects are displayed in craftshops or galleries.

The new spirit of invention has brought widespread developments in ceramics. There are several reasons for this. Within western society generally there has been a move towards a political conservativism, with great emphasis placed on monetarist values, on individual enterprise and competitiveness rather than on wider social issues. While this has influenced all the arts, in the visual arts this has affected both the market and the objects made: there has been a particular concern with purchasing collectable items, which can be displayed rather than used, and may also be seen as an investment. Potters responded to the market, and some started to make such pieces.

There have also been other significant changes. The deaths, of Bernard Leach in 1979, of Hans Coper in 1981 and of Michael Cardew in 1983, all stimulated the sales of their pots; in the leading auction houses prices rose dramatically. Pieces which had hitherto sold for hundreds of pounds or dollars were now sold for thousands. Ceramics suddenly had significant investment potential. New galleries opened to show the work of established potters, as well as to promote up-and-coming younger makers. Some painters have also been attracted to ceramics, often working in collaboration with potters. In Britain interesting work has been produced by Bruce McLean and John Hoyland, in the US by Keith Haring and Frim Kess. The buoyant market has been a particularly significant aspect of ceramics in the US, with galleries with international reputations showing the work of potters alongside paintings and sculptures. Some dealers, notably Garth Clark, have specialized in ceramics. While it is only a very small number of potters who can command prices sufficiently high to maintain gallery status, their work, technically innovative and artistically adventurous, has had a profound impact on ceramics as a whole.

Technological developments

Technological changes have taken place on a broad front. Most of the machinery used by potters, whether throwing wheels, pugmills, slab-rollers or kilns, has been redesigned. Most items have become smaller in size, lighter in weight and more efficient in use. By far the largest change has occurred in kilns. The introduction of ceramic fibre, the highly effective lightweight insulating material, has enabled kilns to be built which have up to half the size of those using traditional brick insulation whilst having much the same amount of packing space. Equally, the saving in the amount of fuel needed has brought down firing costs and enabled a reasonably-sized electric kiln to be fired off a domestic supply. Gas-fired kilns have also been made much more efficient, while for raku firing a simple metal bin, lined with ceramic fibre, has made the process widely available at low cost. Techniques which had previously been cumbersome and difficult now became accessible and relatively easy to handle, offering new and exciting possibilities; potters have been quick to take them up.

Studio pottery reconsidered

One of the first areas of ceramics to be reassessed was that of studio pottery, brought about by the move away from its '70s image. This image was characterized by pots made for use in the kitchen and living room, for serving or cooking food, with well-considered shapes which celebrate clay as the chosen material, throwing on the wheel being the preferred method of making. Glazes tended to be dark or neutral, with a minimum of decoration. These pots suggested a particular lifestyle with an

Bottle forms, thrown and modelled, wood-fired stoneware, tallest about 10 inches. John Leach, 1986.

Middle Container form, earthenware, about 15 inches long. Jacqui Poncelet, 1985.

Bottom Bowls, thrown with painted decoration, reduction fired stoneware. Andrew McGarva, 1986.

awareness of the environment, of concern with natural foods and a rejection of purely materialistic values. Such potters as, in Britain, John Leach, Andrew and Joanna Young, David Frith, Richard Batterham and potteries such as Dart Pottery and Highland Stoneware, have continued to refine and develop their production of such ware, making pieces to a high standard with skill and ingenuity. Other potters, faced with falling markets and diminishing sales, reassessed their work and moved away from the muted colour textures of reduction-fired stoneware towards brighter more vibrant shades, with all-over decoration.

In Britain one of the first potters to experiment with colour and decoration was Janice Tchalenko (born 1942). Trained as a potter on the studio pottery course at Harrow College of Technology in the late '60s, she had set up a workshop in south London making domestic pots fired to stoneware temperatures in a gas kiln. Glazes were tenmoku, brown and dark greens, and shapes reflected the twentieth-century traditions of studio pottery. Contact with painters, such as Roger Hilton, and with Jacqueline Poncelet and Glenys Barton – potters who had trained at the Royal College of Art in London – brought a new awareness of the possibilities of ceramics. Equally, visits to the Middle East and to France made her familiar with pottery traditions other than those of the Far East, as did an interest in mass-produced enamelled metal forms with stencil decoration. With the help of a Crafts Council grant she simplified her shapes and made a more limited range, concentrating on thrown tall jugs and on teapots. Decoration, inspired by French medieval slip decorated jugs, of trailing glaze over the surface of white base glaze, produced rich colours and a lively animation of the surface of the pot. Form and decoration were integrated in a new way. A collaboration with textile designer John Hinchcliffe pushed her ideas forward so that large, flat press-moulded dishes could almost be used as canvases for experiments with colour and pattern.

An immediate success, Tchalenko's work caught the spirit of adventure of the time, merging a bold decorative approach with technical innovation. Recognized as a decorator with a facility for enlivening three dimensional form, her richly-coloured and patterned pots have encouraged a renewed interest for her in domestic pots, but now produced in much smaller quantities, more highly finished, and decorated with bright colours and all-over designs. Some potters stencil or trail on decoration, while others, such as Andrew McGarva, paint elaborate but freely interpreted motifs based on tin-glazed earthenware onto reduction fired stoneware with great success.

Other potters, including Sandy Brown (born 1941), produce freely-thrown plates, cups and saucers and the like with bright colours painted, splashed or trailed onto the white ground. In contrast David Garland, born in the same year, who trained as a painter, makes domestic items in earthenware with bold striking decoration of cobalt blue and iron brown on a white slip base. A similar clarity and sureness is evident in the modern equivalents of traditional shapes in the work of Takeshi Yasuda.

American developments and influences in Europe

In the US potters have responded to oriental and to medieval ceramics with energy and skill. Betty Woodman (born 1930) has been inspired by Renaissance forms and the colours of Tang earthenware; she makes individual pieces which combine thrown and handbuilt form with a beguiling ease. John Glick, one of the most innovative of the new wave studio potters, has not only developed bright colours for use on plates, dishes, lidded boxes, teapots and so on, but has evolved new methods of making which combine clay slabs with extruded sections as well as forms thrown on the potters wheel. Stylistically, the work has an attractive hybrid quality with the mixture of different making processes. While drawing on traditional work, Glick has produced a lively and inventive range of shapes with surfaces ideal for decoration. His pots, and his combined experimental, alternative-technology-engineering approach, have had an influence on potters round the world. He has written on his methods and has given workshops to potters.

Teapot, thrown and modelled, oxide decoration, oxidised stoneware, 7 inches tall. Takeshi Yasuda, 1987.

In Britain, the Scottish-born potter Archie McCall has successfully drawn on his ideas. Jane Hamlyn has also adapted some of Glick's forming methods into her own work. For some years she has been making well-considered saltglazed stoneware at her workshop in Nottinghamshire; in recent years her approach has been more experimental, involving not only the use of extruded sections for the walls of dishes and the like, but also the use of coloured slips to introduce greens, pinks and blues into the usual limited range of saltglaze colours. Working with saltglaze has caught the attention of potters round the world,

Above Dish, with painted and trailed decoration, reduction fired stoneware, about 12 inches long. Archie McCall, 1987.

Left Pillow Pitcher – zig Zag, thrown and modelled, earthenware with clear gaze, 18½ inches tall. Betty Woodman, 1985.

Jugs, thrown and decorated, saltglaze, tallest 7 inches. Jane Hamlyn, 1985.

pieces domestic in size and context, such as teapots and jugs, Keeler has concentrated on the idea of the form, and through a series of clever manipulations he has emphasized 'essence'. Teapots, though flattened and with exaggerated spouts or handles, become elaborations of the idea. Expert making, using thrown, slabbed and extruded sections, ensures that there is little if any evidence of handmaking, so the almost mechanical precision becomes a vital part of the quality of the piece. Sprayed layers of metal-coloured underglazed colours give mottled slate blues, greys or dark green saltglaze surfaces with a semi-matt shine. Little or no decoration embellishes the shapes, which rely entirely on their form and the saltglaze for their success. Keeler continues to be among the leading potters in Britain, maintaining a particular excellence in concept and execution.

Jar, saltglaze, stoneware, 14 inches tall. Janet Mansfield, 1981.

despite the problems involved. Robert Winokur, in the US, and Janet Mansfield, in Australia, have both found individual styles, using uncomplicated shapes which bring out the qualities of the firing.

Saltglaze has remained an important part of the work of Walter Keeler (born 1942). Attracted by the refinement and smooth perfection of eighteenth-century Staffordshire lathe-turned pots, with their clean cut profile and crisp decoration, and by the mechanical strength of metal containers such as oil cans, Keeler has sought to incorporate these qualities in his own saltglaze pots. Still making

Top Jug form, saltglaze, about 8 inches tall. Walter Keeler, 1986.

National potters, international styles

Established potters such as Lucie Rie, Janet Leach, David Leach, Colin Pearson and Ruth Duckworth have continued to develop subtle refinements in forms and in their decorative approach. Lucie Rie, now in her late 80s, throws bowls, vases and bottle forms, producing new volcanic glazes and metallic surfaces. Widespread international acclaim, and a major retrospective exhibition at the Sainsbury Centre, Norwich and at the Victoria and Albert Museum, London, in 1982 has brought renewed interest in her pots, which in their emphasis on form rather than applied decoration, and on glaze and body colour, epitomise all the subtle possibilities which can be achieved at stoneware temperatures in the electric kiln.

At the Leach pottery, St Ives, Janet Leach (born 1918) throws powerful individual bottles which, though greatly informed by the qualities of spontaneity and the process of making and firing of the traditional Bizen pot, of Japan, have an individual feel and belong in the contemporary world of studio pottery. Bottles, seemingly freely-thrown, are pushed or modelled so that areas of emphasis are changed, with a quieter section counterbalanced by busier interaction. Placed in or near the firebox of the kiln, the pieces take up the effect of the process and become encrusted with small lumps of ash, or marked with an orange flash. Other bottles, or vase forms, thrown from a black-firing clay, are decorated with a dramatic swish of glaze which accentuates movement and shape.

David Leach, at Lowerdown Pottery, Devon, has gradually ceased making purely domestic wares in favour of individual one-off thrown pieces. His bottles, with the full swelling form, either with painted floral abstract decoration or a matt crackle glaze, are characteristic.

Handbuilt ceramics

While throwing on the wheel is still a major and important crafting method for many, particularly for potters who produce in relatively large quantity, others have turned their attention to other methods of making. Slipcasting, the technique widely used in industry, has been taken up by potters in Britain and the US. Such west-coast American potters as Richard Shaw (born 1941) and Kenneth Price (born 1935) continue to produce finely made pieces with wit and ingenuity. Richard Shaw's use of fine slipcast forms such as books or playing cards in porcelain, assembled into still life groups and

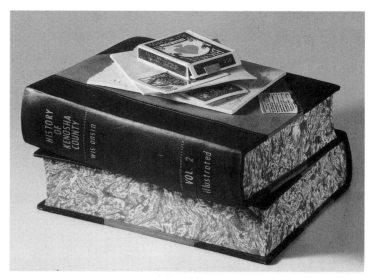

Jar in two volumes, porcelain, slip cast, with decal overglaze. Richard Shaw.

covered with transfer (decal) decoration, has resulted in some fascinating *trompe-l'oeil* pieces. Much of the success of Shaw's work lies in its expert handling of the processes of ceramics, exploiting its versatility and drawing on the traditions associated with high art ceramics and the meticulous ornateness of such royal factories as Sèvres and Meissen. If Shaw calls on long-established processes, his choice of imagery is totally up-to-date, combining pop elements of Warhol's soup cans with the illusionistic façade of much modern life.

In Britain potters such as Carol McNicoll (born 1948) have used the successes of slipcasting to produce more sculptural forms. After studying at Leeds Polytechnic and the Royal College of Art, McNicoll set up a workshop in London, making in slipware items which imitate other processes and materials. Teacups and saucers, for example, may look as if they are slab built from folded clay, but are in fact slipcast in plaster of Paris moulds. More complex decorative dishes with structures which echo wood or metal are made in much the same way: pieces are cast and then assembled, either in the mould or subsequently. These individual forms, with their concern for the processes of ceramics and also for more sculptural requirements, are some of McNicoll's stronger work. Though still made for the home, most could function as dishes or containers of some sort; they cross many boundaries and demonstrate the adaptability of ceramics in the hands of a creative potter. McNicoll has also designed items such as vases and ashtrays, which look humorously handmade, for factory production. Along with bowls and jugs designed by Janice Tchalenko, these pieces have been produced for sale at reasonable prices in retail shops across Britain.

The particular making method, so important to McNicoll but not immediately evident in her work, is also reflected in the sculptural container forms of Richard Slee (born 1946). For his decorative forms he uses handbuilding or press moulding brought to a high degree of precision. His shapes – a particular favourite is the cornucopia – suggest excess and plenty, an overabundance of treats. References in his work are not only to the classical tradition but to elements of nineteenth-century forms. Bright industrial-style glazes enliven his pieces. His pots give an intelligent commentary not only on the process of ceramics but also on the activity of art pottery.

Left Optical Jar, with built and painted stoneware. Elizabeth Fritsch. (City Art Gallery, Manchester)

Vessels, coil built, burnished, tallest about 11 inches. Magdalene Odundo, 1985. (Birmingham City Museum)

The vessel and the figure

A particular feature of ceramics in the '80s has been a concern with the vessel. This is usually handbuilt, often by coiling, is rounded in form, is a one-off even if part of a series, and though these pieces acknowledge the functional traditions of pottery they seek to have a presence in the modern world. The vessel is not only a description of a container, but also suggests mystical or even religious connections. Vessel makers include such established figures as Ewen Henderson, Elizabeth Fritsch, Alison Britton and Jill Crowley in the UK and Paul Soldner, Peter Voulkos and Ruth Duckworth in the US, but there is also a wide range of younger makers whose concern is as much with the process of potting as with the aesthetic consideration of the final piece. Building forms by coiling and then honing down the shape to a flat surface has continued to interest Elizabeth Fritsch (born 1941). Her shapes tend to be flattened or to incorporate some element of directional change which can only be achieved by careful consideration. The thin-walled vessels with the smooth finish are ideal for the painted decoration of coloured slips. Geometric bands or complex, almost op-art, patterns, precisely painted, animate and change the shape. Slow to produce, Fritsch makes few pots a year, and her pieces are widely regarded as collectors' items.

Building up shapes from slabs and coils is also the method used by Alison Britton (born 1948). Since becoming well known for her jug forms with painted figurative decoration, she has remained with the concept of function in that all her pieces are containers, but has pushed such an idea to the extent where no precise label can be applied. The forms have got larger and now seem more slab-like, but the shapes move in and out in a complex way; some recall jugs, others have a more figurative feel. Decoration is now less naturalistic, and splashes of colour or trails of slip have introduced a new element of freedom.

Ewen Henderson (born 1934) makes forms which have become less vessel-orientated and more sculptural in feel, with the bubbled and volcanic surfaces adding depth and mystery. A similar degree of freedom is evident in the humanoid forms of Jill Crowley (born 1946). She left the Royal College of Art in the early '70s and has made figurative sculptures which combine character and comment. Recent work has included limbs and hands.

In Britain the Royal College of Art has been an important school for the development of new ideas and for the reappraisal of the work of the potter. Jennifer Lee (born 1955) evolved a series of precise, rounded coil-built forms which have elements of Fritsch's skilled working and Anglo-Saxon coil-built funerary vessels. Colour mixed into the clay bleeds and runs into adjacent areas, and the overall muted effect, enhanced by a final polish of the clay surface, is one of subtlety and richness. Martin Smith (born 1950) graduated from the Royal College of Art in the mid-'70s and since then has had an abiding concern with the vessel. He has built a series of shapes in red earthenware which have references to architecture and the forms of building without in any sense seeking to portray or replicate them directly.

An interest in traditional making methods but with an awareness of ceramics in the modern world characterises the coil built pots of Magdalene Odundo and Fiona Salazar. Since leaving the Royal College of Art both have worked with red earthenware, building up precisely controlled shapes. Odundo's recall the traditional work of Nigerian potters, Salazar's South American shapes and decoration. Surfaces are rubbed smooth and burnished to give them a dull gloss; some are fired in sawdust to achieve dappled colour changes. Slow to make, and finished with great care, Odundo's and Salazar's pots are among some of the finest.

The processes of sawdust or saggar firing which leaves a distinctive, almost primitive mark on the vessels, have interested many potters. The work of Judy Trim and Elsbeth Owen in the UK, Richard Hirsch, Roberta Marks and Byron Temple in the US, and in France Pierre Bayle, should be mentioned.

Raku, particularly on a large scale, is another technique which has found new favour. In the UK the thrown and coil-built bottle and bowl forms of David Roberts have made imaginative use of the medium. In particular his large scale work, and the white crackle glaze, has resulted in some excellent pots. Wayne Higby, in the US, has developed a fascinating range of landscape bowls with intricate inlay and glaze finish.

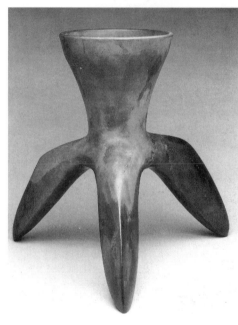

Top Bottle forms, coil built, sawdust fired, tallest 12 inches. Judy Trim, 1986.

Middle Ceremonial Vessel No. 4, V series, blue-purple, raku fired. Richard Hirsch, 1984.

Bottom left Vase, earthenware, coil built, burnished and decorated, wax polished, 10 inches tall. Fiona Salazar, 1985.

Bottom right Sawdust Vessel, slab and coil technique with underglaze pencil and pastel, raku fired, 17 inches tall. Roberta B. Marks, 1983.

Top Bottle, coil built, burnished and smoked. Pierre Bayle, 1981.

The diversity of approach of ceramics in the '80s is nowhere better demonstrated than the taut forms of Sarah Radstone, in the ceramic sculptural constructions of Gillian Lowndes, in the fine agate pieces of Dorothy Feibleman and in the handbuilt forms of Angus Suttie (born 1946). After training at Camberwell School of Art, Suttie set up his studio in central London, making coiled and slabbed forms which related to the figure. Freely built teapot forms, often with written messages of love and sexual desire, are brightly coloured with earthenware glazes. More recently the use of higher firing clays and more sombre colouring on forms which have more obvious structure recall the handbuilt pots of South America; handles make linking bridges, and more controlled use of the clay links freedom and a spontaneous method of working with a more vigorous analysis of intention.

In the US potters have concerned themselves not only with making use of the latest technology, but with issues, whether around such specific political concerns as atomic warfare, old age or the history of the American Indian, or with defining a new role for ceramics. Richard Notkin's small-scale, almost miniature, pieces combine precision and traditional skills with a sharp observation and ironic comment on the ever present danger of nuclear war. His 'Cooling Towers' and 'Cube Skull' teapots, only 6 in long, are based on the fine red Yixing wares of China. With an atomic explosion on the lids, they comment on the dance of death involved in atomic weapons.

The figurative element in Notkin's work is also taken up by potters as diverse as Viola Frey, who produces virtually life-sized figures which have a disturbing presence, Peter Vandenberge, whose large coil-built head portraits mix caricature and presence, Robert Brady's huge stoneware, matchstick-thin figures, and in the work of Judy Moonelis. Expressionist and extrovert in feel, her figures suggest the powerful feelings of relationships as they writhe and twist, involved in some dark and secret bond, on the significance of which we can only speculate.

Middle Raku bottle, coil built. David Roberts, 1987.

Bottom right Double Cooling Tower Teapot, No 10, fine red earthenware, slipcast, 8 inches tall. Richard Notkin, 1986.

Bottom left Bowl form, agate, coloured porcelain clays, 5 inches across. Dorothy Feibleman, 1987.

GLOSSARY OF TECHNICAL TERMS

Albany clay Naturally occuring clay found near New York which melts to form a smooth dark-coloured glaze at stoneware temperatures.

Alkaline glaze Contains soda or potash in some form and when small quantities of copper oxide are present gives a rich turquoise colour.

Amphora Pot form used in Mediterranean countries for holding liquids. Characterized by two handles linking the neck to the body of the pot.

Arabesque Ornamentation derived from a mixture of formal geometric and foliage patterns, characterized by flowing linear designs of leaves and scrolls.

Barbotine decoration Made by trailing thick slip on to the surface of a leather-hard pot.

Biscuit Pottery which has been fired once without a glaze in the biscuit-firing. It is usually porous and fairly soft.

Body General term for various clays from which pots are made.

Bone china A type of porcelain, made in England, from china clay, bone ash and flint, which is pure white and translucent.

Burnishing Sometimes known as polishing, made by rubbing the surface of unfired pots with a smooth surfaced tool such as a stone or a bone. The particles of clay, pressed flat and smooth, take on a dull gloss.

Carinate Pottery shape made by joining a rounded base and straight in-sloping walls.

Celadons General term for Chinese wares with green glazes, where the colour was obtained by small amounts of iron in the glaze. Sometimes known as green wares.

China clay Pure white clay, sometimes known as kaolin, of theoretically pure composition. Essential for the production of fine porcelain.

China stone Form of feldspar, known as petuntze, used by the Chinese for the production of fine porcelain. Modern equivalents are cornwall stone and cornish stone.

Clay Plastic malleable earth occurring over much of the earth's surface. It must be carefully prepared to remove foreign matter and be mixed evenly throughout.

Cobalt oxide A metal oxide which gives blue over a wide temperature range. Imported from Persia into China where it was known as Mohammedan blue or Sumatran blue.

Colouring oxides Various metal oxides when painted on or mixed into a glaze give different colours. Copper oxide gives green, manganese oxide gives brown or purple, iron oxide gives brown or green, cobalt oxide gives blue.

Combing Incised parallel-line decoration made by a toothed tool such as a piece of comb.

Delftware English term used originally to describe tin-glazed earthenware made in Delft, Holland, and sometimes used to describe all tin-glazed ware made in England.

Earthenware General term used for pottery fired to temperatures up to 1150°C (2101°F). Characterized by glaze and body remaining as quite separate layers.

Enamels or on-glaze decoration Glazes prepared in frit form to melt at low temperature which allows a wide range of colours. Painted on to a fired glaze and refired in a muffle kiln.

Faience (Egyptian paste) An artificially made clay body prepared from clay and sand to which a fluxing agent has been added, which was capable of being moulded into small objects or pots. The surface became glossy when fired and, if dusted with copper oxide, turquoise. A term also used by the French for tin-glazed earthenware.

Feldspar Naturally occurring mineral consisting of alumina, silica and a flux of potassium or sodium. Melts at 1250°C (2282°F) to form a simple glaze.

Flux Essential glaze ingredient which causes other ingredients to melt and fuse to form glaze. Different fluxes affect colouring oxides to give a wide range of colours.

Frit Artificially produced glaze or body material made by heating two or more raw materials together until they melt to render them insoluble or non-poisonous. The mixture is shattered by being poured into cold water and subsequently ground to powder.

Galena An impure lead ore used by potters to make lead glazes.

Glaze A smooth waterproof glossy surface applied to pots, discovered in the Near East about 1500 BC, about the same time as glass.

Green wares General term for pots before they have been fired.

Incised decoration Pressed or cut into the surface of a pot or tile.

In-glaze painting or maiolica painting Technique of decorating pottery, brought to perfection by the Italians in the Middle Ages, in which colouring oxides are painted on to unfired opaque white tin-glaze.

Kilns Sometimes known as the potter's oven, they are structures in which clay forms are fired until they become pottery. Developed originally in the Near East, they separate the fire from the chamber which holds the pots.

Kwaart Technique used by the Delft potters to imitate Chinese blue and white porcelain in tin-glazed earthenware by using a clear transparent glaze over the white opaque glaze. This gave a greater gloss and depth to the colours.

Leather-hard Term to describe the half-way stage between wet and dry clay when it behaves like shoe leather. Stiff enough to support its own weight but sufficiently pliable to bend slightly and be carved. The stage at which turning is carried out on unfinished pots.

Levigation Process of preparing clay of fine particle size by reducing it to liquid and decanting finer particles which remain in suspension while heavier particles sink to bottom. Technique used by, among others, Greeks and Romans.

Liu-li A glass frit probably of lead and sand, imported into China from the Near East in the Han dynasty (206 BC–AD 220).

Lustre A type of colouring decoration achieved by painting metallic pigment on to a fired glaze and refiring in a reducing atmosphere which gives an iridescent effect.

Maiolica General term, used first by the Italians, for tin-glazed earthenware decorated with oxides painted on to the unfired glaze.

Majolica A corruption of maiolica used during the nineteenth century for moulded earthenware with relief patterns decorated with coloured glazes or maiolica painting.

Monochrome pottery Usually made in one colour or has decoration painted in a contrasting colour.

Muffle kiln Protects pots from flames in a flame-burning kiln. Essential for production of enamels.

Natron A mineral found in the Near East containing sodium oxide (Na_2O) which acts as a flux in a glaze or in faience.

Opacifier A substance, usually a metal oxide such as tin oxide, which, when added to clear glazes, suspends itself and renders the glaze opaque and white.

Oxidizing atmosphere Conditions inside a kiln when a clean bright flame burns with plenty of oxygen available. The resulting pots are often bright coral red and iron-glazes yellow or brown.

Paddle and anvil Tools used for hand-built pottery. The anvil, often in the form of a stone, supported the pot wall inside while the paddle was beaten against the outside wall. Used in Indus Valley and America among other places.

Plastic Wet clay which can be moulded or worked without breaking is described as being plastic.

Polychrome pottery Decoration painted in two or more colours usually with coloured slips or oxides.

Porcelain High-temperature ware which is white and translucent. The body is made by mixing china clay, china stone and quartz together. Sometimes known as hard-paste porcelain.

Potash A form of potassium oxide (K_2O) found in wood-ash. Acts as a flux in glaze or in faience.

Quartz A form of silica (SiO_2) such as sand, which when mixed with a suitable flux will form a glaze. Flint is a more finely ground form of silica.

Raku A method of firing pots quickly using an open body. Used extensively since the eighteenth century in Japan and more recently in Britain and the USA.

Reducing atmosphere Opposite to oxidizing atmosphere in a kiln. Oxygen content is kept to a minimum by burning damp fuel or closing air inlets. The resulting pots are often dark brown or black and iron-glazes green or blue.

Resist Decoration where one area is painted in a substance such as wax which resists colouring pigment or glaze when applied to the pot and therefore fires a contrasting colour.

Rouletting Two sorts of decoration. In antiquity made by allowing a tool to 'chatter' against the side of a leather-hard pot revolving on the wheel. Also used to describe the pattern made by a relief-decorated revolving wheel held against a turning pot.

Saltglaze A thin glaze achieved by introducing common salt (NaCl) into the kiln at high temperature. The chlorine as a poisonous gas goes up the chimney and the sodium vapour forms a glaze on the surface of the pots.

Sgraffito Decoration scratched through a layer of slip to show the body of contrasting colour.

Slip Clay which has been softened down in water and put through a sieve to make it smooth. Usually has consistency of cream.

Slipware Pots and dishes decorated with different coloured clay slips and usually finished with a transparent lead glaze.

Soft-paste porcelain A European imitation of Chinese porcelain made by mixing white clay with a frit or a flux such as bone ash or talc, which vitrifies at earthenware temperature to give a white translucent body.

Sprigging Decorating technique in which relief-moulded decoration is applied to the leather-hard pot. Used extensively by Wedgwood in the production of his Jasper wares.

Stoneware Pottery fired to a high temperature, about 1250°C (2462°F). Body is vitrified and glaze and body partially fused together.

Tenmoku Term used to describe black oriental glazes which break light brown on rims and ornament.

Throwing Art of building up pots on the fast-spinning potter's wheel using centrifugal force.

Turning Process of removing surplus clay from thrown pots by returning them, when leather-hard, to the potter's wheel and trimming with a metal tool.

Underglaze painting A technique of painting colouring oxides on to unfired pottery which may or may not be subsequently glazed. The term is used occasionally to describe the technique of painting on to unfired glaze.

Viscous A glaze which when melted remains stiff and does not run down the pot is so described.

Vitrified Like glass, fused together.

MUSEUMS WITH POTTERY COLLECTIONS

UK

Aberdeen University Anthropological Museum
Brighton Museum and Art Gallery
Bristol City Art Gallery
Cambridge Fitzwilliam Museum
Cambridge University Museum of Archaeology and Ethnology
Durham Gulbenkian Museum of Oriental Art and Archaeology
Glasgow Art Gallery and Museum
Hastings Public Museum and Art Gallery
London Bethnal Green Museum
 British Museum
 Museum of London
 Martinware Pottery Collection, Pitshanger Manor
  Museum, Ealing
 Percival David Foundation of Chinese Art
 University College Department of Egyptology
 Victoria and Albert Museum and extensive Art Library
 Wallace Collection
Newcastle Laing Art Gallery
Norwich Castle Museum
Nottingham City Museum and Art Gallery
Oxford Ashmoleam Museum of Art and Archaeology
 Pitt Rivers Museum
Salisbury and South Wiltshire Museum
Stoke-on-Trent City Museum and Art Gallery

*Museums and Galleries in Great Britain and
Ireland* is a full detailed list of Museums,
published annually by Index Publications,
available from stationers and bookshops.

USA

Baltimore Museum of Art
Boston Museum of Fine Arts
Chicago Art Institute
Cincinnati Art Museum
Honolulu, Bernice P Bishop Museum
Houston Museum of Fine Arts
New York, Brooklyn Museum
New York, Metropolitan Museum of Fine Art
New York, Museum of Primitive Art
Pasadena Art Museum
Pennsylvania Art Museum
Santa Fe, Museum of Navaho Ceremonial Art
Washington DC, Smithsonian Institution

BIBLIOGRAPHY

General

CAIGER-SMITH, A. *Tin-Glaze Pottery,* Faber & Faber, London 1973

CARDEW, M. *Pioneer Pottery*, Longman, London 1969

CHARLESTON, R. J. (Ed.) *World Ceramics,* Paul Hamlyn, London 1968

COOPER, E. *Handbook of Pottery,* Longman, London 1970

CUSHION, J. and HONEY, W. B. *Dictionary of European Ceramic Art*, Faber & Faber, London 1952

DODD, J. and ROGERS, A. *Exploring Pottery*, Odhams, London 1967

GODDEN, G. British Pottery, Barrie & Jenkins, London 1974

HAGGAR, R. *Pottery through the Ages*, Methuen, London 1959

HILLIER, B. *Pottery and Porcelain 1700–1914*, Weidenfeld & Nicolson, London 1968

HODGES, H. *Artifacts*, John Baker, London 1964
The Technology of the Ancient World, Arthur Lane, London 1970

HOLLAND, F. *Fifty Years a Potter*, Pottery Quarterly, London 1950

HONEY, W. B. *Art of the Potter*, Faber & Faber, London 1955

LEACH, B. *A Potter's Book*, Faber & Faber, London 1940

LEWENSTEIN, E. and COOPER, E. *New Ceramics*, Studio Vista, London 1974

MITCHELL, L. *Ceramics – from Stone Age to Space Age*, McGraw-Hill, New York 1963

RIETH, A. *5000 Jahre Topferscheibe*, Jan Thorbecke Verlag KG, Konstanz 1960

ROSENTHAL, E. *Pottery and Ceramics*, Penguin, London 1949

WOODHOUSE, C. P. *The World's Master Potters*, David & Charles, London 1974

The Far East

BRANKSTON, A.D. *Early Ming Wares of Ching te chen*, Lund Humphries, London 1971. First issued by Henry Vetch 1938

CHEWON, K. and GOMPERTZ, G. ST G. M. *Korean Arts,* Volume II. *Ceramics*, Korean Ministry of Public Information, London 1961

FRANKS, SIR A. W. *Japanese Pottery*, 3rd edition, Victoria and Albert Museum Handbook, London 1912

GARNER, SIR HARRY *Oriental Blue and White*, Faber & Faber, London 1964

GOMPERTZ, G. ST G. M. *Chinese Celadon Wares*, Faber & Faber, London 1958

GRAY, B. *Early Chinese Pottery and Porcelain*, Faber & Faber, London 1953

HETHERINGTON, A. C. *Early Ceramic Wares of China*, Ernest Benn, London 1922

HOBSON, R. L. *The Art of the Chinese Potter*, Ernest Benn, London 1923
British Museum Handbook of Pottery and Porcelain of the Far East, British Museum, London 1937

HONEY, W. B. *Ceramic Art of China*, Faber & Faber, London 1945

JENYNS, S. *Japanese Porcelain*, Faber & Faber, London 1965
Ming Pottery and Porcelain, Faber & Faber, London 1953

KORJAMA, FUJIO (Ed.), *Japanese Ceramics*, Oakland Art Museum, California 1961

LAUFER, B. *Chinese Pottery of the Han Dynasty*, American Museum of Natural History, New York 1909

MEDCALF, C. J. B. *Introduction to Chinese Pottery and Porcelain*, Cresset Press, London 1955

MEDLEY, M. *The Chinese Potter*, Phaidon, Oxford 1976

MILLER, R. A. *Japanese Ceramics*, Toto Shuppan Co. Ltd., Tokyo 1960. Distributed by Charles E. Tuttle and Co., Rutland, Vermont, and Tokyo, Japan

SANDERS, H. H. *The World of Japanese Ceramics*, Kodansha International Ltd, Tokyo 1967

WU, G. D. *Prehistoric Pottery in China*, Kegan Paul, Trench Trubner and Co., London 1938

Prehistory and the earliest civilizations

ALDRED, C. *The Egyptians*, Thames and Hudson, London 1961

ALLCHIN, B. and R. *The Birth of Indian Civilization*, Penguin, London 1968

EYLES, D. *Pottery in the Ancient World*, Doulton, London 1950

POULIK, J. *Prehistoric Art*, Spring Books, London n.d.

CHILDE, G. *What Happened in History*, Penguin, London 1964

HUTCHINSON, R. W. *Prehistoric Crete*, Penguin, London 1962

PORADA, E. *Ancient Iran*, Methuen, London 1965

SINGER, C., HOLMYARD, E. J. and HALL, A.R. (Eds.). *History of Technology*, Volumes I–III. Oxford University Press/Clarendon Press, London 1954, 1956, 1957

Greece and Rome

AMERICAN SCHOOL OF CLASSICAL STUDIES AT ATHENS. *Pots and Pans of Classical Athens*, Princeton, New Jersey 1958

BEAZLEY, SIR JOHN. *Attic Black Figure Vase Painters*, Oxford University Press, London 1956
Attic Red Figure Vase Painters, Oxford University Press, London 1942

Etruscan Vase Painting, Oxford University Press, London 1947

CHARLESTON, R. J. *Roman Pottery*, Faber & Faber, London 1955

COOK, R. M. *Greek Painted Pottery*, Methuen, London 1960

COUNCIL FOR BRITISH ARCHAEOLOGY RESEARCH REPORT NO. 6. *Romano-British Coarse Pottery*, London (n.d.)

LANE, A. *Greek Pottery*, Faber & Faber, London 1956

NOBLE, J. V. *The Techniques of Painted Attic Pottery*, Faber & Faber, London 1956

OSWALD, F. and DAVIES PRYCE, T. *Terra Sigillata*, Gregg Press Ltd., London 1966

STANFIELD, J. A. and SIMPSON, G. *Central Gaulish Potters*, Oxford University Press, 1958

Islamic pottery

BUTLER, A. J. *Islamic Pottery*, Ernest Benn, London 1926

HOBSON, R. L. *A Guide to the Islamic Pottery of the Near and Far East*, British Museum, London 1932

LANE, A. *Early Islamic Pottery*, Faber & Faber, London 1958

Later Islamic Pottery, Faber & Faber, London 1957

POPE, A. U. *An Introduction to Persian Art since the 7th Century AD*, Peter Davis, London 1930

POPE, A. U. *Survey of Persian Art*, Volume II, Oxford University Press, London 1938

WALLIS, H. *Persian Ceramic Art* (two volumes). Privately printed, London 1891

European pottery

ARRIBAS, A. *The Iberians*, Thames and Hudson, London 1968

FORTNUM, C. D. E. *Maiolica*, Clarendon Press, Oxford 1896

FOTHINGHAM, A. W. *Lustreware of Spain*, Hispanic Society, New York 1951

Talavera Pottery, Hispanic Society, New York 1944

HONEY, W. B. *European Ceramic Art* (two volumes), Faber & Faber, London 1952

LIVERANI, G. *Five Centuries of Italian Majolica*, McGraw-Hill, London 1960

MORGAN, C. H. *The Byzantine Pottery (Corinth)* (American School of Classical Studies), Harvard University Press, Harvard 1942

PENKALA, M. *European Pottery*, A. Zwemmer Ltd., London 1951

PICCOLOPASSO. *The Three Books of the Potter's Art* (translated and edited by RACKHAM, B. and VAN DER PUT, A.), Victoria and Albert Museum, London 1934

RACKHAM, B. *Italian Majolica*, Faber & Faber, London 1952

RICE TALBOT, D. *Byzantine Glazed Pottery*, Clarendon Press, Oxford 1930

SAVORY, H. N. *Spain and Portugal*, Thames and Hudson, London 1968

SOLON, M. L. *Ancient Art Stoneware of the Low Countries and Germany*, privately printed, London 1892

Italian Majolica, Cassell and Co., London 1907

STEVENSON, R. B. K. *The Great Palace of the Byzantine Emperors*, Oxford University Press, Oxford 1947

TATLOCK, R. K. *Spanish Art*, Burlington Magazine Monograph II, London 1927

THEOPHILUS. *The Various Arts* (edited by DODWELL, C. R.), Nelson, London 1961

WALLIS, H. *The Byzantine Ceramic Art*, Bernard Quaritch, London 1907

Italian Ceramic Art, privately printed, London 1897

America

BARBER, E. A. *Pottery and Porcelain of the USA* (3rd edition), G. P. Putnam, New York 1909

"Rise of the Pottery Industry in the USA", from *The Popular Science Monthly*, Vol. XL, No. 2, 1891, and No. 3, 1892

BIVINS, JOHN JR. *The Moravian Potters in North Carolina*, The University of North Carolina Press, 1972

BUSHNELL, G. H. S. *Ancient Arts of the Americas*, Thames and Hudson, London 1965

BUSHNELL, G. H. S. and DIGBY, A. *Ancient American Pottery*, Faber & Faber, London 1955

COE, M. D. *The Maya*, Thames and Hudson, London 1966

Mexico, Thames and Hudson, London 1965

GODDARD, P. E. *Pottery of the South-western Indians*, American Museum of Natural History, New York 1928

GUILLAND HAROLD, F. *Early American Folk Pottery*, Chilton, New York 1971

HOOD, G. *Bonnin and Morris of Philadelphia*, University of North Carolina, 1972

HOYLE, R. L. *Peru*, Thames and Hudson, London 1966

LOTHROP, S. K. *Treasures of Ancient America*, Skira, London 1964

MASON, ALDEN J. *The Ancient Civilization of Peru*, Penguin, London 1964

SPARGO, J. *The Potters and Potteries of Bennington*, Dover Publications, first published 1926; republished New York 1972

VAILLANT, G. C. *Artists and Craftsmen in Ancient Central America*, American Museum of Natural History, New York 1935

Aztecs of Mexico, Penguin, London 1962

WILEY, G. R. *An Introduction to American Archaeology*, Volume I. *North and Middle America*, Prentice-Hall Inc., New Jersey 1966

English pottery until 1800

CHURCH, A. H. *English Earthenware*, Victoria and Albert Museum Handbook, London 1911

Some Minor Arts, Seeley and Co., London 1894

COOPER, R. G. *English Slipware Dishes*, Tiranti, London 1968

GARNER, F. H. *English Delftware*, Faber & Faber, London 1948

GODDEN, G. A. *British Porcelain*, Barrie & Jenkins, London 1974

JEWITT, L. *Ceramic Art of Great Britain* (2nd edition 1883), J. S. Virtue & Co., London 1877

KIDSON, J. R. and F. *Leeds Old Pottery* (first published 1892), S.R. Publishers and *The Connoisseur*, London 1970

MCVEIGH, P. *Scottish East Coast Potteries 1750–1840*, John Donald, Edinburgh 1979

RACKHAM, B. *Medieval English Pottery*, Faber & Faber, London 1947

RACKHAM, B. and READ, H. *English Pottery*, Ernest Benn, London 1924

TOWNER, D. C. *English Cream Coloured Earthenware*, Faber & Faber, London 1957

Australia

HOOD, K. and GARNSEY, W. *Australian Pottery*, Macmillan, Melbourne 1972

GRAHAM, M. *Australian Pottery of the 19th and early 20th Century*, David Ell Press, Gladesville, N.S.W. 1979

Modern pottery from 1800

BEARD, G. *Modern Ceramics*, Studio Vista, London 1969

BEMROSE, G. *Nineteenth Century English Pottery and Porcelain*, Faber & Faber, London 1952

BIRKS, T. *Art of Modern Pottery*, Country Life, London 1967

BIRKS, T. *Hans Coper*, Collins, London 1983

BIRKS, T. *Lucie Rie*, Alphabooks/A & C Black, London 1987

CALLEN, A. *Angel in the Studio*, Astragal Books, London 1979

CASSON, M. *Pottery in Britain Today*, Tiranti, London 1967

CARDEW, MICHAEL *A Pioneer Potter*, Collins, London 1988

CLARK, GARTH *American Potters*, New York 1981.

CLARK, G. and HUGHTO, M. *A Century of Ceramics in the United States 1878–1978*, E. P. Dutton, New York 1979

CLARK, GARTH and WATSON, OLIVER *American Potters Today*, Victoria & Albert Museum, London 1986

COYSH, A. W. *British Art Pottery*, David & Charles, London 1976

DAVIS, HARRY *The Potter's Alternative*, Collins, London 1988

DONHAUSER, P. *History of American Ceramics*, Kendall/Hunt, Dubuque 1978

DORMER, PETER *The New Ceramics*, Thames & Hudson, London 1986

FOURNIER, ROBERT *Illustrated Dictionary of Pottery Decoration*, Prentice Hall Press, New York, 1986

GAUNT, WILLIAM and CLAYTON-STAMM, M. D. F. *William De Morgan*, Studio Vista, London 1971

HASLAM, M. *English Art Pottery 1865–1915*, Antique Collectors Club, London 1975

HASLAM, M. *The Martin Brothers*, Richard Dennis, London 1978

HETTES and RADA. *Modern Ceramics*, Spring Books, London 1965

HUGHES, G. B. *Victorian Pottery and Porcelain*, Country Life, London 1959

IOANNOU, NORIS *Ceramics in South Australia 1836–1986: From Folk to Studio Pottery*, Wakefield Press, Adelaide 1986

JEWITT, L. *Ceramic Art of Great Britain 1800–1900*, first published 1878; revised by G. Godden, Barrie and Jenkins, London 1972

KLEIN, A. *Moderne Deutsche Keramik*, Franz Schneekluth Verlag, Darmstadt 1956

LANE, PETER *Studio Ceramics*, Collins, London 1983

LEACH, B. *Hamada*, Thames and Hudson, London; 1976 Kodansha International, Japan

LUCIE-SMITH, E. *World of the Makers*, Paddington Press, London 1975

NAYLOR, G. *The Arts and Crafts Movement*, Studio Vista, London 1971

PELICHET, E. *La Céramique Art Nouveau*, Les Editions du Grant-Pont, Lausanne 1976

PLEYDELL-BOUVERIE, KATHARINE *A Potter's Life 1895–1985*, Crafts Council, London 1986

PREAUD, TAMARA, and GAUTHIER, SERGE *Ceramics of the Twentieth Century*, Phaidon, Oxford 1982

ROSE, M. *Artist Potters in England*, Faber & Faber, London 1970

WAKEFIELD, H. *Victorian Pottery*, Herbert Jenkins, London 1962

WILDENHAIN, M. *Pottery Form and Expression*, Reinhold, New York 1962

Magazines

American Ceramics, 15 West 44 Street, New York, N.Y. 10036

American Crafts, 401 Park Avenue South, New York, N.Y. 10016

Antiquaries' Journal, Society of Antiquaries, Burlington House, Piccadilly, London

Apollo, Bracken House, Cannon Street, London EC4

Archaeological Journal, British Archaeological Association, London

Art Journal, (published 1849–1912), London

Atelier des Métiers d'Art, 18 Rue Wurtz, 75013 Paris

Burlington Magazine, 10 Elm Street, London WC1

Ceramic Review, 21 Carnaby Street, London, W1V 1PH

Ceramics Monthly, 1609 Northwest Boulevard, Box 12448, Columbus, Ohio 43212, U.S.A.

The Connoisseur, Chestergate House, Vauxhall Bridge Road, London

Crafts, Crafts Council, 12 Waterloo Place, London, SW1Y 4AU

New Zealand Potter, 15 Wadestown Road, Wellington, New Zealand

Oriental Art, 12 Ennerdale Road, Richmond, Surrey

Pottery in Australia, 48 Burton Street, Darlinghurst, N.S.W. 2010, Australia

Real Pottery, Northfield Studio, Northfields, Tring, Herts.

La Revue de la Céramique et du Verre, 61 Rue Marconi, 62880 Vendin-Le-Vieil, France

Studio Potter, P.O. Box 4954, Manchester, New Hampshire 03108, U.S.A.

Transactions of the English Ceramic Society, Shelton House, Stoke Road, Stoke-on-Trent, Staffs.

INDEX